THE
HOME FRONT:
SHEFFIELD IN
THE FIRST WORLD WAR

THE
HOME FRONT:
SHEFFIELD IN
THE FIRST WORLD WAR

Scott C. Lomax

Pen & Sword
MILITARY

First published in Great Britain in 2014 by
PEN AND SWORD MILITARY
an imprint of
Pen and Sword Books Ltd
47 Church Street
Barnsley
South Yorkshire S70 2AS

ISBN 978 1 78159 296 0

Printed and bound in England
by CPI Group (UK) Ltd, Croydon, CR0 4YY

Typeset in Times New Roman by
CHIC GRAPHICS

Pen & Sword Books Ltd incorporates the imprints of
Pen & Sword Books Ltd incorporates the imprints of Pen & Sword
Archaeology, Atlas, Aviation, Battleground, Discovery, Family
History, History, Maritime, Military, Naval, Politics, Railways, Select,
Social History, Transport, True Crime, and Claymore Press, Frontline
Books, Leo Cooper, Praetorian Press, Remember When, Seaforth
Publishing and Wharncliffe.

For a complete list of Pen and Sword titles please contact
Pen and Sword Books Limited
47 Church Street, Barnsley, South Yorkshire, S70 2AS, England
E-mail: enquiries@pen-and-sword.co.uk
Website: www.pen-and-sword.co.uk

Contents

Acknowledgements

This book is the culmination of a vast amount of original research. Without the assistance of the following people this research would have been less thorough; the staff at Sheffield Local Studies Library, Sheffield Archives, Keith Howard (the Club historian for Sheffield Wednesday Football Club), and Don Alexander and Lesley Cowley who responded to a request for information I made in the local media. For their kindness in providing photographs and information about the City Battalion I am most grateful to Andrew Jackson, Jill Rowlands and Donald Wiltshire.

I would also like to thank Lisa Hooson and the staff at Pen and Sword Books for publishing this detailed account of one of the most important periods of Sheffield's 20th century history. Finally, thank you to my wife for her support and assistance, especially with proofreading.

The following sources have been invaluable in my research:

Binfield et al, 1993. *History of the City of Sheffield 1843-1993 Volume II: Society* Sheffield, Sheffield Academic Press Ltd.

Chapman, A. W., 1955. *The Story of a Modern University: A History of the University of Sheffield*, Oxford: Oxford University Press.

Dalton, S., 2004. *Sheffield Armourer to the British Empire*, Barnsley, Wharncliffe Books

Gibson, R. and Oldfield, P., 2006. *Sheffield City Battalion: The 12th (Service) Battalion York and Lancaster Regiment: A history of the battalion raised by Sheffield in World War One*, Barnsley, Pen & Sword Books Ltd.

Keeble Hawson, H., 1968. *Sheffield The Growth of a City 1893-1926*, Sheffield, J. W. Northend Ltd.

Lloyd George, D., 1938. *War Memoirs of David Lloyd George*, London, Odhams Press Ltd.

Norton History Group, 1995. *Norton in Wartime: An account of life during wartime in a village on the southern boundary of Sheffield*, Sheffield, Norton History Group.

Sparley, R. A., 1920. *History of the 12th Service Battalion York and Lancaster Regiment*, Sheffield, J. W. Northend Ltd.

Sheffield City Council minute books for the period 1914-1919, available at Sheffield Local Studies Library.

Sheffield Year Book for the period 1914-1919, available at Sheffield Local Studies Library.

Tweedle, G., 1995. *Steel City: Entrepreneurship, Strategy, and Technology in Sheffield*, Oxford, Oxford University Press.

The Yorkshire Telegraph and *Star* (referred to here as the Telegraph and Star)

The Sheffield Daily Telegraph (referred to as the Telegraph)

A wide range of original documents have been consulted, including private letters from the battlefields to loved ones back home, letters from Sheffield residents relating to events in the city, postcards, business documents and police letters and memorandums. These were viewed at Sheffield Archives and where referred to the Archive reference is provided.

Introduction

Much has been written about the First World War and the involvement of the people of Sheffield on the front line. The efforts of those who returned home during or following the hostilities and those who made the ultimate sacrifice, dying on foreign soil having fought for King and country, whilst not always fully appreciated, have been written about previously. A great deal has been written about the Home Front of the Second World War. However, very little has been written about the experiences of people living in Sheffield in the immediate run up to, during, and immediately following, the First World War. General information regarding this period has featured in books about Sheffield's history but until now there has been no book dedicated to this important period of Sheffield's past.

It is apt that as we mark the centenary of the outbreak of the war, whilst paying our respects to those who were killed serving our country, we recognise also the impact that the war had on those at home and the civilian efforts which made victory possible.

Of course, it is necessary to include information about those brave men who hailed from Sheffield and found themselves on the battlefields or on the seas. However, this will largely be confined to the recruitment process, ending when the men left the city, although some information about their conditions, morale and, occasionally deaths, is provided in a bid to show the impact on those who remained in Sheffield.

The book *The Home Front in World War One: When Sheffield Went to War* provides detailed information to form the first definitive account of the experiences of Sheffield's citizens during the Great War. It details: the run up to war and Sheffield's reaction to its outbreak; the war fever which led to thousands of Sheffield's men answering their country's call; the efforts of those who could not fight; Sheffield industry and how Sheffield workers were instrumental in creating the weapons and tools that helped Britain win the war; Sheffield's role in treating and entertaining wounded soldiers; the role of the University of Sheffield and the effect of the war on education; the role of women in the munitions factories, working on the trams and in producing goods for the troops; the defence of the city; a Zeppelin raid over Sheffield which killed, maimed, destroyed and created fear in the minds of those in the city. For the first time in its history, Sheffield realised that the horrors of war were not confined to overseas battles but that they could be witnessed and experienced in their own neighbourhoods; Belgian refugees and how they were treated by citizens of their adopted city; conscientious objectors; prisoners of war held in the city; food shortages and the use of rationing; the Armistice and peace celebrations; and the influenza epidemic which killed thousands of people in Sheffield as the war came to an end; and the social and economic legacy of the war, which helped mould the city what it is today.

All of these themes are discussed at length in the following chapters. Above all this book details the human experiences, thoughts, concerns, fears and hopes of Sheffield during one of the most important periods in the city's history.

CHAPTER 1

Sheffield in 1914

Prior to the outbreak of war Sheffield was, as it is today, a major city with a large population. In 1911 there were 454,632 inhabitants according to the Census of that year. It was estimated that by 1914 the population was 476,971, with the city covering an area of 24,886 acres. Having been granted city status only 21 years before the first shots of the war were fired, it was a young city but one which was rapidly growing as industry and technology developed, requiring improved infrastructure and an increased workforce. There were 107,742 houses within the city boundary, of which around 92 per cent were rented.

Sheffield was a conservative city, politically and, as in most places during the early 20th century, in its views. In June 1914 the *Telegraph and Star* ran a disparaging article about the 'youth of today' with their 'vanishing manners', pursuit of money with little or no regard for anything else, and general attitudes. In July 1914 Baden Powell attended the Sheffield Scout Rally and announced to the crowd his belief that the Scout movement would help resolve the problem of hooliganism.

Women had no rights to vote, and with only a small number of exceptions could not work. Although the Sheffield Corporation overtly attempted to assist the poor, in reality little was done to improve the lives of those living in the slum areas of the city, as will become apparent

Sheffield had a Conservative Party led council, with 32 Tory councillors, 30 Liberals and two Socialists having been elected in the 1913 election. The Conservative Party had gained a majority only by the Lord Mayor's casting vote. There were no elections during the war, with the seats of retiring councillors being filled by someone of the same party; in most cases the councillors continued to serve but some members had to be co-opted.

The health of the city, especially the poor, was in a serious state. The death rate in Sheffield was 16.3 per thousand and the birth rate 27.3 per thousand. Those aged under five were particularly prone to an early death, with six percent of those aged between one and five dying in 1912 and 12.7 per cent dying under the age of one between 1910 and 1914, though due to investment in child welfare throughout the war this figure began to slightly fall.

In May 1914 according to the City Hospitals Committee there were 165 admissions to the City Hospitals for scarlet fever of which eight people died, 55 admissions for diphtheria of which there was one death, an admission for scarlet fever and whooping cough with that patient dying and eight deaths for phthisis. During that month 781 cases of consumption received treatment. With such a large number of contagious diseases the death rate for May 1914 was slightly above the average.

In a one week period at the close of June and the beginning of July two died of diphtheria, 46 died of measles and 52 died of tuberculosis. During July 71 infants under the age of two died of diarrhoea and enteritis

The health issues affecting predominantly the poorest sector of the city were in no small part due to the conditions in which they lived. In June 1914 many properties on several of Sheffield's streets were deemed, by the Medical Officer of Health, as being 'in a condition so dangerous or injurious to health as to be unfit for human habitation'. It was stated they should cease to be occupied unless significant improvements could be made. The streets included Hoyle Street, Waller Street, Bright Street, Matthew Street, Burnt Tree Lane, Leadmill Road, Bernard Street, Shepherd Street, Ellis Street, Newhall Road, Crookesmoor Road and Radford Street. Excessive damp, structural problems, poor lighting and a lack of ventilation were the chief concerns of the Medical Officer of Health.

Although published in 1937, and researched and written in the immediate years previously, an account by George Orwell who visited slum housing in Sheffield, gives an insight into the size and conditions of housing which formed a major proportion of the 92 per cent of rented homes in the city. In his book *The Road to Wigan Pier*, Orwell described a house on Thomas Street, which was 'Back to back, two up, one down (i.e. a three storey house with one room on each storey). Cellar below. Living-room 14ft. by 10ft., and rooms above corresponding. Sink in living-room. Top floor has no door but gives on open stairs. Walls in living-room slightly damp, walls in top room coming to pieces and oozing damp on all sides. House is so dark that light has to be kept burning all day...Six in family, parents and four children...'

The size would be typical of those in which Sheffield's poor lived in the run up to, and during, the First World War. The conditions in 1914 would have been little different to when Orwell visited two decades later.

In 1913 15 per cent of all houses in the city were of the 'back to back' type (accounting to approximately 16,000 houses) with a common yard system. In such conditions disease could spread easily. More than 20 per cent of the city's houses had privy middens and a further 20 per cent had ash pits for refuse.

At the July 1914 council meeting Councillor Barton spoke of the housing conditions and in particular the 'scarcity of houses in the city suitable for working-class occupiers and the failure of private enterprise to supply them'. He requested that an assessment should be made of how many new houses could be built on corporation land and whether land could be acquired in the suburbs to build 2,000 new homes in the immediate future.

Meanwhile, as thousands lived in overcrowded slums, the council approved further money being spent on the extension of the Town Hall which had by then cost £11,553 more than originally thought. The work cost £54,389 and the extension did not allow any additional staff to work in the building but reduced overcrowding in the offices. There were plans for new baths and modernisation of the sewers but once war was declared these spending plans were shelved. Needless to say the work on the Town Hall continued.

In addition to poor quality housing that impinged human health, the water supplies were a major source of ill health. By the summer of 1914 a clean water supply covered an area of 134 square miles, serving 491,808 people in Sheffield and the surrounding districts. However, there were many homes which were not supplied.

In addition to improved access to clean water, efforts were made to increase electricity so that more businesses could benefit from the relatively new source of power. In June 1914 20 applications were approved for extensions to the electricity supply and the number of telegraph lines was also increased.

Industry was always causing health problems. Some industrial chimneys, the Health Committee noted, were producing 'excessive emissions of black smoke' in 'such quantities as to be a nuisance or injurious to health'. Sheffield's steel industry, chiefly focussing on cutlery manufacturing, was already well established, with approximately 98 per cent of all of British manufactured cutlery being produced in Sheffield. Eighteen companies were prosecuted for excessive emissions but it was becoming increasingly realised that domestic chimneys were also contributing to a deteriorating environment, though no action was intended to be taken about this. Apparatus had been erected in Attercliffe Burial Ground, Hillsborough Park, Meersbrook Park and Weston Park, to assess air pollution across the city. In July there was 27.53 metric tons per square kilometre at Attercliffe, 6.92 metric tons per square kilometre at Hillsborough Park, 7.36 metric tons per square kilometre at Meersbrook Park and 9.63 metric tons per square kilometre at Weston Park, giving an average across the city of 12.86 metric tons per square kilometre of pollutants, which was higher than in London, Hull and Manchester.

It was estimated that 25 per cent of the sunshine was cut off by smoke in certain areas of the city.

Many streets, such as Dane Street, Blaco Road, Thurley Place, Twelve O'Clock Street, Martin Street and Alfred Road, were recorded as being in an 'unsatisfactory condition so as to be a nuisance and injurious to health', due to excessive litter, filth, waste from damaged sewers and human effluence where there was a lack of sewerage, and blocked or absent drains resulting in pools of stagnating water, with large areas infested with vermin. By July more drains were determined to be defective on Middlewood Road, Granville Lane, Granville Street, Park Hill Lane, Parkwood Road and South Street.

A byelaw was passed, to come into force on 1 December, prohibiting anyone from spitting on the street, with those found guilty of breaching the law being fined a maximum of 40 shillings. The law was due to end on 1 December 1916.

Today Sheffield has a reputation for the state of its roads, with it having been called 'pot hole city' in the local press. It may surprise readers to learn that in 1914 most roads in the city were paved in granite and even wood. Consequently they were often too muddy to travel along following rain and in the summer they were covered in thick dust.

The authorities believed that in terms of traffic control Sheffield was an example to others. The Chief Constable announced in April that Sheffield could be considered a pioneer in its methods of street traffic control.

Although slum areas covered large portions of the city, including Attercliffe, Burngreave, Pitsmoor and Hillsborough, in 1914 there were green open spaces that could be enjoyed if time could be found in between the long working hours and the chores of domestic life. There were 177 acres of recreation grounds as well as parks, 16 bowling greens, 11 grass and six gravel tennis courts and a nine-hole golf course in Abbey Lane, which later became used for allotments. In 1914 a second golf course was opened at Tinsley Park Wood.

CHAPTER 2

The Run Up to War

The mercury in thermometers showed high temperatures during June 1914, with what was described as 'tropical weather' by some and a 'heatwave' by the majority. The temperatures were so high that it was considered by reporters writing in the Sheffield newspapers 'too hot for certain occupations'. A reporter in the *Telegraph and Star* referred to June as 'flaming June' and there had been articles in that same newspaper advising mothers how best to protect their babies from the extreme heat.

This heatwave was not only affecting Sheffield, or Yorkshire, and not even just Britain. Large areas of Europe were suffering. Readers of the *Telegraph and Star* learnt that an Italian man by the name of Louis Costaz, who was living in Paris, had been so affected by the heat that he had, allegedly, turned mad and had threatened his neighbours with a revolver. He had then barricaded himself in his apartment and when the police arrived and attempted to shoot him, Costaz shot himself in the head.

This act of seeming insanity was pale in comparison to another incident that had happened just days earlier. The world was to become focussed on another shooting, this time more than 1,100 miles away from Sheffield, in the city of Sarajevo in Bosnia Herzegovina.

On 28 June 1914 the heir to the throne of Austria-Hungary, Archduke Franz Ferdinand, and his wife Sophie were inspecting the army in Sarajevo. A group of seven young Bosnian Serbs, members of an organisation known as the Black Hand had planned to assassinate the Archduke as he drove along the Appel Quay; the main road in the city. One of the men threw a bomb at the car but it missed the vehicle and that man was arrested. The visit was then abandoned, with the intention that the Archduke would return home, but the driver of the car was unaware of that plan and so the journey continued along a route that had been well publicised. It was when the car turned into Franz Josef Street that the Archduke met his killer. There stood Gavrilo Princip, gun in hand. Princip pulled the trigger and the bullet hit the heir in the neck, rupturing his jugular. A short struggle followed during which Sophie was shot and killed. Within a short period of time the Archduke had bled to death.

The following day the *Telegraph and Star* reported on the tragic incident:

> 'A great Prince and his noble wife have been swept out of life in a gust of criminal passion as meaningless as any act of lunacy can be, yet we can in no wise absolve the murderer...the personal element of the crime stands out more saliently than the political meaning and issue, though the latter may ultimately be of more intrinsic importance to the world.'

Upon hearing the news, according to the newspaper, Kaiser Wilhelm of Germany had exclaimed 'Mein Gott, Mein Gott'. Undoubtedly few of Sheffield's populace would have shared the Kaiser's concern, although they would have felt some degree of horror, but none would have predicted what was to follow and the speed at which events would unfold.

On 30 June Sheffield folk read in the same paper that two hundred Servians had been slain in revenge for the Archduke's assassination, creating what was to be described as a 'veritable sea of blood'. The city of Sarajevo was a 'town in flames'. Anti Servian demonstrations were also held throughout the country.

'Just how far this Servian danger penetrates Bosnia it is impossible to tell, but it is feared that it will be difficult to stop the trouble. Now martial law has been proclaimed provisionally in order at least to make an end of bomb throwing and revolver shooting by reckless agitators,' wrote the editor, but still people in Sheffield could be forgiven for failing to realise any relevance it would have to their own lives.

In Sheffield, and across much of Britain, there was a more pressing concern. On 1 July large parts of the country were hit by a huge storm. Sheffield was particularly affected, with many of its lower lying streets being flooded and several houses struck by lightning. The storm began at around 6pm and lasted into the early hours of the following morning. The Wicker was described as being like a great river, with the relatively small number of cars on the roads only being able to travel with considerable difficulty. In north Derbyshire a woman had been struck by lightning whilst holding a pair of scissors and in Warwickshire a tornado had caused tremendous damage and took several people off their feet. In Sheffield, according to the local newspapers, a staggering one million tons of rain had fallen in the city in a period of just half an hour. The storm hit again the following day, with more heavy rainfall hitting the city over a period of eight hours. There had been hailstorms in nearby Mosborough.

A woman was killed in the storms in Weston-on-Trent. The inquest into her death found that death was 'from a visitation of God'. At a time when religion played more importance in society than at present many of those living in Sheffield could be forgiven for thinking that the storm was an act of God and the superstitious amongst them probably felt that it was on omen, a portent of things to come. Storm clouds had gathered in both a literal and metaphorical sense.

CHAPTER 3

The Outbreak of
War

Following the burial of the Archduke and his wife, the tragedy of Sarejevo was given little mention in the Sheffield newspapers and so the people of the steel city probably began to allow the awfulness of the crime to enter the backs of their minds. There was, during July 1914, the more pressing concern of troubles in Ireland, referred to as the 'Ulster Situation', which were based on the arguments of whether four or six Ulster counties should be excluded from Home Rule for six years. In March 1914 the Curragh Mutiny had taken place and there was general disloyalty among the British army in Ireland. The army could not be relied upon to impose Home Rule upon Ulster. Weapons were bought from Germany during April 1914 and that same month the Home Rule legislation was passed in the House of Commons, with it due to come into force in September 1914.

On 21 July King George V addressed a conference at Buckingham Palace to try and resolve the 'situation'. Interestingly alongside an article in the *Telegraph and Star* about the first day of the conference was an article about the swastika and how it had become a popular good luck charm. The conference ended on 24 July, with some suffragette demonstrations causing disruption, and it was quickly determined to have been a failure. Its dominance in discussions within the House of Commons and in the media is somewhat remarkable given that a far greater threat was growing in Europe.

Indeed it was only once the conference had ceased that there seemed to be concern that there was a situation in Europe of growing seriousness.

The first indication for many Sheffield people that a wider conflict overseas could occur was in the evening edition of the *Telegraph and Star* on 24 July when an article appeared under the headline 'NOTE TO SERVIA'. The article related to a letter from the Austria-Hungary authorities sent the previous day. The note had accused Servia of being responsible for propaganda against the Austria-Hungary system of Dual Monarchy and for being somehow responsible for the assassination of the Archduke and his wife, the crime having been planned in Belgrade and the weapons used having been obtained from Servian officers and officials, with the assassins having been given assistance in entering Bosnia by the chiefs of the Servian Frontier Service. The note demanded that Servia officials, under Austro-Hungarian supervision, arrest all of those on Servian soil who made the assassination possible. The German government was keen to make it clear that it had not been involved in the writing of this letter to Servia and that it would only involve itself if another power became involved in the conflict, in which case it would fulfil its obligations as an ally. The article added that Germany felt that the situation was extremely serious.

The following day the Sheffield newspapers revealed that war was becoming increasingly likely as the deadline for Servia to respond to the Austro-Hungarian note fast approached. Sheffielders read that, 'Unless Servia complies with the demands contained in the Austro-Hungarian Note by six o'clock tonight, war may break out at once, making easily possible a conflict of the Great Powers.' There was still hope that Servia would agree to the terms of the note as long as it did not offend the prestige of Servia. It was believed Russia would side with Servia and it was understood the Russian army was being mobilised. It was feared that this would lead to the involvement of Germany and France. Earl Grey told the House of Commons that the situation was 'extremely grave'.

Meanwhile in Ireland there was what the *Telegraph and Star* described as a 'disaster' which it acknowledged diverted attention away from the problems in Europe and brought the horrors of battle much closer to home. 'Blood has been shed, and it is difficult to see how the new state of things created by this disaster will work out,' the paper stated on 27 July. The belief was that the 'gunrunners' fired the first shots, with British troops retaliating, killing three civilians and injuring a further 38.

On the same day as the reports of bloodshed in Dublin there was an account of an attack by Servians against Austrians, which was an engagement considered by the *Telegraph and Star* to be of 'some importance', with great efforts being made by the Foreign Office in London and the officials of other European governments to avert what was looking to be increasingly inevitable. The reporter who wrote the article believed that 'although there is ominous prospect of a European blaze the outlook may be said not to be without hope'. Servian troops had fired shots against Austro-Hungarian soldiers. Servian troops had also blown up a bridge over the River Danube. It was hoped, however, that Russia's intervention in a diplomatic rather than military manner could avert catastrophe. Yet it is most probable that the majority of Sheffield people were more concerned with the events in Ireland than in a country overseas that few would have heard of.

All hope failed, however, and the following day Austria declared war on Servia, having received only an unsatisfactory response to their demands.

Inevitably, as in all wars and other conflicts, there were many people who believed that Britain should not intervene in a situation involving countries where the vast majority of British people had never been to and in all likelihood had not even heard of. A letter from an anonymous correspondent to the *Telegraph and Star*, who referred to themselves as PAX (Latin for peace), probably summed up the thoughts of many people living in Sheffield. The letter, printed on 29 July, stated:

'Sir, - I notice in some papers it is assumed that if war breaks out further on the Continent we shall be involved in it. I hope not.

This is no affair of ours, and if Russia takes any action that will involve her and France in war with the Triple Alliance, I maintain that we ought to stand aloof. Of course if we have a binding agreement we must fulfil it, but I cannot find that we have.

No doubt we should be bound to join if there were any aggressive action taken against France or Russia, but that does not seem possible in the present circumstances. Austria has a perfect right to protect herself against the stings of the Servian nest of hornets, and there seems to be only one way of doing it, but I hope we shall not go to war on that account. Yours, etc., PAX.'

On the same day as the letter from 'PAX' Austrians living in Sheffield were advised that they were likely to be requested to return to Austria to serve their country. It was estimated that there were approximately 12,000 Austrian reservists living in England in July 1914 but Mr PR Kuehnrich, the acting Consul for Austria in Sheffield, did not know how many were residing in Sheffield. He could only say, 'There are some here.' He added that some men failed to register themselves after leaving Austria and so it could not be estimated how many were in the city. An amnesty took place for any man who had previously deserted his military duties provided they voluntarily returned to Austria without delay. There was at this point no request for French or German residents in England to return to their own countries but German men living in Sheffield were advised to immediately return to Germany if that country entered the war.

Meanwhile troops in Russia had partially mobilised as the Czar prepared for war. Mr Asquith, the Prime Minister, told the House of Commons that the situation was one of extreme gravity and all efforts were being made to prevent the war spreading.

There was an immediate consequence in Sheffield to the news that war had begun in Europe. Food prices began to rise, especially in the case of sugar and flour. Sugar supplies were low because the new sugar crops were not due for another month or so, and there had been no need to buy large quantities. However, given that sugar supplies came largely from Germany and Austria, with France and Russia also being large suppliers, the increasing hostilities were having an impact. As for flour, supplies were short prior to the threat of war and the situation was made worse because Russia and Austria were the key suppliers to Britain. With no surplus existing because of the poor state of the crop, supplies were immediately short and so prices had to rise. There were concerns that the price of butter would rise, because Russia was a key supplier. With the exception of flour and sugar, however, the people of Sheffield were not too badly affected at this early stage. A leading member of a Sheffield provision and grocery company told the *Telegraph and Star*, 'At present the position is not alarming so far as the ordinary consumer is concerned.' Sheffield millers had a meeting to establish what they could do to keep flour costs from escalating. A 'gentleman qualified to speak' told the *Telegraph and Star* that the public should not be concerned. 'The public should not get excited and make a "run" on their grocers and provision dealers,' he said, 'If trade goes on normally all will be well, but if everybody rushes in to buy up quantities of goods, the stocks of the retailer will be depleted and by force of competition he will have to charge more.'

However, Sheffield people still would not have expected the situation in Europe to affect them in any other way than in the supply of some foods. Many were too concerned with their own lives and circumstances to be interested in growing tensions and violence hundreds of miles away.

On 30 July the *Telegraph and Star* summed up the views of those who were taking an interest in the European situation and the concern of the Prime Minister that the situation was 'grave'. The paper stated:

'News concerning the crisis continues to justify Mr Asquith's choice of words, and the situation remains extremely grave, though as we write it is not yet necessary to abandon hope that the war will be confined within a limited area.'

The partial mobilisation of Russian forces was described as being 'a highly dangerous move' because this would lead to a German mobilisation. 'The position is of such extraordinary delicacy that the slightest thing may upset the balance of affairs, and plunge Europe into the greatest war of all time,' it was said, although readers were encouraged to keep 'steady heads'.

In a prediction that would be proven to be very wrong, the editor continued, 'We cannot think that Europe will consent to be dragged into war on such a flimsy pretext as the defence of Servia from the just consequence of her actions...No one wants war, except the heedless crowds who clamour for it on the slightest pretext...'

The mention of the word war, and the hint that Britain could become involved, despite the attempts to reassure the public, led to escalating worries. Fearing a crisis, people began to panic buy provisions, reducing the stock of shops and driving prices up. On 30 July flour, sugar and bacon prices rose dramatically. Butter was described as being 'dearer than it has been at this time of the year for twelve or fourteen years' though this was not entirely due to the war; there being a 'natural scarcity'. The war was said to be having a 'serious effect' on the prices of various commodities, the newspapers reported. The wholesale price had risen 2s per sack of flour for each day since the first hint of the potential for a wider European crisis. It

This photograph is believed to show queuing for provisions at the beginning of World War I, 189-193 Crookes. No. 189 was Mrs Esther Ward, No. 191 was Sarah Ann Morton, and 193 was Imperial Meat Company. (*Photograph reproduced from the Picture Sheffield Collection, courtesy of Sheffield Local Studies Library*)

was anticipated that the price of sugar would rise again and that 'supplies will be exceedingly difficult to get'.

Still, there were hopes that a European conflict could be entirely averted. 'FINAL EFFORTS FOR PEACE – Hopes of Averting a European War', was the headline of the *Telegraph and Star* on 31 July. 'The international situation continues extremely delicate today. Peace and war tremble in the balance, and the scale may turn at any moment,' the paper stated. However, readers were given hope with Russia and Austria having resumed talks. The London and provincial stock exchanges, including the one in Sheffield, were closed until further notice due to the uncertainty of war and the effect on the financial markets. The public were becoming ever more alarmed at food prices, though the grocers and other shopkeepers in Sheffield were reported not to have 'the panicky feeling'. The public were advised 'Don't be panicky' because it was hoped the crisis 'will quickly pass'.

As August began an increasing number of people in Sheffield were beginning to recognise the impact of what was happening overseas. The editorial in the *Telegraph and Star* on 1 August explained that events were moving 'darkly' and tried to stop its readers from jumping to assumptions that war was now inevitable. 'News must be taken as it comes and judged on its merits, and we are doing our best to do this, without on the one hand pandering to panic, or on the other undervaluing the importance of the news,' it said. The situation was described as 'terrible' and its significance was 'only just beginning to dawn on the average man'. The feelings of Sheffield people were described, with that average man, according to the newspaper, 'We believe that he regards war with no favour, but he has not yet grasped what it may mean to this country, and indeed it is almost impossible for anyone to figure to themselves the possible consequences.'

On the likelihood of war, given that forces were mobilising in several countries in Europe, it was said that Europe was on the brink of war. 'It must become a matter of the extremest difficulty to prevent war, even if there is any further possibility of so doing. Thus, unless there is a contradiction of the news we are writing, we have arrived at the very brink of the precipice towards which we have been stumbling for days.'

All hopes were on talks between the countries and a German ultimatum to Russia and France which required a response that day.

Meanwhile two Royal Field Artillery Brigades from Leeds and Sheffield were carrying out tactical manoeuvre practice, involving the movement of heavy guns over sand hills. The King's Own Yorkshire Light Infantry were practicing in Whitby but were hampered by rain. Although this was part of their annual training there was an increased emphasis on the possibility that their services could be used in war.

As Europe moved closer to the 'brink of the precipice' food supplies were reduced further and prices continued to rise. Fruit had never been cheaper although traders were warned that they should place orders from overseas at their own risk in case the shipments could not arrive. 'The general public are taking things very calmly,' a head of a large Sheffield grocery firm told the *Telegraph and Star*, 'But there are a few people who are wanting to make ridiculous purchases.' Several customers were buying as much as they could physically carry in anticipation of supplies entirely running out and some were concerned of an invasion and were stockpiling.

On the evening of 2 August the Admiralty issued an order for the reserves of the fleet to be mobilised and the Sheffield Territorials were ordered to return to Headquarters, with all the training camps traditionally held annually during the summer period closed.

That same day the editorial of the *Telegraph and Star* explained why the orders had been issued, announcing what everyone had feared. 'WAR! Germany and Russia at war' ran the headline, though despite the outburst headline readers were told, 'It is necessary that we should keep our heads.' There would be plenty of food and so people should not panic, the article continued, as meat prices sharply increased in price. They should 'face the future with the high heart that has always characterised our Imperial race'.

Any doubts that Britain was to be brought into a war in Europe must now surely have fled the minds of those living in Sheffield who were keeping even only one eye on the latest developments.

On 4 August Germany invaded Belgium with the intention of passing quickly through that country into France, conquering France and then turning towards Russia, as part of its Von Schlieffen Plan.

Yorkshire Telegraph and Star 'First Shots in European War' (*Photograph reproduced from the Picture Sheffield Collection, courtesy of Sheffield Local Studies Library*)

Germany had not reckoned on the resistance of the Belgian forces, however, which were almost immediately supported by the British Expeditionary Force, with Britain declaring war on Germany that same day, declaring war on Austria eight days later. Later that day the Sheffield newspapers began to make it clear that they were to be the primary source of news about the war. With Sheffield newspapers receiving news through a private wire they were able to provide the latest news.

Ten Sheffield school trainee teachers on a study course were trapped in France, being prevented from leaving the country when the war began. They finally made it back to Britain on 16 August.

People in Sheffield and elsewhere in Yorkshire were warned that there would be dark times ahead, although no one could anticipate at that early stage of what horrors and hardship were to follow. The situation had never been experienced in history before and the technology available had never been used in a conflict on such a large scale, therefore there had to be a large amount of uncertainty. Readers 'must be prepared for a time of serious difficulty, and even of distress…Those who can offer personal service must do so, and the rest of us must be content to do our duty as we find it.'

The paper tried to reassure its readers that Britain would not be invaded by foreign forces but the following day when there were reports of a Naval battle in the North Sea just off the coast of Scarborough, Sheffield folk must have begun to wonder whether an invasion was on the cards. Concerns were also increased that same day when news arrived that two Sheffield soldiers had been lost at sea days earlier. Private JW Morton and Private JW Rhodes, who were both members of the 4th York and Lancaster Regiment, had sailed out in a boat as part of a training exercise and had not been seen since. Although it was not believed they had been captured or killed by enemy fire, with it being reported to have been an almost certain accident involving high waves, the news shocked Sheffield coming at such a time that there were growing fears about the loss of life. To hear that two of the city's sons had probably lost their lives suddenly brought what had been a conflict in another country far away, a war with local implications.

CHAPTER 4

Joining the Colours

On 5 August there were reports of further naval battles on the Thames and the North Sea and the fear of invasion spread. In order to try and prevent enemies encroaching upon Britain via the coast, and to allay fears, the Sheffield Artillery under the control of Colonel Clifford VD moved quickly to the coast near Grimsby. The Engineers under the control of Colonel Bingham went to East Yorkshire to carry out trenching and make entanglements to hinder invaders. Although many still questioned why Britain should be involved in the war, the threat of invasion was the spur for a feeling that Britain needed to fight for its survival.

It quickly became apparent that if Britain was to be fully engaged in the European War, as it was becoming known, there would need to be a massive increase in the number of troops available to the military. Sheffield University advertised for recruits for the Special Reserve of Officers and the Territorial Force. Anyone wishing to be recruited was advised to attend the Headquarters of the University Contingent, which was at the Department of Applied Sciences. From 8 August there were parades each day between 10am and noon at the university.

With thoughts of glorious battles involving chivalry and heroism, based on vivid imagery from childhood stories, there was a desire amongst a large proportion of young men to enter the war. There was tremendous enthusiasm among Sheffield folk to join the war. With there having been no major conflict in the lifetimes of most, there was an entire lack of knowledge of what war entailed. It was widely believed that hostilities would not last long and so they were keen to join from the outset before the war ended in order that they should be involved and it was this enthusiasm which became known as 'war fever'.

The Glossop Road baths had consisted of two swimming pools for men, one for women, a slipper bath, Turkish, Russian, electric and medicated baths. The men's first class bath could be transformed into a hall, as it was every winter. The building as a whole could also be transformed into a public hall. From 5 August this function of the baths came into being when the military took it over for mobilisation purposes.

An appeal was made for any man aged between 19 and 30, who was of good health and wanted to serve his King and country, to enlist. On 7 August it was announced by the Secretary of State for War, Lord

When war broke out Lord Kitchener announced that 100,000 men were needed to fight in the army. This figure continued to rise as the war intensified and men who were killed or wounded needed replacing. (*The Author's Collection*)

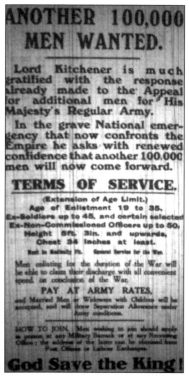

An advertisement made in the Sheffield newspapers appealing for more men to join the army. (*The Author's collection*)

Kitchener, that the country required 100,000 men and so anyone wanting to serve was urged to visit the Recruiting Office in their district for information. The Recruiting Office in Sheffield was at 10 St George's Terrace. The enrolment process involved filling in an enlistment form, passing a medical examination and taking an oath of allegiance. The medical examinations were held at various locations, including 315 Middlewood Road. At first an average 200 men presented themselves at the Recruiting Office each day, with men committing themselves for the duration of the war. Soon other recruiting offices opened in Attercliffe, Brightside, Heeley and East Parade.

Although the appeal was well responded to, there was a need for even more men and due to the enthusiasm shown by those men aged above 30 who had the relevant skills and experience, on 12 August it was announced that anyone aged between 19 and 42 could enlist for the duration of the war with anyone above the age of 30 who had been previously refused being encouraged to visit the Recruiting Office once again. Men aged up to 42 who were too old to serve in the regular forces were able to sign up for the Special Reserves.

Skilled men in certain trades were requested to enlist for a year. Trades which were particularly sought were bakers, blacksmiths, fitters, turners, motor-lorry drivers and tailors.

Sheffield motorcyclists responded well to an appeal by Colonel Bingham for volunteers to serve with the Sheffield Territorial Engineers. Between 20 and 30 men who owned motorcycles responded within a day of the appeal and were appointed. Dozens more men applied but the positions had already been filled.

The York and Lancaster Regiment and the King's Own Yorkshire Light Infantry were the two major regiments that men from Sheffield joined when they enlisted, with the 4th (Hallamshire) Battalion forming a territorial battalion, which also drew men from the city.

Other military units Sheffield men joined included the 1st, 2nd and 4th Troops, 'A' Squadron, the Queen's Own Yorkshire Dragoons (who camped at Market Weighton), the West Riding Divisional Royal Engineers, the 3rd West Riding Brigade Royal Field Artillery and the 3rd (West Riding) Field Ambulance.

The Field Ambulance was created in April 1908 and consisted of eight officers and 167 men at the outbreak of war. When war broke it was divided into groups, with some going to Aldershot for further training and the remainder being sent to Grimsby to help defend the East Coast from invasion. It later provided medical support in France, including at the Battle of the Somme.

Some Sheffield men who had joined the Army found their new home in Hillsborough Barracks. The Barracks had been built at a cost of approximately £100,000 and was located on land with Penistone Road to the north and Langsett Road to the south. The officers' quarters were at the south side where there was an imposing battlement in 'Tudor style' with an impressive gateway.

Norfolk Barracks on Edmund Road was the home of the Artillery. The Engineers had their headquarters at Glossop Road in what was later known as the Somme Barracks. The Hallamshires were based at Hyde Park in Sheffield. The Royal Army Medical Corps were housed at Brook House on Gell Street.

With war come casualties and it was quickly recognised that there was inadequate provision for the treatment of soldiers and sailors who were wounded or who were suffering from illness.

The wounded began to arrive in Sheffield on 2 September following the Battle of the Mons. The previous day Britain's first wounded had arrived but were transported to new university buildings in Birmingham. The long trains carrying the wounded would become a familiar sight to Sheffield, as they pulled into the Midland Railway Station.

When casualties were brought to the city by train they were transferred to one of a number of hospitals. Civilian hospitals were commandeered for military use, as were other none medical buildings.

A Special Committee decided on 10 August that Lodge Moor Hospital should allow 150 cases of enteric fever at the request of the military. The hospital was later used for the wider needs of the military. As a result tents had to be erected for civilians recovering from illnesses such as scarlet fever and diphtheria.

The Northern General Hospital was created to be a Base Hospital on the outbreak of war. It was first located at Brook House on Gell

Today the Hillsborough Barracks has been renovated, with a supermarket, fast food outlet, hotel and other establishments making use of the former military institution. (*The Author*)

The Royal Army Medical Corps were based at Brook House on Gell Street. (*The Author*)

Street but later occupied the Sheffield Teachers' Training College on Collegiate Crescent/Ecclesall Road.

In 1915 the Wharncliffe Hospital in Middlewood became a war hospital. It had originally been a lunatic asylum from its opening in 1872 until it was taken over by the military, opening as a War Hospital on 1 April 1915. Between that date and its closure in July 1920 37,000 wounded soldiers were treated.

Established as a children's hospital in 1916, the Sheffield Union Hospital, which was also known as Fir Vale Hospital, also provided medical treatment for more than 15,000 soldiers.

Towards the end of 1914 the hospital at Winter Street was also taken over by the military, resulting in temporary accommodation for civilian sufferers of diseases such as tuberculosis at Crimicar Lane. Those who were not as badly affected were sent home.

Believing that the war would be short-lived the corporation gave allowances to its staff who had joined the forces, in order to encourage them to play their part in active service. Their jobs were safeguarded so that they could resume work upon return and their families were given an allowance which at the height of hostilities cost the corporation £487,000 per year. The allowance covered half the wages for married couples and originally a quarter of the wages for unmarried couples, if the men had signed up before 31 December 1914. The allowance had increased in line with the Government's separation allowance with an additional grant being made in cases of acute hardship. Other large companies in Sheffield also promised to safeguard the jobs of anyone who signed up and provided half of their wages for the benefit of their families. Many companies also actively encouraged their staff to enlist, partly as a public relations exercise to show that the businesses were doing their part for the war.

Sheffield seemed determined to fill its quota of the 100,000 men needed nationally. So keen were Sheffield men that the recruitment stations failed to cope with the huge numbers of men who presented themselves each day. On 2 September the *Telegraph and Star* reported that, 'The daily experience in Sheffield seems to show that the five recruiting stations are not quite sufficient to deal adequately with the crowds of Sheffielders who are eager to enlist.'

Six hundred men had enlisted on 2 September but critics claimed there would have been 2,000 new recruits that day if the recruiting offices had been more adequately staffed.

A man signing himself as 'LOYALTY' wrote to the paper detailing the difficulties he had observed and experienced. He wrote in response to an appeal by Colonel Walker for more recruits. 'If Colonel Walker, instead of appealing for recruits, would use his influence in expediting the enlistment of men who are daily presenting themselves outside the recruiting offices only to be turned away after waiting eight or nine hours without food, and never had a ghost of a chance of getting inside to see the recruiting officer, he would be helping Lord Kitchener far better than he is at present doing.' He related a story of a man who had visited St George's Terrace Recruiting Office and had waited outside from 8:30am until 5pm but was not seen. 'He says he shan't go any more.'

Others recounted similar tales. RD of Heeley, informed readers, in a letter that is worthy of reproducing at length, that:

'One cannot walk twenty yards without being informed by various strikingly worded announcements that "Your King and country need you", "Men are urgently required for His Majesty's Army", "You should fight for civilisation", etc, and in spite of the croakings of many blatant, but certainly strangely inactive "patriots" the youths of Sheffield have given ear to the call, and sacrificing to an extent much greater than most people realise, have attempted to respond actively to the slogan.

The word "attempted" is necessary, in face of the following facts: On Tuesday morning at 9:30 several athletic, respectable and willing youths, eager to carry out all which the posters call on us to perform, took up their stand outside the Heeley Recruiting Office, behind a number of similarly inclined young fellows who had already arrived.

As a first reward for their offer of all they possessed, viz themselves, they were allowed to stand in the roadway a trifle of about 3½ hours, during which time the staff managed to attend to about half a dozen cases. Then, as patriotism did not offer much consolation to the inner man, our party retired for lunch, and returned to find the queue had not moved in the least. What a monument to the system of the "office".

However, wishing to see the matter to the bitter end, they endured a further wait of about four hours, during which period the number of men actually enrolled would not exceed a dozen, and finally gave it up as a bad job, having stood for 7½ hours without getting near the office door. Needless to say it demands a patriotism really monumental to submit to such treatment as this.

The aforementioned is not an isolated case, as witness the fact that several men lost a day's wage and endured about ten hours of alternate sickening waits and rushes for the office door at one of the central recruiting stations, without being attended to.

Treatment like this can have only one effect upon these enthusiastic and self-denying young fellows, as nothing can damp enthusiasm so effectually as the "ennui" and "fedupness" which is resulting from such lack of system.

If "Britain wants men", let her take steps that these brave youths who volunteer may at least given what Britons so cherish, namely, a sporting chance.'

That same day a letter by R Storry Deans (also of Heeley and one suspects this was RD writing two letters to emphasise his argument) stated:

'May I suggest that instead of keeping the volunteers for the Expeditionary Force standing outside, they should be invited inside, to wait until they can be examined. Some men I know have stood outside for two and three days. Heeley men, at the Heeley recruiting office, might easily be accommodated inside.

I spoke to them to-day, and many of them were exceedingly weary of the long wait, which is most depressing to lads of active habits.'

To try and alleviate this problem large firms held recruitment meetings on their premises, with medical officers, magistrates and recruiting officers present 'so that men wishing to join Lord Kitchener's army will be able to enlist straightaway, and will thus be saved the inconvenience and annoyance which are being experienced by many who have applied to the Recruiting Depots...'

At William Hutton and Sons Ltd on West Street, Herbert Hutton spoke of the causes of the war and the importance of a formidable number of troops. He asked for volunteers to follow the example set by their 17 colleagues who had already enlisted. The result was that 80 men volunteered themselves, of whom 24 were married, most for the full duration of the war. A request was made that they should all serve in the same regiment so that they could face the enemy in friendly company.

On 3 September 370 enlisted during a meeting at Messrs Mappin and Webb's works, with 90 of the new recruits of that firm, with the remainder from other firms who had attended the meeting. Mr G Locker Lampson MP and other notaries had addressed the crowd. The high number was obtained in just four hours. They, like all others who followed the call, were given an enthusiastic send off.

To meet the unwavering demand eventually other offices opened across the city, including 'The Jungle' (a disused ice rink on Hawley Street) on 4 September and the Corn Exchange. The use of The Jungle and the Corn Exchange, according to press reports, 'proved excellent, the recruiting officials being able to deal with the men as they presented themselves for enlistment without the least delay'. Soon almost one thousand new recruits were obtained on a daily basis. Meersbrook Vestry Hall was later offered and proved to be much more suitable than the other offices which had been used. The original offices at St George's Terrace, Attercliffe, Brightside, Heeley and East Parade continued in their use. Extra doctors were called upon to speed up the medical examinations.

Men on government orders in the factories were advised not to enlist, for example those producing shells and other munitions, weapons and tools which were needed by the troops. Those who could not sign up for this reason still wanted to do more for their country. At the Darnell Works a meeting was held during a lunch hour to establish how they could help, with a further meeting to resolve how much of their wages they should give to the war fund. Sheffield's other firms carried out similar meetings, agreeing to form subscriptions to raise funds for the military.

Meanwhile despite the increased number of Recruiting Offices and the relaxation of the rules affecting the age of the men who could join the forces, there was still a need for more soldiers and sailors.

On 8 September Lord Charles Beresford MP, Admiral, addressed a crowd of 10,000 at the Artillery Drill Hall at the Norfolk Barracks, urging them to join. The speech resulted in 150 new recruits.

The local newspapers continued to appeal for people to enlist. However, the feelings of those who did not want to join soon became apparent. One correspondent to the *Telegraph and Star* on 2 September believed that if men were to join the army they should be better looked after:

'It is high time that the British people awoke to the fact that the call for men to fight for the country should be backed by willingness on the part of the country to pay them well. At the moment we are appealing to the patriotic sentiment of all classes to join the King's Army in one or other of its branches, and to risk life and limb, to say nothing of hardship and discomfort; and in addition to these we are asking many of them to sacrifice things dearer than life. We offer our heroes our blessing and wages contemptibly small. This willingness to fight is hampered by concern for wives, children and other dependents. These things ought not to be.'

He added that men should not be penalised for joining the armed forces, with a reduction in pay for those whose employers did not wish to provide an allowance and often with families to support. 'We could not offer every man the wages he is getting now, but we might at least offer him a living wage, and security for his future in case he is disabled.' He finished by saying that if men were well paid they would be able to be in good health and better spirits so that the war would be brought to an end sooner. 'Let recruiting be placed on a business footing. Offer men decent pay and the prospect of adequate pensions if disabled, and amend the arrangements for enrolling them, and there will be no difficulty in getting them,' he wrote.

On 10 September 1914 what was commonly known as the Sheffield City Battalion was officially established. Its original name was the Sheffield University and City Special Battalion of the York and Lancaster Regiment, but it soon became formally known as The Sheffield City 12th (Service) Battalion of the York and Lancaster Regiment.

It had been founded at the instigation of Herbert Albert Laurens Fisher, who had become Vice Chancellor of the University of Sheffield only two months earlier, and who was proving to be a key part of Sheffield's war effort. The idea had first been conceived by two students of the university and had been taken up by Fisher for further consideration. The Battalion was established with the support of the Lord Mayor, the Chancellor of the University the Duke of Norfolk and Dr George Franklin, Senior Pro-Chancellor, who presented themselves to the War

The Vice-Chancellor of the University of Sheffield who was a driving force in the creation of the City Battalion, gave lectures about the importance of the war before becoming the MP for Sheffield Hallam and an important figure in Lloyd George's wartime coalition Government. *(The Author's Collection)*

Office to request permission for the establishment of the Battalion. Its intention was to provide a battalion comprising men from the 'professional classes' and it was students and staff from the university who were particularly sought. It was hoped that a battalion would be similar to those in Liverpool, Manchester and Birmingham, which were known as Pals Battalions which worked on the principle that men of similar social standing, who hailed from the same city, would be able to work better together and have a higher level of morale. It was anticipated that some of the men would be friends or colleagues and would therefore be happier.

The formation of the Battalion was first announced by Fisher at the end of one of his war lectures at the Victoria Hall. He told the assembled crowd that formal approval was expected within days but that in the meantime names could be taken for those interested in joining the following afternoon.

The Battalion began taking names at the Town Hall of those who would like to enlist a week before the Battalion was given the official authority from the War Office to come into being. Although one thousand men were needed for the Battalion to be formally recognised, 1,500 forms were produced in the hope that there would be the full complement of men in one battalion and the makings of a second. A room in the Lord Mayor's parlour was set aside for the enrolments. A high calibre of men presented themselves according to the press, with university students and professional men consisting of almost every profession in the city. According to Richard Sparley, in his 1920 history of the Battalion, the recruits consisted of '£500 a year business men, stockbrokers, engineers, chemists, metallurgical experts, university and public school men, medical students, journalists, schoolmasters, craftsmen, shop assistants, secretaries, and all sorts of clerks'. In just an hour and a half more than 200 names had been recorded, with the intention of calling upon them when the Battalion was given the green light to begin enrolment. By 3 September the number of names reached almost 500. By the end of 7 September 1,303 men had given their names.

Once the approval had been received on 10 September the official recruitment, including the medical examinations, commenced at the Corn Exchange. A 'great rush of applicants' arrived eager to sign up having seen banners and signs reading 'To Berlin – Via Corn Exchange'. Recruiting took place in that building between 8am and 8pm each day, with 600 men passing through the process on the first day.

By 11 September 900 men had fully signed up to be part of the Battalion and within a week of the call to arms 1,500 men had made themselves available, though not all passed their medicals. Those who joined up received 1s 6d.

Although more than the thousand men had signed up, the War Office announced it would not allow a second battalion to be formed.

Training commenced on 15 September at the home of Sheffield

12/505 Ernest Scholey, of the City Battalion. (*Photographs by kind permission of Ernest's granddaughter, Jill Rowlands*)

Officers of the City Battalion. (*Photograph by kind permission of Donald Wiltshire*)

Officers and non-commissioned officers in the City Battalion. In the centre are Colonel Mainwaring (in command) and Major Clough (second in command). (*Photograph reproduced from the Picture Sheffield Collection, courtesy of Sheffield Local Studies Library*)

United Football Club on Bramall Lane under the charge of Colonel Hughes, the Acting Colonel of the Battalion, although eventually new land was sought because the club was displeased with the effect of the training on the state of the grass. They took the Artillery Drill Hall, Norfolk Barracks as their base. Due to a shortage of space they originally lived in their own homes and received wages of three shillings per day. Those who came from outside Sheffield were put up by residents keen to help, and were generally not charged.

Sir William Clegg, Leader of the Council, issued a tram call urging people to 'Enlist, work, or pay! Do something'. He was a member of a committee set up to oversee the City Battalion and like many prominent members of Sheffield society he wanted to emphasise his patriotism.

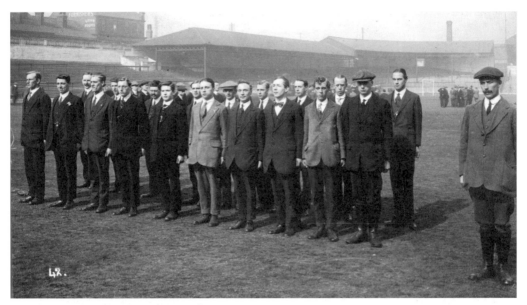

Men being recruited for the war. (*Photograph reproduced from the Picture Sheffield Collection, courtesy of Sheffield Local Studies Library*)

Members of the City Battalion at a learning drill at Bramall Lane. Nearest the camera on the front is 12/1007 Thomas A. W. Newsholme; second and third form the right on the third row are 12/946 J. Hastings and J. F. Wells; farthest right is 12/1163 William Wyatt Bagshawe. (*Photograph by kind permission of Donald Wiltshire*)

Members of the City Battalion during a learning drill at Bramall Lane. 12/505 Ernest Scholey is believed to be the fourth from the right on the front row. (*Photograph by kind permission of Ernest's granddaughter, Jill Rowlands*)

City Battalion drilling at Bramall Lane. (*Photograph reproduced from the Picture Sheffield Collection, courtesy of Sheffield Local Studies Library*)

Sheffield City Battalion recruits at Bramall Lane football ground. (*Photograph reproduced from the Picture Sheffield Collection, courtesy of Sheffield Local Studies Library*)

In addition to politicians, some religious men tried to do their bit from the outset. Five hundred men of the National Reserve were addressed by the Archdeacon Gresford Jones at Sheffield Cathedral on 16 August 1914.

Between August and 30 September 10,719 Sheffield men joined the armed forces. Due to the need for even more men, the rules were relaxed to allow some of those who had failed medicals to once again try and enlist. 'Every man organically bound will be accepted. Red tape is being burnt' Sheffield people were told. Now any man in even reasonable health who was aged between 19 and 38 and was 5'3" in height or taller was eligible.

Those who were unfit could not join. However, there was anger amongst many Sheffield men who wanted to do their bit for their country but were prevented from doing so. One such man wrote to the *Telegraph and Star* in early September 1914 informing their readers that he was 40 years old but had served in the army as an NCO in the artillery. Despite his age he claimed he could swim a mile as easily as someone could walk that distance, he regularly walked 25 miles and cycled between fifty and one hundred miles each day. He was, he said, 'fairly well known in athletic circles' but apparently the doctor undertaking the medical examinations had declared him unfit, which the former soldier attributed solely to his age. He was frustrated that the authorities were turning away perfectly fit and healthy men when they were happily enlisting younger men who were not as fit and lacked military experience.

Those who were too unhealthy to join the forces were often unfairly considered to be shirkers even if they were desperate to sign up. A man of Broomhill, signing himself WCJ, argued there was 'much unfair and extravagant vilification of those unable to serve due to ill health or age'. Some people were sacked if they could not enlist. They were accused of not being patriotic when in reality they were being turned away.

Although most companies actively encouraged their staff to answer their country's call, with some firms promising to keep the jobs open and some paying an allowance, there were companies who were not so keen to see their employees leave. On 18 November the prosecution of an apprentice for enlisting without his employer's permission failed.

CHAPTER 5

The Munitions
Factories

The thousands of Sheffield men who answered the nation's call provided a significant proportion of the manpower which was believed to be needed to bring the war to a successful, and hopefully swift, conclusion. However, these men needed weapons and ammunition if they were to have any worth.

Heavy industry and the steel industry in particular played a major role in Sheffield prior to the war commencing. It would be shown that the First World War, whilst disastrous for the city in many ways, was a great stimulus in terms of the steel industry, with there being more work available than could be handled by Sheffield's firms despite tremendous expansion. 'Business as usual' was the rallying cry for Sheffield industry but if anything Sheffield industry was far more busy than usual. It is true to say that Sheffield industry, in particular the steel industry, benefited tremendously by the war, with several firms actually making vast profits.

Prior to the hostilities beginning Camell-Laird & Co Ltd had been struggling to stay afloat but immediately prior to war commencing it began to receive orders for armour plate and warships. Consequently the company grew and flourished, doubling its income by the end of the war to almost £8 million. It could be argued that if the war had never happened Camell-Laird would have ceased to exist.

The workforce of Hadfields Ltd, which was to become Sheffield's largest firm, more than doubled during the war, rising from 5690 in 1914 to almost 13,000 in 1918, gaining more than £1 million in net profits by the end of hostilities.

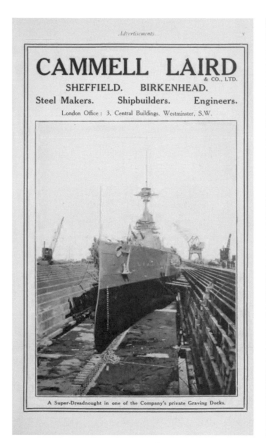

An advertisement for Cammell Laird and Co, Ltd, promoting their munitions, in Brassey's Naval Annual 1915. (*The Author's Collection*)

An advertisement for Hadfields Limited promoting their artillery shell production and "ERA" steel, in Brassey's Naval Annual 1915. (*The Author's Collection*)

By the end of 1916 nearly 11,000 workers were employed on Vicker's site on the banks of the River Don. On 27 September 1918 the company increased its capital to £12,000,000, and in 1919 it was able to record its capital worth as being £20,663,237 as opposed to £7,015,000 shortly after the war began.

The above three companies were only three of nearly 200 companies involved in the steel trade operating in the city and it was believed 150 of these were directly involved in steel production.

Although many of these were quite small, 20 of the companies together employed around 20,000 in the days before the war began and it has been estimated that the remaining companies employed approximately the same again. With such large business, Sheffield was already firmly on the map with regards to steel. The war was to see its position further cemented with an estimated 100,000 people employed in the steel factories by 1918.

Sheffield would, in 1918, be described by the Corporation as 'The World's Arsenal' and looking at the different products produced in the city it is not difficult to see why.

Shells, machine guns and rifles were produced in huge quantities, with 25,000 tons of steel being produced each week for the war effort by 1915. The War Office needed 55,000 shells each week, with this figure rising as the war went on, and a high proportion of these were produced in Sheffield. Bayonets, swords, body armour, seven million steel helmets, tools to dig the trenches, surgical instruments used to help treat the injured, the materials used to build the ships, even the cutlery and razors used by the troops, were all produced in Sheffield. Steel was also manufactured for the railways, which were to become increasingly essential for transporting troops and supplies to the battlefields. It has been said by Tweedle that 'In almost every area of war material…Sheffield steel was on the front line on both land and sea.' In fact it could be argued by producing the means of war, it was Sheffield that won the war.

In October 1914, not only were the factories producing munitions for the British forces, but they were also producing some of the 50 guns needed per week for the French Government, with the Vickers gun being a popular weapon of choice.

Although most munitions factories expanded rapidly throughout the war, it was not all good news for Sheffield steel manufacturers, with those owned by Germans suffering a rapid and dramatic drop in trade, as will be discussed in a later chapter, with the exception of Kayser Ellison who went to great lengths to show patriotism and encourage its staff to join the armed forces. Sheffield industry tried to steal trade from Germany but it was busy carrying out its own work.

A Sheffield manufactured Vickers machine gun, shown set up for anti-aircraft purposes. (*The Author's Collection*)

It was also not good news for manufacturers of high quality, commercial products such as silverware. Due to most manufacturing fulfilling government contracts for the military, there was a lack of raw materials and also a lack of demand for higher value products. Traditionally these companies had traded in Europe and due to trade restrictions the demand had massively reduced.

Stainless steel began to become widely produced and used. It had been first produced by Brown Bayley's, John Brown's, Sanderson Bros & Newbould, Hadfields, Osborn, Howell's and Firth's. In fact it was to become so popular, especially for cutlery, that in 1917 restrictions were imposed preventing its use for anything other than aeroplane engines. The restriction was not lifted until after the war.

It was thought that only approximately one thousand men were out of work at the height of production due to the high demand for workers to work around the clock producing the means of war.

However, there was some evidence that men who tried to work in munitions were turned away. At an early stage in the war one Sheffield man tried to enlist in the forces but was too unfit so he attempted to work in munitions, to do his bit for the war effort, but he was turned away. This led to tremendous frustration for the men who wanted to play their part in the war but could not do so despite the huge demand for soldiers and workers.

One major problem which quickly developed was that skilled employees of the factories joined the army, leaving a serious skills shortage. The River Don works, for example, lost 1,000 employees in 1914. Although people began to fill the places vacated by the new army recruits, those new employees were inexperienced.

As further demand for munitions increased as the war continued and increased in its ferocious nature even more workers were needed and these had to be brought from elsewhere. This led to the problem of a shortage of housing. In August 1914 the Estates Committee were asked to prepare a scheme to complete the Wincobank estate. That year only 515 houses had been built despite the city's growing population prior to the outbreak of war. In the summer of 1915 approximately 500 houses had to be demolished due to the expansion of munitions factories. The corporation refused to build any new homes for workers who had recently moved to the area to work in the factories, claiming that it only had a responsibility to providing housing for permanent residents.

The Lord Mayor and the chairman of the Local Munitions Committee met with the Minister of Munitions to demand funding for accommodation. In August 1915 it was approved to build 67 houses at Wincobank but this was woefully inadequate. The government agreed to fund temporary accommodation and the corporation decided to build permanent houses on behalf of the government on the agreement that the corporation would assume full responsibility for them once the war was over. These houses were to be erected by 31 July 1916.

The temporary accommodation consisted of 238 houses, 57 hostels and 12 colony blocks at Tyler Street and 111 houses, 35 hostels and four colony blocks on Petre Street. Such accommodation was intended to cater for 4,631 workers. Additionally land at Tinsley was developed, with 163 houses, 38 hostels and 12 colony blocks. After the war this temporary accommodation was converted into corporation housing.

In order to facilitate workers getting to work from the houses which were becoming further away from the factories, investment had to be made into transport. Although plans to extend the tram system were shelved when the war began, the number of buses run by the corporation increased to 25, with some private companies running their own transport for their staff. Buses had been favoured since before the war, after a committee carried out a fact-finding mission abroad to see how different countries ran their public transport.

There was a massive expansion of factories but there was a lack of land and infrastructure. Companies had to grow beyond their capabilities. The scale of the growing demand was such that it was incredibly difficult to supply.

And still, there was a shortage of workers as the number of men joining the armed forces increased. Women would eventually be employed, as will be discussed. Many Belgian refugees worked in the munitions factories and, on 30 July 1917 approximately one hundred Australians started work in Sheffield's factories.

To encourage hard work and high productivity wages for those working in the factories increased during the war for most companies. The number of working hours also increased, with shifts throughout the day and night. Large numbers of Sheffield workers had more money than ever before.

Soon after the war began it became apparent that even with expanding factories and longer working hours there was a tremendous shortage of the means of war being produced. In December 1914 the country required 50 rounds per gun per day for the 18-pounders, 40 rounds per gun per day for the 4.5-inch and 25 rounds per gun per day for the 4.7-inch. Until March 1915 only approximately one quarter of the required amount were being produced. It led to the situation in

THE MUNTIONS FACTORIES

March 1915 where three days into the battle of Neuve-Chapelle the forward movement of the troops had to come to an end due to a shortage of ammunition. It was what David Lloyd George called in his war memoirs, 'The Great Shell Scandal'. The Board of Trade, which had the responsibility for labour and munitions, in consultation with the War Office, was clearly failing. In an attempt to massively increase the amount of munitions needed for the war effort, a new Government department, the Ministry of Munitions was created and Lloyd George became its first Minister.

The Ministry of Munitions attempted to increase the amount of munitions by:

a) checking the enlistment of skilled men, requesting the army to release those who had joined up who were skilled in the munitions factories

b) Ensuring that workers work their full hours and ensure they work to their maximum levels of performance, also ensuring that they remained working in the same factory to maintain continuity of staff and skills

c) Ensuring a more rigid control of establishments selling alcohol in industrial areas

d) Training and employing women to undertake work in the factories

e) Ensuring all available labour was well used in order to meet demands, by transferring all workers to the cities where they could work in established munitions firms or by spreading production across the country.

The Munitions of War Bill received Royal Assent on 2 July 1915. In June efforts were made to bring back any skilled munitions workers who were in the armed forces, but it was stipulated by Kitchener that only men who were not yet overseas could be released, though this was extremely difficult; as Lloyd George remarked it was 'like getting through barbed-wire entanglements without heavy guns'. Around 50 members of the City Battalion were identified to return to the munitions factories but in the eventuality some of these were reserved by the army due to them being specialists in warfare, possessing skills such as being able to use machine guns.

One of the earliest decisions made by the new Ministry was to order 12,000 Vickers machine guns from Sheffield firm Vickers, although weapons from other companies in other cities were also popular. The number of machine guns produced nationally was 287 in 1914 but had risen to 120,864 by 1918, with a large proportion being produced in Sheffield by the Vickers company.

The reforms by the Ministry of Munitions helped alleviate many of the problems in producing the vast quantities of munitions needed to win the war by bringing factories under Government control and ensuring that war work took priority over non-essential production. Over time, especially with the introduction of women workers into the factories, the labour problem was almost eradicated.

On 15 December 1915 the House of Commons worked late into the night to advance the Munitions of War (amendments) Bill. It was agreed that an employer should not be able to sack an employee within six weeks of the employee commencing work, unless a sufficient reason is given otherwise he could be eligible for a large fine. It allowed for compensation to be given to a worker if he or she was dismissed with less than a week's notice, unless there were reasonable circumstances which did not allow such notice to be given. A leaving certificate had to be given by the employer when a worker was sacked or suspended for more than three days, in order to allow the employee to obtain another job, unless the Munitions Tribunal believed that the worker deliberately got sacked. It allowed for the Minister of Munitions to regulate the number of hours worked by women. A minimum wage for women, to ensure they were not paid low wages, was something that would be considered further. There was criticism of those who were carrying out quality control inspections, with pawnbrokers, barbers, butchers and bakers being used to inspect shells, causing the inspections to be regarded as a 'laughing stock'. An example was given of a gardener who was employed as an inspector but his knowledge of machinery was limited to the workings of a lawnmower. It was argued that it would not be possible to give greater training and monitoring for inspections because to do so would cause extra burdens on the Ministry of Munitions, though the Department would endeavour to get rid of those who were not properly qualified.

Interestingly there was a shortage of the means of transporting raw materials and completed munitions to and from the factories. This problem increased as the railways became used more to transport troops and mail to and from the front line. Trams were sought to transport materials at night around the city. Previously horses had been used as a means of transport, but horses were being used on the battlefields. One novel way of transport was adopted by Thomas Ward's, who obtained an elephant from a circus.

Lizzie Ward, as the elephant was known, became a familiar sight over the course of two years from 1916 as she carried heavy loads of steel around the city.

Given the shortage of horses, Thomas W. Ward used a novel means of transporting raw materials and finished goods to and from his works. The elephant was known as Lizzie Ward. (*Photograph reproduced from the Picture Sheffield Collection, courtesy of Sheffield Local Studies Library*)

What was working in a munitions factory like? In her poem *Cry from the City*, the Sheffield poet Renshaw describes 'dingy Sheffield with its smoke-dark streets' with 'labours without ending' and 'furnaces that throb and surge the whole night through'.

In her poem *From Town to Country* she described her view of the factories further:

'Crowded city streets where road cars race,
With deafening screams, where great gaunt chimneys stand
Like labouring demons in a smoke-dark land
Belching forth crimson flames, where every face
Is hard and strange with lifes grime fever pace
Mirrored smoke, wrapped in desolate mists
Uncared for alleys swerve and interlace
… women labour, sorrowing for their dead'

The factories were noisy, often filled with smoke and the smell of chemicals, with large numbers of people working in poorly lit, filthy workshops for long hours with few breaks, usually standing up in tremendous heat.

The Munitions of War (Amendment) Act of January 1916 sought to control wages and conditions of the workers. Although factory owners were educated about improving the conditions there was no requirement for them to do so. Often a broken basin and a jug of cold water were the only washing facilities provided. Overalls were not always provided. There were usually no dedicated places to eat, with staff eating their meals whilst stood at their machines.

In November 1915 a reporter from the *Telegraph* watched workers at one of the city's munitions factories, leaving the city centre at 4:30am and heading towards Brightside for a long shift in one of the factories there. He witnessed the 'knocker up'; a woman tapping on windows of workers to tell the workers that it was time to rise for a day's work. The reporter remarked that 'war work is a wonderful thing'; jobs were created including the knocker up and keepers of shops which opened early, newspaper sellers with newspapers being sold 'like hot cakes'. Whilst the workers were rising it was remarked that half the city slept whilst half the city worked, the sleepers not knowing how the other half lived and the workers not caring what the sleepers thought.

As for the factories themselves:

'Here was a shop with long lancet windows all flaring with light, here a huge red glowing light playing on escaping steam and furnishing it with reds and browns, dull greys and yellows all fluctuating like the changes in a kaleidoscope. Sounds of toiling hammers came across those sullen walls, the screaming of steel in agony, the smashing of heavy presses. It was the sounds rather than the sights which struck one. Once we saw a funnel of exhaust steam driven right across the breadth of the road against the opposite house walls, where it shivered like the shivering of a wave on a breakwater, and through the many windows of one vast shop one could catch sight of the busy shafting, the multitude of wheels, and could imagine the scene below, the army of men busy at their lathes and the miles of ordered machinery.'

At the end of one shift the workers, with only men being described in the article, were said to quickly rush to the tramcars in such a hurry to get home. So many workers had finished their night shift that they could not all fit on one tram and had to wait for another, disappointed that they would not reach their beds as early as they had hoped.

Fires and explosions became increasingly common as the outdated machinery had ever increasing burdens placed upon it. Sometimes machinery would be running all day and night, all year round, with only short breaks at Christmas. As such it became prone to failure. The explosions and fires caused important working time to be lost, thousands of pounds of damage and more importantly injuries and death.

A small number of examples highlight the problems, but hundreds more accidents fill the company records. During the summer or autumn of 1918 one employee was trapped on a high chimney at the Vickers River Don Works. The two men who saved him, Edward Colwell and Frederick Linley, were awarded the Edward Medal on 16

September that year. He was fortunate but others were less so. On 23 October 1917 William Gill was burned alive in his crane cage at Vickers. On 30 January 1918 William Henry Brookes was electrocuted when he grasped a live wire at Swift, Levick & Sons. Richard Finch collapsed at the Vickers River Don works in early 1918. He was pronounced dead on arrival at hospital. It would be desirous to have a memorial to all those who died as a result of their valuable work in the munitions factories, in the service of their country.

CHAPTER 6

German 'Aliens' and Anti-German Feeling

In the 1911 Census 390 residents of Sheffield were listed as being of German birth. Although this number was only a tiny proportion of the population of the city, it was viewed to be a sizeable minority and increasingly a sizeable danger.

Early into the war, on 14 August 1914, the editor of the *Telegraph* wrote, under the heading of 'The German Amongst Us', that it must be hard to be a German living in Sheffield and that they should not all be judged as being the enemy; 'A large number of them dwell amongst us in perfect good faith, and are quite harmless and in great trouble. Others, it must be admitted, are anything but beyond suspicion.'

Others were more judgmental. 'Why have enemies walking among us?' Sheffield people were heard to ask, with those enquirers arguing they should be interned to prevent them from helping invaders.

Those sentiments, which were expressed across the country, were answered to the satisfaction of the enquirers when all those of German birth who had not become British citizens were arrested and taken to a barracks in Sheffield to assess their potential risk. They were recorded as 'alien enemies' and those considered to pose a risk to security were detained at the barracks, but those for who no evidence of any national security risk could be identified were released on the proviso that they did not travel more than five miles from the city without a permit, that they presented themselves to the authorities each day and that they should have telephones removed from their homes so that they could not communicate overseas.

In late October 1914 all 108 German and Austrian citizens of military age living in Sheffield were requested to report to the Central

Police Station where they were arrested once again and were held for two days in the city's police cells. Most surrendered themselves but those who did not found themselves being hunted by the police. They were then taken by train to York where they were kept in the city's Exhibition buildings before being transported to other internment camps across the country where they remained until 1919 when they were repatriated. The Isle of Man was the largest of these camps, with 25,000 German and Austrian detainees. In May 1915 another series of arrests were made, as those who had been too young previously came of military age. At this same time German and Austrian women were sent to their countries of birth.

As the war escalated and more men in Sheffield were killed anti-German feeling increased in the city. On 10 May 1915 the *Telegraph and Star* claimed Germans were a 'breed of bestial savages animated only by a terrible lust for blood'. It was demonisation at its strongest.

All were being tarred with the same brush, irrespective of the prominence which some Germans locally had held before the war started. Professor Julius Freud of the University of Sheffield was interned and eventually forcibly sent back to Germany. Due to its German owners business at Poldi Steel Works was temporarily brought to an end and by the end of the war Bohler Bros no longer existed. In 1915 Seebohn & Dieckstaht changed its name to Arthur Balfour & Co. Whilst this was partly due to Balfour becoming the largest shareholder, it was in no small part due to the anti-German feeling and the need to be seen to be English.

Kayser Ellison only managed to survive by displaying its loyalty to Britain through appealing for its workers to join the war effort.

Paul Kuehnrich, who ran a steel manufacturing business, was accused of working for the Germans and was continually harassed by the authorities. It was even suggested that he had a secret army at his home and was a friend of the Kaiser. There was absolutely no evidence to suggest such a thing but unsurprisingly such claims were not good for his business or personal life. Naturally other Sheffield steel companies were keen to see anti-German feelings and lies spread in order to increase business for themselves.

Sir Joseph Jonas, of Sir Joseph Jonas and Colver Ltd, faired even worse than Kuehnrich. Despite having formerly served as a Mayor of Sheffield, he was arrested under the Official Secrets Act in 1918 for passing information to the Germans. Indeed he had passed information about the workings of rival firm Vickers about their rifle manufacturing, to a representative of a company in Essen and Berlin but this disclosure of information had taken place in 1913, at a time when the threat of war was non existent, and the disclosure of information was strictly business, albeit rather dirty business. He was found not guilty of the main charge at his trial at the Old Bailey in July 1918, but was convicted of passing on commercial information to the Germans, was fined £2,000 and censured, and he had his knighthood revoked which he considered to be the greatest punishment of all.

On 7 December 1916 Max Emanuel Hohenwarth, was jailed for six months. He was described as a 'dangerous German subject'.

German butchers who had shops in the city, including on the Wicker, had their shop windows smashed, as did those who had other businesses in the city, including those of AG Friedrich, Herman Zeihar and George Haimeman. Their homes were also occasionally targeted.

At the October 1916 meeting of the Sheffield council a letter was read out from the Honorary Secretary of the Tottenham Committee. The letter called for the council to support the internment of all enemy aliens, irrespective of age or gender. The councillors decided to take no action with regards to the suggestion despite the increasing view amongst the voters that such action should be taken in light of the recent air raid on the city. As will be shown in a later chapter, following that raid in September 1916 there was a feeling of a need for revenge; 'the killing of as many Germans as possible, so that the earth may be rid of their fiendish wickedness'.

In 1917 to maintain and increase anti-German sentiments the Tramways Committee was asked whether it would put up posters in trams on an occasional basis to remind Sheffield folk of the evil acts being perpetrated by Germany. The idea, though tempting to some, was not put into practice.

In addition to German civilians who were imprisoned due to being born of a country to which Britain was at war, Sheffield found itself detaining German prisoners of war. In buildings along Greenhill Road in Norton, and towards the end of the war at the former City Battalion camp at Redmires, the prisoners were kept.

They were forced to carry out road works and undertake construction work. On 28 February 1917 300 prisoners of war were transported to Meadowhead, Woodseats to undertake some construction work. They were even to build air force buildings and other works for the war effort, improving Sheffield's response to German attacks.

On 24 September 1917 Thomas Leenane, a Sheffield labourer, was imprisoned for a month for giving a German prisoner of war a tin of milk. On 19 October 1917 Ralph Whawell was sent to prison for six months for giving the German prisoners at one of the city's camps six loaves of bread and on 3 April 1918 Florence Mayors was fined £5 for trying to give a letter to a prisoner of war in the city.

Despite them being the enemy, some people of Sheffield evidently wanted to help the prisoners. Perhaps seeing them in the flesh, recognising that they were as human as the Sheffield men fighting abroad, they were able to see through the caricatures and propaganda created by the Government and displayed frequently in the media and so felt a degree of sympathy.

One prisoner did not receive any sympathy, however, when he was caught trying to steal potatoes from a farm. The farmer saw the attempt and fired at him, slightly injuring the prisoner.

As the brutality against British prisoners of war in Germany became known, including British soldiers being tied to trees and flogged, there were debates in parliament as to whether German prisoners of war should receive brutality in revenge. This was considered in Sheffield. 'That the Germans are a race apart from other Europeans is shown by their brutal mentality,' wrote the *Telegraph* on 7 May 1918, before adding that it was the opinion of that paper that the only way to secure good treatment of British prisoners was to 'punish helpless prisoners in our hands' and it was to be encouraged that German prisoners in Sheffield should be treated harshly.

Not all Germans wanted to be at war with Britain. An interesting story was told in the *Telegraph and Star*. The story originated from a soldier, Private Frank Barnes of the 2nd Royal Warwicks. Barnes and his comrades were marching through some woods when they encountered a horrific sight; there were 30 Germans, with five English who had been shot dead, some also with their throats cut. Barnes and his company found the Germans in a farmhouse which was packed with troops. A battle commenced, with the Germans quickly being overcome by the British use of the bayonet. Some of the Germans managed to escape but a large number were taken prisoner. Amongst the Germans was one who spoke excellent English and he addressed his captors. 'Excuse me, but is there anyone here who comes from Sheffield?' the prisoner asked. Barnes was somewhat taken aback and informed the German soldier that he was from Sheffield. He was further amazed to discover that his prisoner too hailed from the city. 'Damn fighting,' the German said, 'Let me get back to England and my wife and children. I have been trying to get captured for several days and have only just succeeded.' Prior to Britain entering the war, due to being of military age, he had been forced to leave England to join the German army.

CHAPTER 7

Belgian Refugees

When Belgium was invaded by Germany on 4 August 1914 there was an exodus of approximately 250,000 refugees. Thousands flocked to Britain in need of safety, and Sheffield immediately offered to home refugees and treat their wounded soldiers, with around 3,000 residing in the city at some stage during the war.

The government advised that individuals and organisations should only offer assistance in terms of free or subsidised accommodation and welfare to those who had no means to help themselves.

On 17 October 240 wounded Belgian soldiers and 55 Belgian refugees arrived in Sheffield. On 28 October a further 178 wounded Belgian soldiers arrived, and by 4 November 660 Belgian refugees were living in Sheffield and its district. That figure continued to rise in the following months, with a small but regular influx for much of the war. The newcomers found life in Sheffield very unusual. Many Belgians, especially those in the small towns and villages, had never met anyone from England let alone visited the country. There was a great culture shock but of course a great gratitude that they had somewhere safe to live. The issue was where they could live at a time when there was already a chronic housing shortage which was causing overcrowding for those who had always lived in the city. Any attempt to house such a large number of people required money.

The wounded were taken to the 3rd Northern General Hospital, The Royal Infirmary and St John's Hospital in Dore.

On 28 November a request was made for the Boys' Brigade, Boy Scouts and other such groups of boys, to collect funds for the Belgian refugees, approaching people in the streets to request donations.

The university provided a hostel, known as the University Belgian Hostel, also known as Stephenson Hostel. It was formed from two

BELGIAN REFUGEES

Buses carrying Belgian casualties arriving at the 3rd Northern General Hospital, Collegiate Crescent. (*Photograph reproduced from the Picture Sheffield Collection, courtesy of Sheffield Local Studies Library*)

Nurses at St John's (Abbeydale) Private Hospital where wounded Belgian soldiers have been treated. (*Photograph reproduced from the Picture Sheffield Collection, courtesy of Sheffield Local Studies Library*)

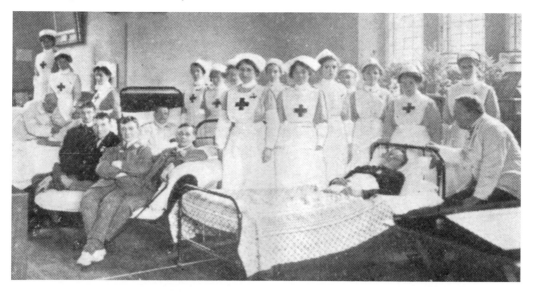

houses and was intended for between 16 and 18 guests but it was stipulated that they had to be of 'the educated class who may be glad to use our university'. Appeals were made for donations of money and furniture. It opened in November 1914 and closed during the summer of 1916. In addition to Belgian refugees it housed wounded soldiers until they were fit to return to active service.

Several receiving bases were created, including Firvale House which could accommodate up to 150, Ecclesall Union was able to accommodate 45, Shirle Hill could accommodate 90, St Vincents Home, Solly Street was home to 12, and Norfolk Base (owned by the Midland Railway Company) which could house 180. These were for temporary accommodation for when refugees first arrived in the city and were occupied until longer-term accommodation could be found.

St. Vincent's Home for Belgian Refugees, Shirle Hill, Cherry Tree Road formerly the home of Sir John Brown. (*Photograph reproduced from the Picture Sheffield Collection, courtesy of Sheffield Local Studies Library*)

Belgian Refugees at Shirle Hill, Nether Edge. (*Photograph reproduced from the Picture Sheffield Collection, courtesy of Sheffield Local Studies Library*)

Many large houses were offered including Westbrook House on Sharrow Vale Road which was described as 'a commodious residence' capable of being home to 50. It had electric lighting, three large kitchens, a large sitting room, a large dining room and numerous bedrooms. In addition lots of people who were lucky enough to have a spare room made those rooms available to house one or more of the refugees.

Churches made efforts to do their part for the Belgians, with several forming committees in a bid to raise funds to pay for accommodation, furniture and some subsidence for the refugees to be able to live on a day to day basis.

The Upper Chapel Belgian Refugees' Fund (the papers of which are at Sheffield Archives, reference UCR/215-243) existed between November 1914 and August 1916. At a meeting of the congregation on Wednesday, 18 November 1914 it was unanimously agreed that a scheme of hospitality for Belgian refugees should be provided. Soon after the call for donations 94 names were on a list of regular subscribers. In the first two weeks a princely sum of £100 was raised.

A cottage in Johnson Street was provided to the fund for the purposes of housing a family. It was provided by George Hunt who gave it free of rent for five or six people. An appeal was made for furniture for the house. Negotiations were also held to secure a tenancy for housing for two or three families who would preferably be trades people and a house in Brandreth Street in the Upperthorpe area of Sheffield was taken on.

With the preparations made, shortly before Christmas 1914 it was decided the time was right to move in some refugees. On 22 December a delegation of the committee met two Belgian families, comprising ten individuals, at the Midland Railway Station and escorted them to the house on Brandreth Street where they enjoyed a high tea, consisting of coffee rather than tea on account of the shortages. One of the families, a 'superior working class' family from Antwerp, consisting of a husband, wife, son, a cousin of the wife and her husband and two unrelated friends, occupied the cottage.

Weekly visits were made to the homes to monitor the refugees with the eventual aim that a husband and wife from one of the families would assume the responsibility. Catering was provided for the first few weeks in order to assist the refugees in settling in. A weekly allowance of four shillings was provided for adults, and two or three shillings for children. Those of a 'better' class were given six or seven shillings for adults and five shillings per child. Those who were in employment did not receive any allowance and once sufficient income had been generated from work, the family was asked to move on.

Some training was paid for, for those refugees who wanted to learn trades. A 'well known Sheffield lady' provided funding for education for two children. Equally, the refugees over the course of their stay tried to provide education to residents of Sheffield. One refugee offered any resident of Sheffield French lessons but he had to give up the lessons due to ill health. Music lessons were provided and a man by the name of Georges, from a village near Malines in Belgium, who had worked as a charcutier and café keeper in his homeland, tried to offer the people of Sheffield his culinary experience in the form of an interview in the *Telegraph* in which he described, in some detail, the recipes for Belgian waffles and several varieties of soup which were highly nutritious but could be produced at very low cost.

Eventually the adult male members of the families in the house acquired work and began to support themselves, and so it was required that they then found their own accommodation in order to make space for families who had no means of supporting themselves. Over the course of the war some returned to Belgium to embark on their military duty. Those who had moved on wrote to the committee expressing their thanks for the hospitality.

On 11 January ten more refugees moved into the house. Throughout the period in which the house was used for accommodating refugees; it was home to between seven and 12 individuals.

Eventually a second cottage, also on Johnson Street, was rented for the same purpose due to a reasonable amount of money being raised. By January 1917 £662 and 2s had been raised and £520 1s 2d spent by the committee.

The fund was wound up in 1919. The final family, who had arrived in December 1918 left in March 1919.

After the war donations continued to be paid to organisations until all the money raised had been spent. Donations were made not only to Belgian refugees but also to the Unitarians of Hungary and the French Protestants, with each organisation receiving £50.

Another fund was set up by the Belgian Sub Committee, a Sub-committee of the Stocksbridge Relief Committee (the papers of which are at Sheffield Archives, reference CA68/11).

The sub-committee first met on the evening of 20 November 1914 at the Works School where the use of a house offered by a Stocksbridge resident was discussed. On 16 November a letter from GC Knowles had been sent promising the use of a house on Alband Road for the 'Homeless Belgians'. The house had two cellars, two bedrooms, a 'house room', an attic, a toilet, a bath and hot and cold water. He normally charged rent of 6s 6d per week 'but in sympathy with the most urgent cause your committee have in hand I beg to offer you my little help by granting you the house free of rent for 3 calendar months from this date November 16, 1914'.

The offer of the house was accepted but the sub-committee was unsure of the type of refugees it should house. It sought information from Wakefield as to whether they 'should have refugees of the educated class' and if so whether a family (women and children preferred) was ready to be sent immediately. Also the authorities in Sheffield were contacted to determine what class of refugees they had and for their details.

In order to minimise the expenditure on the house, Messrs S Fox & Co were approached to give free gas, but it is unclear whether it was provided. The local authorities were asked to forego the General District Rate and Poor Rate. Collections were made for furniture which was to be insured for £100. Collections of money and other donations were held at the council offices in Stockbridge, with weekly and monthly subscriptions.

On 1 December it was agreed the house should be cleaned in preparation of the arrival of a family, and three beds were placed in each bedroom.

The distress committee was then asked to send 'one family of Belgian Refugees or failing a family women and children – not more than six persons'.

A family was identified and on the evening of Saturday 2 January 1915 a selected group of members of the sub-committee greeted the new arrivals at Sheffield Midland Station and conveyed them to the house.

Weekly visits were made by a member of the sub-committee to obtain a list of things required by the household, and an allowance of £2 2s for the family was provided each week, to be granted every Saturday from 9 January. It was agreed with the owner of the house that once the period of free rent had elapsed, after three months of the house being offered, a rent of 5s per week was to be paid by the committee.

On 19 June the family moved out to support themselves and a new family was introduced to the house. On 4 November 1915 the refugees were instructed to start paying their own rent of 6s 6d per week and in order to raise this money, take in lodgers.

In April 1916 a letter was received from the family who had been residing in the house, thanking the committee for their assistance and advising that they were now living in Sheffield. It was at that time decided that no more refugees should be brought to the house.

Remaining funds, and the proceeds from the sale of the furniture, were donated to the National Committee for Destitute Belgians in Belgium.

In addition to the house some people offered to take in Belgian refugees into their own homes and the sub-committee assisted with the costs of this.

As well as assisting the Belgians who found themselves residing in Sheffield, there were efforts to raise funds for those who were forced to remain in their own country. On 1 October 1915 an appeal was made by the Lord Mayor of Sheffield, who had opened a fund for Belgians who were starving in their own country. The Lord Mayor was satisfied that the need was urgent, with the real prospect of all Belgians being in a condition of starvation during the winter of that year. He felt the plight of the Belgians in Belgium was important and that the efforts they were making in assisting British troops in the battles taking place in that country was essential to a successful outcome to the war. He was concerned that the Germans might easily be able to shoot a starving population. He believed it was necessary for the nation to raise £60,000 each week to avert this.

Services were provided to the refugees in Sheffield including clothing manufacture and repair at a shop at 84 Wicker. Although there was great hospitality towards the Belgians, and a great enthusiasm to hear stories of their country which few Sheffield people will have ever visited, and an expectation that in exchange for free or subsidised accommodation they should open their new homes to anyone wanting to visit and to be entertained, there was also some resentment towards the Belgians. This will become apparent in a later chapter in relation to the request for shops to sell horsemeat in the city, with horsemeat being a popular food source among the Belgians. There was a reluctance by some councillors to introduce new laws and regulations for people who were only temporary residents.

Generally, however, the refugees were well received, and were a valued part of the community. To mark their gratitude, in addition to the several letters given to those who welcomed them to the city, in March 1918 Arthur Balfour, the Sheffield Consul for Belgium, was presented with a portrait of him in oils.

Following the war most of the Belgian refugees returned to their homeland. However, some decided to stay including those who married local residents. Forty-four failed to return home; a memorial at the City Road Cemetery bears the names of that number of refugees and Belgian soldiers, who died whilst in the city.

A memorial at the City Road cemetery commemorating the lives of 44 Belgian men and women who died in Sheffield during the First World War. (*The Author*)

CHAPTER 8

Education

Today the role of the city's two universities is very clear, with large facilities, campuses and a student population in the city into the tens of thousands. In 1914 the newly founded University of Sheffield began to have an important role in the city and would quickly have a significant role in the war effort.

The University of Sheffield opened in April 1909 and by August 1914 had faculties of Medicine, Law, Pure Science, Applied Science, Arts and the University Training College for Teachers.

When the university reconvened after the summer break of 1914 Britain had been at war with Germany for two months. During this period many students had decided to give up their studies and had signed up to the armed forces. Medical students were generally prevented from signing up until they had qualified but students of other disciplines joined in with the enthusiasm of going to war. Medical students were required to assist in the treatment of wounded soldiers, with all medical students working part time at the Northern General Hospital when it opened in May 1915.

Stark figures of graduates from the university reveal just how much of an impact the war had on people studying at the university. In 1913 34 men and 24 women graduated. In 1914 43 men and 17 women graduated. The number of those who began their courses in 1914 was so small, with some of those leaving during their courses, that in 1917 only five men and 21 women graduated. By the autumn of 1916 the number of students slowly began to increase, however, with 17 men and 20 women graduating three years later.

The war was something which, although everyone spoke about, there was a large proportion of people who did not understand its causes or the need for Britain to involve itself in what was considered to be a European crisis. The Vice Chancellor of the university, Fisher, gave lectures on 31 August, and 1 and 2 September. The lectures were entitled 'The Causes and Issues of the War'. The first lecture was held at the university's Firth Hall but there was such interest, with huge crowds packing the hall, that future lectures were delivered in the Methodist Victoria Hall. Lectures were held intermittently throughout the war and they were seen to have such value that the authorities of other towns and cities across the country requested the Vice Chancellor to speak to their people. Fisher was so popular in his support for the war and his determination to use the wide resources of the university for the good of Britain that he was approached by the Government to become the President of the Board of Education and Minister of Education in December 1915 when Lloyd George formed his coalition government. He resigned from the university in December 1916 in order to take up the post. Just days later he became an independent Member of Parliament for Hallam, upon CB Stuart Wortley being elevated to the House of Lords. Fisher was unopposed in the election.

There were other members of staff, and guest speakers from other universities and institutions, who gave lectures. On 22 October a lecture was delivered by the Honourable RH Brand about the finance of the war and on 29 October Dr Charles Sarolea gave a lecture about Belgium's plight.

Due to the war student life, as it had once been, ceased, with no athletics, few sports and few other social activities. The running ground was abandoned and turned over for grazing.

In 1917 the corporation reported on the hard work of the staff in helping keep the university functioning with their 'almost undiminished vigour' and 'zealous and self sacrificing work of the teaching departments'. The university had faced tremendous challenges with the loss of academic staff. Indeed a third of staff joined the forces, with those who remained having taken on some form of war work. Women graduates were approached to become Chemistry lecturers in a bid to keep the Chemistry Department running. The Architecture Department was not so lucky and had to be closed towards the end of the war.

EDUCATION

The university did not lose all of its staff voluntarily because of the war. Professor Julius Freund, the Head of the German Department, was interned because he was an 'alien'. To stop the department from closing students of German were taught by an English lecturer.

A large amount of voluntary work was undertaken for the benefit of the wounded and refugees.

Five hundred women worked at the Western Bank buildings which formed the Sheffield University Hospital Supply Depot, producing 456,247 articles for use at hospitals in Sheffield, across England and in battlefields and hospitals in France and Belgium. Men also worked in the woodworking section. All labour was voluntary and the costs of the raw materials were funded by voluntary subscriptions. Articles produced included splints, bed screens and bed rests.

A Surgical Appliance Branch was created at St George's Square where around 50 volunteers worked to produced surgical and orthopaedic articles for nearly 500 wounded soldiers.

More than 1,000 men who were unable to fight were trained in the engineering workshops to turn shells. Women were eventually trained in the Department of Metallurgy to analyse metals and they were sent to work in the steelworks.

New methods of production for munitions were researched and developed to help keep up with the demand for munitions. In October 1914 a Scientific Advisory Committee was founded to research such techniques. Tests on the strength of sword blades and the coatings of metals were part of the university's work.

New materials were researched and created. Alloys and gauges were produced at the university by its metal research and production teams. A Department of Glass Technology was set up in 1917 to carry out work studying refractories, which are fireclays and other materials used to line furnaces. The new department also helped alleviate the shortage of glass by finding new, cheaper and more efficient methods of production.

Importantly the Chemistry Department produced local anaesthetics that were of invaluable use in treating the wounded in the city's hospitals and on the battlegrounds.

In addition to the university, schools suffered with some teachers in most schools enlisting and some female teachers joining the

Women's Auxiliary Services. This resulted in a shortage of teachers and inevitably the education of a generation suffered.

There was therefore a need to recruit and train more teachers and this need increased as the war continued. In order to find the required number of new teachers, most of whom were to be women, they had to be brought from other towns and so needed accommodation. On 11 July 1917 the United Methodist Church Conference at the Surrey Street Church resolved to close the Ranmoor Theological College for the duration of the war because despite its financial situation looking very healthy, and the sterling work it had carried out, there was currently only one student. The principal of the college, the Reverend J. S. Clemens, was retiring and so it was felt the time was right for a temporary closure. It was decided that the college should be offered to the Sheffield Education Committee, who had expressed interest, to form a hostel for the 60 female students of the Sheffield Teachers' Training College.

Education suffered even further when, in 1915 to meet the demand for workers given that thousands of men had left their jobs for the military, boys were allowed to leave school at 13 due to the shortage of labour. The *Telegraph* described this as 'an educational back-step, the necessity for which is regretted as generally as it is admitted, is one of the direct consequences of the war'. Until 1918 the employment was poorly organised, but in that year the Minister of National Service had put better plans in place and an appeal was made for every boy of secondary school age to give up at least three weeks of his summer to assist with the harvest and for some boys to continue beyond the school holidays with the potato harvest. It was a way in which those who were not yet of military age could serve their country.

There were nonetheless some improvements to schooling. On 30 September 1915 a new department for junior school students at the Western Road School providing space for an additional 450 students and a new infants department at Morley Street School allowing for 444 pupils opened. There was no formal opening of the schools due to the war. The schools, described as 'light and airy and well adapted for their purpose' helped increase the number of pupils in corporation schools to 64,267 with almost five hundred pupils in private schools.

EDUCATION

The standards of education appeared generally good and attendance levels were often found to be worthy of compliment. On 22 December 1915 at the Prize Day at the city's Sale Memorial Boys' School, the Reverend S Woods complimented the boys on their attendance which was very little different to previous years although some of the older and more capable boys had left school to undertake work. Certificates were awarded for swimming and awards given for assisting the war effort with collecting money. Money had been raised for an ambulance and cigarettes for wounded soldiers. The girls at the school were awarded certificates for swimming and domestic economy and were congratulated for providing entertainment at the Base Hospital and for giving hospitality to soldiers from the Lydgate Lane Hospital.

At the Prize Day at Wicker School, Holy Trinity Church, on 23 December 1915, the Lord Mayor, (Councillor FA Warlow) handed out the prizes. Albert Harland, one of the co-managers of the school, gave the advice of the former British Prime Minister William Gladstone, which summed up all that could be asked of this generation, 'When you run, run as fast as you can. When you jump, jump as high as you can. When you work, work as hard as you can.' He expressed concerns about the wellbeing of the children and urged the parents to ensure their homes were as well ventilated as the school was, and that the children should be sent to bed at a reasonable time in order that they should be able to give their full concentration at school. The children performed entertainment, cheering, singing and reciting. They were described by the *Telegraph* as 'radiant with happiness'.

Children from all schools in the city performed entertainment for soldiers at hospitals, and occasionally at the schools, raised funds and provided comforts, as will be shown in the following chapters.

The education and general welfare of orphans and homeless children became increasingly recognised. On 17 December 1915 the Sheffield Catholic Hostel also known as the Sheffield Boys' Working Home was reopened by the Duchess of Norfolk, before opening the King Edward Memorial Hospital for Crippled Children in the Rivelin Valley. After an enlargement the Catholic Hostel housed 50 boys, most of whom were orphans, with seven young boys whose fathers were in the army and whose mothers were either dead or had been convicted of neglect. It was hoped to make further extensions to accommodate 100 boys. The hostel had an evening school enabling the development of skills that could be used in work. It also helped train boys in war work. The Bishop of Leeds, who presided over the opening ceremony, said he could not think of a better means of housing the boys by allowing them to have accommodation that was more like a home than mere lodgings, with staff who could fulfil the roles of parents. Its aim was to help and support the boys and whilst there was a serious problem of girls without homes, it was felt that the boys would be more likely to turn to crime if they did not have somewhere stable to live. It would make them good citizens and workers. It was hoped more could be created across the country for every denomination.

Despite some accounts in newspapers, little would have been known by Sheffield folk as to what life was really like on the front line. Constance Ada Renshaw of the Pupil Teacher Centre wrote several poems and anthologies (Sheffield Archives: SY 628/F and SY 482/F), many of which concentrated on the War, including *England's Boys* (published 1916), *Battle and Beyond* (1917) and *Lest We Forget* (1937) which relate to the hostilities of the First World War.

A soldier wrote in the *Telegraph* that Renshaw was 'universally admired and it was the general feeling that she had grasped the spirit of the soldier and expressed his thoughts and emotions in action'. Another reader, a woman who had four sons in the army, admired her poems. 'As I read the poems, I felt very near to my boys,' she wrote.

The following are some extracts from Renshaw's poetry:

England's Boys
'When England called, a hundred thousand boys
Came singing down the roadways of the world
The trumpet blared, the banner was unfurled;
The earth breathed battle and its lusty joys
What dreams of mail-clad steeds in prancing pose
And flash of moonlit armour near the sea
Stirred their child-souls to strenuous chivalry
And swept them into battle from their toys!
Back, back they come, boys with the mouths of men

Still singing but with purpose in their eyes,
And dimly-blending dreams of dead Romance
"England!" they cry – and hunger for her skies
But some will never see her skies again
… And some laid their lives for her in France.'

Our Soldiers
'Brave sons of empire keep untiring guard,
Across the world while blinding searchlights flash
On all the glories man has made and marred,
Dawn steals o'er lonely desert and raided plain
The scorching sun, and shell's mud spattering crash
Bring pitiless thirst, and torturous death again.'

Human Nature
'When the warrior staggers bleeding,
And the quivering landscape blurs,
Swift he sees, with sense receding
Tumbling waves of wind swept furze
'mid the cannon's rending thunder
And the shrapnel's battle tune,
Hardy soldiers gaze in wonder,
Mute before some faded moon.'

Our Answer
'Sad, battle weary men with eyes grown red
choking poison fumes
all the hellish horrors of the dark
shell scarred battle fields
where torn men twist and red eyed boys grow old'

In addition to providing information, sometimes information about the horrors of the war and how British men were living in horrific conditions and dying in battle, the poems also helped increase morale. Her poem *The Great War* was about how although the war was not yet over it would one day end and that the Germans would face their punishment.

CHAPTER 9

Life Goes On

Despite the war and the urgency to join the armed forces, and in no small part because of the war and the need to keep up morale, elements of ordinary life continued in Sheffield.

In early September the Lyceum Theatre presented a production called *Who's the Lady?*', which was described as being a 'really funny piece' and was 'one of London's biggest successes'. The Sheffield Weekly News Cycling Club organised matinees with the Lyceum Theatre to raise funds for the Lord Mayor's Relief Fund.

The Lord Mayor's Relief Fund had been set up a week after the outbreak of war. The Fund was set up by the Lord Mayor of Sheffield, GE Branson, and was aimed 'for the relief of Sheffield, if and when the necessity arises'. With thousands of men joining the armed forces, there were thousands of families who lost income and now faced hardship of varying levels of severity.

At the Theatre Royal *The Fatal Wedding*, a play about New York life was performed. At the Sheffield Empire the Zigeuner Quartet performed a musical ensemble. The comedian Chas R Whittle performed comedy songs, the ventriloquist Tom Edwards gave a humorous performance of a surgery operated by a bloodless surgeon, Arthur Ferris gave humorous character studies, the comedian Harold Baker, The Zanfrellas who were novelty equilibrists, a comedy sketch called *A Savage Encounter* by Fred Edwards and May Yates, Adele Moraw 'the Gay Parisian' and the latest war films could all be enjoyed at the same venue.

Oswald Williams, believed to be the only stage illusionist in the country headed the bill at the Hippodrome. FV St Clair performed his good voice and 'phenominal quickness of thought'. He would ask a member of the audience to name a subject and he would instantly sing a verse about that subject. *They built Piccadilly for me* was performed by JW Ricksby, Tsambo and Tambo tambourine artists, sangfroid athletes The De Wynne Bros, singers and dancers the Soho Trio, Rosie Lloyd, Will Poluski junior, and the Whittakers performing a 'clever burlesque' of *Dick Whittington* were also enjoyed along with the war news and pictures.

The Cinema House on Fargate presented *The Penalty of Beauty*, and *The Dream Ship*. Comedy and topical films, including dramas *The Unexpected*, and *The Seagull* were shown.

The Electra Palace on Fitzalan Square showed *When the Right Call Came*, *The Countess Veschi's Jewels*, *Max on the Briny* which had 'abundant humour', *The Devil Fox of the North*, *Bronco Billy and the Mine Shark* and war pictures and news. The Tivoli Picture House provided 'excellent vaudeville artists'. The Union Street Picture Palace, Hillsborough Kinema House, Globe Picture Palace, Spital Hill Coliseum, Unity Picture Palace and the Greystones Picture Palace were also showing 'capital programmes'.

That other popular form of entertainment, football, proved to be a matter of great debate. There were arguments over whether it should be stopped during the war. John Charles Clegg said stopping it would cause panic. Clegg was a former Sheffield Wednesday player and Chairman and was in 1914 the Chair of the Football Association. He was also responsible for the creation of Sheffield United's ground on Bramall Lane. John Charles Clegg was the older brother of Sir William Clegg, Leader of the Council, who had also played for Sheffield Wednesday and was capped for England twice, before injury ended his footballing days. He then became a lawyer and represented the notorious Sheffield killer Charlie Peace, before turning full time to politics. There was therefore local political pressure to ensure football continued.

Both Sheffield United and Sheffield Wednesday continued to play in the Midlands League, but professionalism was abandoned as players were no longer paid and had to find employment. Players who had to work on Saturday mornings often missed their matches as a consequence, which resulted in 'guest players' being required.

Nonetheless in the early stages of the war the crowds of spectators at football matches formed ideal target audiences for recruitment speeches. During the afternoon of 5 September 'great patriotic demonstrations' took place at Bramall Lane when 'special efforts' were made to try and encourage football spectators to enlist. A band played patriotic music, following which the fans were addressed by Mr GH Bibbings. The 'mad Kaiser' had plunged the whole of Europe into 'a welter of sacrifice', and that they should not underestimate the gravity of the situation. He told the crowd that if they did not want the German flag to fly victorious then they should commit themselves to ensuring the British flag flew supreme. He praised the efforts of those who had already enlisted and were making a difference, especially the navy who had stopped the German fleet and the 9th Lancers whose charge against the Germans would 'ring through history'. The Empire was responding to the call, he announced, 'Would the men of Yorkshire be the last to reply?' To this there were loud cries of, 'No!' He said he had received a letter from the Prime Minister's secretary informing him that Asquith desired for men to leave the football grounds and join the war effort. Bibbings added, 'Leave the football to those of us who are crocked; we will look after it while you do the nation's duty.' Councillor Arthur Neal also spoke to the fans, encouraging them to enlist. All of those who wanted to enlist were marched to the recruiting offices after the match, with the band leading the procession.

There were questions asked in the House of Commons to establish whether it was possible to tax football fans who were not wearing military uniform so that they paid their entrance to the matches and paid the same amount to the Government's war fund, to encourage men to use their time more wisely. It was argued that football fans were being singled out and that if football fans were penalised for watching their favourite sport then so should the spectators of other sports. Calls to end other sports were not so frequently made and indeed the King himself announced he fully intended to have his horses race for the full racing season. There were some who argued that the working class, which was the class providing the majority of the troops and all of the war work in terms of producing munitions, was being attacked, with the higher classes being allowed to continue enjoying their pleasures.

Soldiers fighting overseas were grateful that football was continuing. They received newspapers sent to them by friends or relatives. They missed football and wanted to hear about it. It was a connection to home, something to talk about and follow, especially as the war continued and the troops began to miss home. Sheffield soldiers obtained their sports information, as many South Yorkshire sports fans today, through the *Green 'Un*. Private J Ward of the British Expeditionary Force, who was of Allen Street in Sheffield, wrote 'It will please your readers to know how the *Green 'Un* travels in warfare. The one I got on December 1 and read at daybreak, before the close at night must have passed forty hands.'

The worry of war resulted in a lack of money and a reluctance for people to spend money if they had any. John Atkinson, who owned a clothing shop at 76 to 90 The Moor, held a half-price sale in August, which he extended into September, in order to increase custom. In large advertisements placed in local newspapers he expressed his patriotism in the hope that people would buy from his shop. He was advertising 20/- of clothing for 10/- and 10/- for 5/-.

On 4 September it was reported that produce was arriving in Sheffield in large quantities but there was an absence of buyers, even when prices were significantly reduced. Fruit was now cheaper than any time in living memory. 'It is the shortage of money which is making the shopkeeper tearful and fearful,' said one shopkeeper, who added that the fruit and vegetables were of good quality but still 'trade is quiet'.

It was discussed whether staff who had been 'thrown out of work by the present crisis' could be taken on by the corporation to fill vacancies, but this was not considered advisable at that time. The Finance Committee recommended to the councillors that the places of all employees who may be called for service have their jobs kept open so that they could recommence their work upon their return.

There were growing concerns for those who did not have jobs. A letter sent by the Co-operative and Labour Distress Committee urged that the corporation should create public work as job creation schemes. In September 1914 there were 1,054 men registered on the Distress Committee's list, though that figure began to fall as men began working in munitions or took up active service. However, the number of women, whose husbands were away, increased. In September 1914 289 women sought financial help, though that figure also dropped slightly by November.

On 1 October £10,342 was spent on sewerage works and other works mainly to provide employment. On 6 October it was planned to spend an additional £70,000 on sewerage secondary treatment to create relief work.

Other proposed projects to be commenced straight away included building a major road behind the Blacksmith's Arms at Fulwood, the widening of Fulwood Road and the widening of Chesterfield Road at Meadowhead. By the end of the war the process of obtaining land to widen Fulwood Road was still ongoing.

There was one surprising consequence of war during those early months. On 5 October it was apparent crime had fallen; for the first time in 33 years cases for trial at the Sheffield Quarter Sessions could be dealt with in one court session. There were only 16 cases compared to 73 for the same quarter during the previous year.

On 1 September 1914 the *Telegraph and Star* reported that Germany had withdrawn troops from the French frontier in order to send them to meet the Russians. 'Such an action indicates that Germany is at length feeling the pressure of the task she has undertaken.'

It was updates such as that above which were eagerly followed by Sheffield's citizens. To meet the insatiable desire for news penny specials were sold in the evenings to relay the most important developments which had occurred too late to feature in the main editions. Some newsboys in Sheffield were capitalising on this interest, buying copies of the specials, as they would ordinary newspapers, but sold them to the readers for more than the papers should cost. An appeal was placed in the newspapers for readers to report any such newsboy with a view to prosecuting them for obtaining money through deception.

Although some news seemed promising in the early weeks and

months, seemingly corroborating the optimistic belief that the war would soon be over, news that was most unwelcome began to filter through in the form of accounts of the numbers of men who were losing their lives. People had seen hundreds of wounded soldiers arrive in the city, but it was another month before bodies began to be brought home. On 6 October the first of Sheffield's fallen was brought back to the city. It brought a stark realisation of what Britain had involved itself in. The war was not as glamorous as had been believed.

Some of the first of Sheffield's men to be killed in battle were: Lieutenant HK Peace who died of wounds he suffered on his birthday on 16 October. He had been the first Territorial officer in Sheffield to go to the front line of battle; Lieutenant Roy DP Milner of Totley Hall, a member of the Sherwood Forresters, who died in the battle of the Aisne. '...when leading his little command in the most dashing manner during our first fight. His actions with that of others secured the successful issue of a fight which was of vital importance to the safety of the whole line,' according to his colonel. He died on 20 September; Lieutenant RN Carswell of the University OTC the first representative of the university to be killed in action, though he was not a member of the City Battalion; Harry Allen, a former postman living on Valley Road until war broke. He was killed in the Battle of Aisne. Between the outbreak of war and the end of October 36 Sheffield men were recorded as having been killed.

There were occasional instances of good news amid the tragedy. At the Battle of the Bulwark almost all of the crew of a ship died, but 20-year-old First Class Stoker Fred Goodlad Dufty whose family lived at Carwood Terrace in Sheffield managed to escape before the ship sank.

In addition to death and injury, Sheffield folk read accounts of the conditions that the men were living and fighting in. On 25 November the local papers gave accounts of frozen trenches. There was snow and so no longer was there mud. The conditions were causing 'great hardship to the troops' it was said, with it being almost impossible to keep warm. Severe frostbite was becoming an increasingly common affliction.

Still, the injuries, deaths and descriptions of life in the trenches did not severely dampen the enthusiasm to join the army and navy. Nonetheless, continued efforts had to be made to encourage more men to join up.

One easy way to achieve this was to relax the rules of selecting men. On 26 November 1914 the Government allowed for men to volunteer for training if they were too old or too unhealthy to enlist.

The *Telegraph and Star* called for more men in order to crush the enemy completely, 'While we are confident that the issue of the war, it must never be forgotten that it is highly important that Germany should be brought to her knees before the Allies have had time to grow so tired of the war that they will make it easy for the common enemy to secure peace. … This is why we need men in great numbers. The world will never have lasting peace if the war ends from mere breathlessness on the part of the combatants. It must be a "knock-out" for Germany, and nothing less.'

An early threat to victory was identified, in the form of alcohol. The Chief Constable sent circulars to all licensees urging them to ensure that all recruits were kept sober. For the benefit of recruits, and for workers, to ensure the best was made of them, rules preventing the sale of beer after 9:30pm during the week and 9pm on Sundays were introduced under the Intoxicating Liquor (Temporary Restriction) Act, 1914. Women were not allowed to drink before 10:30am.

On 16 November a mass meeting was held to protest against the new rules which should have come into force two days later but were ultimately postponed because Home Office confirmation was required. There were calls for prohibition. The debate over the ever increasing restrictions on alcohol sales continued in the letters pages of the local newspapers throughout the war.

As the fourth month of the war came to an end there were signs of optimism and some still believed it would be over by Christmas. Such optimism was fuelled by developments publicised in the local newspapers. The *Telegraph and Star* wrote, in an article entitled 'The Outlook' printed on 28 November, 'This weekend brings a more pronounced feeling of confidence than has been experienced for some time; and so far as the situation can be gauged it is a feeling which is fully justifiable. ... The truth appears to be that the Germans and Austrians are retreating more or less in disorder, but are fighting stubbornly at certain points with the object of averting complete disaster...' However, it hinted that the war could last some considerable time, by adding, 'Our ability to wait for a very long period will in all probability be severely tested.'

CHAPTER 10

Over by Christmas

As Advent commenced efforts were being made to step up the military campaign. Locally on 5 December 1,131 men of the City Battalion moved to the purpose-built Redmires Camp where specially built huts provided accommodation. Although they still did not have uniforms or rifles, observers would have noted that the effort to build a camp meant that the end of the war was not considered to be coming in the very near future.

Despite the poor weather large numbers of spectators, forming a crowd of 'remarkable dimensions' according to the *Telegraph and Star*, watched the members of the Battalion march from Norfolk Barracks, led by a military band. Colonel Mainwaring, who was by now in command, led the march. A tram and other traffic were forced to halt for a substantial amount of time as the procession passed.

Redmires Camp was located on high, marshy land that was exposed to the full effect of the elements. On the day they arrived at the camp the men did not receive a warm welcome, with the weather being described by Richard Sparley in his 1920 history of the Battalion as 'wildy and stormy' with rain and snow.

Colonel C. V. Mainwaring who Commanded the City Battalion until September 1915. (*The Author's Collection*)

The men lived in large huts measuring 60ft by 20ft, which were raised slightly off the ground on bricks. Each had a coal stove in the centre, was gas lit, and was capable of accommodating 34 men. It was very much a work in progress, with a large amount of work needed to make the camp fit for purpose. Eventually some basic facilities for sport and recreation helped keep the spirits of the men up, as did the two local public houses which were frequented.

That winter was bitter and two members of the Battalion died before it faced any enemy action. On 8 February 1915 Private Charles Haydn Hanforth died of pneumonia despite treatment at the 3rd Northern General Hospital at Collegiate Crescent. He was buried with full military honours, including a gun salute, at Fulwood Church. Less than a fortnight later, on 20 February, Private JC Ortton died although the cause of his death is unknown.

December was a wet month in Sheffield with only rare breaks from

A group of soldiers of the City Battalion at Redmires Camp. 12/1007 Thomas A. W. Newsholme is fourth from the right on the second row from the front. (*Photograph by kind permission of Donald Wiltshire*)

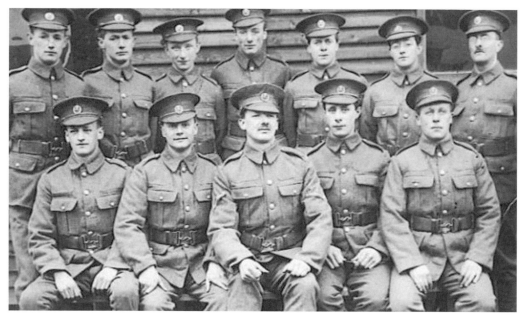

A group of soldiers of the City Battalion at Redmires Camp. (*Photograph by kind permission of Donald Wiltshire*)

The Y.M.C.A. Hut at Redmires Camp. (*Photograph by kind permission of Donald Wiltshire*)

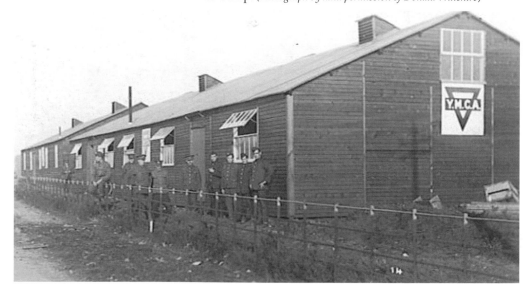

heavy rain. This, and the ongoing war, resulted in a low mood on the Home Front. On 8 December it was noted that people were having breakdowns due to the concern and fear, both for loved ones overseas and the possibility of invasion by enemy forces. Of course, while ever there was fear, someone wanted to make money out of that fear. 'Nerves need nourishment' read an advertisement in the local newspapers, 'So many people are nervous, sleepless, irritable; and rapidly approaching the point of mental exhaustion and physical breakdown.' A new diet was suggested by Sir William Taylor, the late Surgeon General of the Forces, to give elements not supplied in sufficient quantity by regular diets. He recommended Sanaphos, emphasised to be a British product, to nourish the nerves and beat the blues.

The public were being advised to learn the rules of the new Defence of the Realm Act (DORA) which allowed for the military to take any land or buildings for the war effort, prevented people from owning carrier pigeons in case they should be used to send messages to the

Members of the City Battalion at Redmires Camp during the first ration parade. (*Photograph reproduced from the Picture Sheffield Collection, courtesy of Sheffield Local Studies Library*)

enemy, prevented anyone from owning any searchlights or other equipment which could be used to signal enemy aircraft, prevented the use of fireworks, restricted the displaying of light and banned the use of any wireless apparatus capable of communicating with the enemy.

In the same letter which he wrote of the interest in the *Green 'Un*, Private J Ward, summed up the feeling of how the war was progressing as of the beginning of December 1914. He wrote, 'It seems very funny out here that all the boys seem to be in one mind, and that is that they will see their home for Christmas. Well, I prefer to differ with thems [sic] and to rely on Mr Asquith's good old maxim, "Wait and see".'

Details of the war were still being printed in great detail, with the penny specials continuing to inform a fascinated, but concerned public back on the Home Front. People in Sheffield were aware that friends and loved ones overseas were facing a bitter winter and that there was severe bloodshed. The increasing number of troops returning home and being treated in the city's makeshift war hospitals gave a strong sign of the horrors of what was occurring in what was being referred to as a 'battle of human moles'.

The grave of Charles Haydn Hanforth of the City Battalion, who died of pneumonia in Sheffield before he had opportunity to see action against the enemy. (*The Author*)

On 5 December the *Telegraph and Star* warned that the war would not be over soon:

'We must guard against the error of thinking that the war will be over in a few months and must not think that we have, as yet, the slightest justification for any relaxation of the national efforts.'

OVER BY CHRISTMAS

A letter sent from the trenches, written at midnight on 12 December 1914 addressed to the *Telegraph and Star*, and printed in that paper, showed some humour towards the end but described the conditions faced by the troops in the trenches:

'I have been flooded out of my bed, and as this little spot on the table seems to be the only one where no muddy drops are falling from the roof of the dug out, I might as well seize the opportunity to write between now and daylight.

When I wrote last we were frost-bound. It soon thawed, and for the last fortnight we have been victims of rain. To make things pleasanter we have the prospect of eighteen days (over Christmas) before we get back to billets. It is difficult to give you an idea of what stead rain here means. One's lines seem such an orderly, permanent, town-like, and solid series of cubby holes and trenches that when they all start to fall in, and one doesn't know where one is in the dark, it is as if one were trying at home to navigate a pitch-dark London in ruins.

Navigate is the word. The divisional staff have ordered gondolas, and we are going to train the fiercer male eels of Flanders to carry bombs to the enemy trenches.'

Appeals were made for people to donate gifts that could be sent to the troops who would spend Christmas away. Special arrangements were made for parcels at Christmas to ensure troops received letters and gifts to give pleasure to those who could not return. Tobacco, cigarettes and warm clothing were particularly sought. Adverts also appeared in newspapers advertising products that people could buy in order to send to friends or loved ones. Zam-buk was one of the suggested products, with the claim from a soldier that 'a box of Zam-buk out here is like a loaf of bread'. It was ideal for treating cuts, wounds and sore feet.

The best present for most soldiers was the welcome news that they would be given free transport by the Government, from the front line direct to their homes, if they were in a position to return home for Christmas, and free transport back to the battlegrounds. There were concerns from Sheffield women that loved ones in the navy would not be given the same privilege. This was just part of the general annoyance by the relatives and friends of those in the navy, as well as the members of the navy themselves, who felt that all the focus was on the soldiers whilst they were engaged in important military battles on the seas.

Certainly there was a desire for men to join other elements of the forces other than the army although the overwhelming majority of servicemen from the city joined the army, resulting in a natural emphasis towards that force. On 13 December volunteers were obtained for Naval Volunteer Reserve for anti aircraft in Sheffield. Almost four times the number that was needed applied for the positions.

As Christmas approached many soldiers and sailors did come back to Sheffield but not to their homes. Thousands of men were being treated in the city's hospitals.

A Christmas card from wounded soldiers being treated at the 3rd Northern General Hospital. (*Photograph reproduced from the Picture Sheffield Collection, courtesy of Sheffield Local Studies Library*)

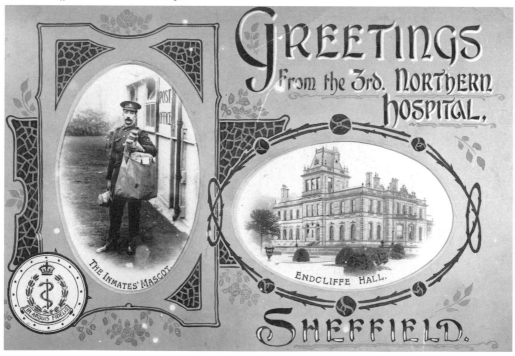

It had been a 'trying year' for the Sheffield Royal Infirmary according to Mr HH Bedford, presiding over the quarterly meeting of the Board of Governors in December. Since August the hospital had been part of a military hospital treating English and Belgian wounded soldiers. This influx of large numbers of patients, often with severe needs, had resulted in huge financial strain. A public appeal was made for funds. An added difficulty was the fact that large numbers of the hospital staff had joined the armed forces, resulting in a skills and experience shortage. The Master Cutler was gratified to announce the workers of his own firm were donating regularly to the hospital along with providing donations to the fund for the maintenance of the wives and children of the Reservists. He hoped other workers would follow their example.

On 14 December a letter from 'Eleven Comrades' was printed in the *Telegraph and Star*. The men thanked hospital staff for the 'kind treatment we have received at their hands. Since we came to the Royal Hospital wounded, we have been cared for in a way that requires the highest praise from the public and army, as well as for the way in which the medical staff throughout gave their time to our wounded soldiers. We would also like to thank the public for the kindness they have extended to us while we have been in the hospital.'

Not everyone was feeling such kindness for the troops, however. On the same day that the letter was printed in the *Telegraph and Star*, it was announced in that same paper that councillors had agreed to withdraw free tram passes for soldiers who were based in Sheffield. It was argued that the privilege was being abused. Large crowds of soldiers, the councillors heard, were staying on trams for 'mere pleasure and amusement' repeatedly travelling from one terminus to another without any intention of disembarking, with such large numbers that the paying public could not step foot on a tram for their own journeys. This was costing the Tramways Committee £300 each week. It was agreed that the free passes would continue for wounded soldiers who were convalescing.

The decision to withdraw passes caused outrage from the public. It was denounced as 'unfair' and 'unpatriotic'. One correspondent argued that Hillsborough Barracks troops were being vilified because they were generally not locals. The councillors had, he argued, only withdrawn the passes when the City Battalion, which was composed of Sheffield men and generally professionals at that, had left for Redmires. This was vehemently denied with the argument that passes had existed before the City Battalion was formed, but this did nothing to appease the angry public who felt the councillors were attacking those who were eager to help defend Britain.

Another correspondent named S Ardken of Victoria Road in Sheffield wrote:

'Are the people of Sheffield so badly off that they cannot afford to give all soldiers free tram rides? Sheffield is making more money out of the war than any town in England.

Surely the town is not going to lie down tamely under the stigma of meanness, the most paltry meanness ever shown, that has been placed on it. It is a disgrace to the Council, that they have been so cowardly and paltry in their dealing with this matter.

We want men, and this is a sample of the shabby treatment that is handed out to them by the rulers of a wealthy city. It is not the citizens wish that they should have to pay out of their miserable allowances towards swelling tramway profits, and it must be stopped at once. ...

It is those who do not wear uniform who ought and must take a back seat, in the stage of National danger. ...

It is an honour for the city to do all they can for such brave and self-denying men, and what a little thing to give free tram rides. Would Sir William want the to pay their fares if the Germans were approaching? As for costing £300 a week, what if it did? But I challenge anyone to prove it.'

The editorial in the *Telegraph and Star* summed up the general feeling:

'What if the glorious privilege of a free ride has been abused? We would send every person who has complained straight into the trenches and leave him there till he learned to appreciate to some extent what the real sacrifices of war are.'

Despite the increasing number of wounded soldiers arriving in the city and the increasingly frequent reports of Sheffield men dying on the war front, more men continued to join the forces. On 15 December 250 more troops were appealed for to join the City Battalion as reserves with the expectation that men would die or be wounded in the main battalion. They received an allowance but were initially required to sleep in their own homes until more accommodation was constructed at Redmires, with that vacated by the main battalion having been quickly occupied by other troops. Despite needing more men, the infrastructure for the troops was clearly inadequate.

As Christmas came ever closer no one could have been in any doubt that the war would not be over by 25 December. This was especially the case when on 16 December the German fleet bombarded the English coast. The Sheffield newspapers reported extensively on the bombardments which had seen considerable damage and loss of life in Hartlepool, with 108 having died in the town by New Year's Eve, with many others still with serious injuries, including some who were critically wounded. In Scarborough buildings had been damaged and destroyed, with lots of residents fleeing to Hull by train and huge crowds forming at the station as people were waiting to get on any train. In Whitby there had been great damage, also, with Whitby Abbey partly destroyed

The editorial in the *Telegraph and Star* on 17 December emphasised the importance of joining the army or navy. 'Now that English lives hath been sacrificed on English soil there can no longer be the slightest excuse for any failure of full realisation of the horrors of war, and the need for a speedy and victorious end to the present campaign...'

In the wake of the tragedy on the East Coast, the Women's Relief Corp in Sheffield appealed for more volunteers to join their ranks. There intention was to relieve men, encourage recruiting, and to be 'trained, prepared and willing to do our share in the event of an emergency'. They were to hold a meeting in January and hoped for more to join their number.

Despite the horrors of war abroad and on the British coast there was a need to try and give some festive fun, if only for the children. A

'Christmas Number' was produced by the *Telegraph and Star*. It was a special paper called 'Christmas Cheer' and it consisted of 28 pages of seasonal stories, pictures, puzzles, a 'Vulcan' cartoon about the war and more. The paper was aimed for family reading, with something for everyone. It was on sale for one penny. 'Christmas Cheer should be in every home.'

The Christmas fair, held on land next to the Midland Railway Station, also added festive cheer. It appeared as if as many people attended the fair as in previous years. The land was occupied with swings, roundabouts and 'other devices provided for the recreation of those people who find congenial entertainment in the mingled melody, noise and bustle that mark the behaviour of the crowd at this always popular resort'.

There was little trade for Christmas a week before the big day, although shopkeepers and market stall holders were hopeful that they would receive some business. There was lots of fruit although the variety was somewhat restricted, and it was generally reasonably priced. New potatoes were a luxury. Other luxuries were kidney beans and asparagus. Salad was priced 'fairly stiff'. There was no horseradish. Other vegetables were 'plentiful'. English turkeys were noted as being in good supply. Birds from France and Italy were on sale during Christmas week, at a price similar to previous years. Rabbits and ducks were also on sale, but there was a 'serious shortage' of fish.

In terms of decoration, there was a small amount of mistletoe from France but there were lots of trees. Most households had a tree and as such large numbers were sold at Sheffield market where there were 'Christmas trees galore'. One trader expected to sell 12,000 trees.

Trade did pick up, with it being remarked in the *Telegraph and Star* a few days later that there were 'no signs of war in the Sheffield markets to-day – unless the term can be applied to the good-natured, but not the less keen, bargaining by which the thrifty housewife endeavours to effect an economy at the expense of the salespeople, who on their part tell a pitiful tale of profits cut so fine that one feels almost ashamed to pay even the price they ask.'

Men were 'conspicuous by their absence' unlike in previous years when marketing brought out the whole family. Where a loved one was overseas many of the women were buying large amounts of supplies to send to the front. Despite the sluggish trade of the previous week, shopkeepers and market stall holders, were now in a good position with it remarked, 'the admission generally made that trade is "not at all bad" may be regarded as the most eloquent testimony that trade has in fact been extremely good.' In the Castlefolds markets many of the stocks were 'practically depleted' quite early in the afternoon. Prices were high, especially for holly and mistletoe, but irrespective of this people were spending their money in order to make Christmas as enjoyable as possible and have a short respite from the darkness of war.

Workers in the steel and cutlery trades were so busy fulfilling Government orders that in most cases they had only Christmas Day and Boxing Day off work, with no holiday over the New Year period. Those employed in the silver and allied trades, however, had very little work due to a lack of desire for luxury goods, and so had an extended Christmas break. Most shops in the city were closed from the Thursday night until Monday morning, enabling shop workers to have a long Christmas weekend.

Married women, whose husbands were in the forces, were kept under close scrutiny as Christmas approached. Their names were given to the Police Headquarters under new Government rules 'to protect the women themselves and to save them from getting into trouble which would endanger their allowances'. The word 'trouble' meant any state of intoxication or immoral behaviour. The women engaging in such behaviour would first be arrested and taken into the care of a 'lady visitor' who would regularly visit to ensure the behaviour had ceased. Allowances would be stopped if they were found to continue such behaviour.

The ongoing argument regarding the consumption of alcohol and the opening hours of licensed premises once again intensified during the festive season. 'A DISGUSTED PUBLICAN' of Sheffield wrote that there was no justice that someone who likes beer should have to return home at 9:30pm whilst lemonade drinkers could remain on the premises until 11 o'clock. He further argued that there should be consistency in the rules. Clubs were open all night selling alcohol. If the rules were to prevent drunkenness and to ensure time was spent on things beneficial to the war effort, then clubs would not sell alcohol. He questioned why those undertaking government work in the factories could not have any pleasures if they had to work late into the evening and did not finish work until after 9:30pm. 'There is unrest amongst the workers in the large East End works [of Sheffield] that their privileges should be taken away.' Other licensees were keen to ensure the public understood that the issue was not about allowing excessive drinking at all hours but that instead it was about ensuring that the city's large number of public houses were not forced to close due to a lack of trade as a result of the 'unfair' licensing laws. It was also argued that to prevent those who were working or the war effort in the factories from any of life's pleasures was an attack on the workers themselves.

At a conference of The General Council of the Licensed Victuallers' Defence League in Leeds in mid December it was reported that in many areas beer sales had been halved due to the regulations.

As Christmas came even closer there was mixed news. The *Telegraph and Star* reported the 'Allies Splendid Work', with 'Trenches Taken Guns Demolished; Advance Everywhere' on 21 December. The following day it reported that a 'Mile of Trenches Taken; Allies Again Make Excellent Progress; Cheery Official Message; Germans Thrust Back at the Bayonet Points'. Again the following day the headline was 'Allies Good Captures' Another Day of Progress All Along the Line'.

However, just as optimism would have been raised in Sheffield, on Christmas Eve the *Telegraph and Star* reported on an enemy plane over Dover. It dropped a bomb but no damage was caused. It was chased away by British air pilots.

In its editorial that day, the *Telegraph and Star* wrote:

'The season at which the Church bids us turn our thoughts to the ideal of peace and goodwill finds the Old World plunged in the most desperate struggle in history. Millions of the best men in Europe and beyond are engaged with the aid of the infernal resources of science, in attempting to kill or maim each other, and sorrow in its acutest forms has descended on thousands of innocent homes. At such a time it would be a mockery to wish our readers a Merry Christmas without reserve, but we may at least express the hope that their children's happiness will be as keen as possible. Christmas is in a special sense the children's festival, and their right to happiness must not be interfered with.'

Children did have some happiness. On Christmas Eve the pantomime *Dick Whittington* was performed at the Theatre Royal. 'The whole show went excellently.' It was remarked upon that it was a very enjoyable pantomime and would have given some welcome distraction, for at least the three and a half hours which it lasted for.

At the Hippodrome, the *Cinderella* pantomime formed a 'pretty spectacle' with 'plenty of good fun, and an altogether pleasant show', although there was some criticism regarding the lack of singing by some of the leading characters, but the character of Pickles was the highlight of the show, with some 'really funny' lines.

Red Riding Hood was performed at the New Tivoli, but no details were provided, undoubtedly it would have given lots of pleasure to the children and any adults who were present.

And for the adults there was plenty of entertainment at the city's theatres, but it was not all fun because fiction was mixed with sobering films showing the latest war news including the reality of the attacks on the coastal towns of Scarborough, Whitby and Hartlepool. An amateur dramatics performance was given at the Lyceum Theatre in aid of Belgian Refugees' Sheffield Fund, with a large audience although many seats were empty. The theatre also hosted a new play by Leslie Barlow-Massicks, a Rotherham writer, entitled *The Bachelor's Defence League* and described as being 'a comedy of tomorrow' which was modern in its story and the outlook on life of its leading characters.

The Empire Theatre had a 'brilliant British burlesque' with ladies in 'full dress and very little dress' representing various nationalities. Dances and singing were performed. Other performances during the festive period at The Empire included singing, dancing, Fred Wildon performing on his phonofiddle, comedy and a matinee on Boxing Day.

War pictures showing the havoc wrought on the English coast during the German attacks were shown also.

At the New Tivoli the 'Melody Maids' performed singing and music, Tom Lees the 'very clever' pianist, a comedian and lots of singers. Other highlights included an educational film showing the industries of Sudan, a drama entitled *A Reformed Santa Claus*, and two comedies entitled *Private Bunny* and *At Three O'Clock*. Special war pictures were also shown. There was a performance on Christmas Day.

A comedy drama entitled *The Man on the Box* formed the principal performance at the Electra Palace. It was described as 'one of the cleverest cinema productions seen in Sheffield recently'. Other 'remarkably good' pictures were also to be shown, as were pictures of 'battered Scarborough' and troops marching through the town following the attacks. Views of the war were shown including pictures of the flooded trenches. Two 'powerful' dramas entitled *The Mysterious Lodger* and *Broncho Billy's Christmas Deed* were performed as was a political 'topical harlequin' named 'The Clown of Europe'.

At Cinema House on Fargate Charles Dickens's *A Christmas Carol* was performed. An 'interesting story' of an American secret service was told in the film *Daphina*, and a film about the wife of a young fisherman eloping with her medical attendant was entitled *The Inner Conscience*. Also shown was a film about the working of the munitions factories, as well as war pictures including the bombardment of Scarborough. Comedy relief was provided in the form of films entitled *The Taming of Mrs Wifles* and *Such a Hunter*.

The Picture Palace on Union Street presented *Detective Craig's Coup*, a picture of 'absorbing interest, showing in a most striking manner into what depth and perils an unsuspecting youth of good heart, but careless, pleasure-seeking disposition may fall'. Two comic pictures entitled *Winky's Jealousy* and *Caught in Tights* offered much amusement. Again the cinema showed the latest war news including pictures of the bombardment of the north-east coast.

The Hillsboro' Kinema House primarily showed the film *Should he Forgive?* which contained 'a story of considerable interest', though the nature of the act that forgiveness was being considered for was not disclosed in the publicity. *The Man With a Future* was also shown, which provided the story of a detective's adventures.

A 'vivid reproduction' of the Passion play was performed at the Don Picture Palace, which was 'of especial interest'. Comedy films of *Two Father Christmases*, *Caught in Tights* and *What's the Use* were also performed. War pictures were shown.

At Walkley Palladium the principal film was a 'stirring war story' entitled *Saved by the Union Jack*, with other drama films entitled *The Tell Tale Scar* and *A Bowl of Roses* along with the comedy *Such a Hunter*.

Greystones Picture Palace and Spital Hill Coliseum also presented well attended films.

The 'Life Targets' in the Wicker provided a novel form of entertainment. Stills from cinema pictures were lined up and members of the public were encouraged to shoot at them, causing 'a great deal of fun'.

In the days before Christmas the *Telegraph and Star* wrote, 'Many optimists prophesised that the war would be over by Christmas. We never took that view, but we are not inclined to plume ourselves overmuch on that fact, though Christmas is so near that the optimists may consider that they have been proved wrong.'

Whilst not over by Christmas Sheffielders who remained optimists could be forgiven for thinking that the end could be soon. Although progress was slow, there was still progress. 'When progress is reported it may mean no more than an advance of a few yards, but it is often none the less significant on that account. Patience is demanded of the spectator of war, as well as of the soldiers at the front,' remarked the *Telegraph and Star* on 21 December. But uncertainty remained, as did the fears of an invasion. Many would have taken comfort in the words of the newspaper that the Germans could not cause damage to Britain. The raids on Hartlepool, Whitby and Scarborough had been intended to put fear and terror into the minds of those at the Home Front, it was acknowledged, but the efforts had been a 'monumental' failure it was claimed, and such efforts would not be repeated without significant loss to the Germans. 'The desire to harm us is not paralleled by ability to inflict injury,' the paper claimed. How wrong these claims would later be shown to be.

The *Telegraph and Star* was somewhat optimistic in its view that 'the common view that the final defeat of the Germans is assured, provided that this country continues to play its part'. Little would they know there would be three more Christmases before the hostilities would come to an end.

Christmas saw a welcome relief for those who had loved ones return from the battlefields but it was a time of heartache and misery for those spending a Christmas in the knowledge their loved ones would never come home.

Others who could not return were Sheffield men who had been captured and were in a prisoner of war camp in Germany. A post card (Sheffield Archives: MD6860) was sent to the Lord Mayor of Sheffield from Ruhleben expressing 'compliments of the season to the Lord Mayor & citizens of Sheffield'. It was signed by 'Sheffielders (Civil Prisoners of War) in Rehleben'. Twenty-four men signed the card,

Prisoners of War, including soldier George T Berry. (*Photograph reproduced from the Picture Sheffield Collection, courtesy of Sheffield Local Studies Library*)

including two men with the surname Waring and two with the surname Mason who were probably related. No information was given about their conditions.

On New Year's Eve 220 more wounded soldiers arrived in Sheffield from La Bassee, arriving by train at 6am. Many had come straight from the battlefields and were still covered in mud. Almost all the men were dirty. Despite this and their wounds they were described as being a 'happy crowd'.

That same day approximately 400 troops of the City Battalion at Redmires Camp commenced their festive break. It was 'like breaking up day at school' it was said. The men were described as being in high spirits. Due to being at camp on Christmas Day they had been granted an extra day of leave and would not have to return until Sunday night.

Each soldier had been given a travel pass to last the duration of the holiday and a shilling. They had been looking forward to returning to their homes because there had been approximately three inches of snow fall over night and it was extremely cold.

After a breakfast they went on parade. Those from Sheffield left straight after. The others marched to Sheffield where they were given free rail travel passes at Sheffield's two rail stations. It was certainly a happy day for one Lance Corporal, who got married as the holiday commenced.

On New Year's Eve the editorial of the *Telegraph and Star* stated:

'Writing a year ago, no one would have prophesised that today we should have been so long in the midst of Armageddon that we had come to regard its horrors as the norm of human life.'

Elsewhere in the paper it was said that the end of the war was unlikely to come 'for some considerable time' but that 'a decisive event would change the whole aspect of the matter'.

It was felt Sheffield should be thankful that it had not felt the horrors of war as much as Belgium which had suffered the brutality of the German invasion, along with tracts of France and Poland. 'The time for the grand advance against the Germans has not yet come, but it is not far off, and already the preliminaries may be observed.' The editor predicted that it would be during early spring 1915 that large numbers of German troops would be moved and great gains made by the Allies. The year closes, he wrote, 'with a memory of blood and tears, and the New Year dawns with a promise of more, but beyond these there is hope.'

CHAPTER 11

The Role of Women

In order to place the role of women during the war into perspective it is first important to give a brief overview of the status of women in Sheffield in the years immediately prior to its start.

Women in Sheffield had long been striving for equality. A suffragette campaign had commenced during the late 19th century but gathered pace following the turn of the century and continued up to the outbreak of war.

In July 1906 Emmeline Pankhurst visited the city and spoke about women's suffrage, later addressing a crowd at Hillsborough.

In November 1907 when Mr Haldane, the Secretary of War, arrived into Sheffield he was greeted by large numbers of women holding posters with the slogan 'Votes for Women'. They presented a petition to him but they were told he would not refer to the issue in his speech later that day and due to his refusal he found his car plastered with suffragette messages. At the meeting, held at the Albert Hall suffragettes heckled Haldane. The group of women were ejected from the meeting and, following a scuffle, fled to Barkers Pool where they made speeches. There is an irony that they heckled the Secretary of War but went on to show their worth carrying out war work.

In 1907 the Sheffield Trades and Labour Council resolved in favour of giving women the vote, as did the Corporation in 1911 when they called on the government to support the female franchise.

In March 1908 a Women's Social and Political Unit meeting was held in Sheffield during the lead up to the General Election. The WSPU began sponsoring election cars to promote their cause, and took to chalking graffiti on pavements.

Two years after her own visit, Emmeline Pankhurst sent her

daughter Adela to Sheffield to be a local organiser for the WSPU and a shop was opened at 26-28 Chapel Walk. In October 1908 Adela attempted to enter the Cutler's Hall, disguised as a waitress, to disrupt the dinner and speech of the First Lord of the Admiralty. She was identified and ejected from the building. She went on to speak outside the Town Hall and at a monument at the top of Fargate. A fight ensued with the police and the crowd, and it spread into Leopold Street.

In April 1909 election offices were set up at 869 Attercliffe Road during a by-election campaign to collect signatures for a petition calling for women's suffrage. During the by-election questions were asked of each candidate as to whether they supported given women the vote.

On 22 May 1909 women were banned from a meeting at the Norfolk Barracks at which Prime Minister Asquith was speaking. The meeting was stormed and a fight followed.

In July 1910 5000 people attended a 'Votes for Women' rally at Crookesmoor Recreation Ground.

In April 1913 a number of bombs were dropped into several postboxes including those on High Street, Fitzalan Square and Surrey Street. That same month the Attercliffe MP Joseph Pointer found the words 'VOTES FOR WOMEN' written in white paint across the front of his house.

In July 1913 during a Women's Suffrage march from Newcastle to London, the marchers called at Sheffield and assembled at Snig Hill where a crowd of an estimated 5,000 people was addressed. The following day they assembled at Fargate, continuing the march towards the capital.

The suffragette cause in Sheffield was assisted by some men including Edward Carpenter, whose work will be discussed in a later chapter. Carpenter wrote letters promoting women's right to vote and occasionally spoke at their events.

Clearly then Sheffield had already seen great efforts of a diplomatic and disruptive nature, made by women in order to increase their reputation and to gain the vote. Little could they have known in August 1914 that a war being fought on the other side of the English Channel, and their response to it, could achieve more for them in four years than all of the campaigning they had undertaken over the course of several decades.

Lloyd George regarded the suffragettes as 'a thorn' and 'terrorists' but it was, he recalled in his memoirs, one of the brightest stories of the war how they became valued members of society, crucial to the success of the war.

When the war began women in Sheffield quickly assumed an important, if not stereotypical role. They were requested to learn first aid in order to help treat wounded soldiers but their major task was to produce clothing for soldiers and they responded to this request with enthusiasm.

On 3 September 1914 ladies were asked to make cardigan jackets, preferably of khaki colour, for the 3rd West Riding Brigade, Royal Field Artillery (Territorials) who were expected to be sent to the battlefields imminently, because winter was only around the corner and 'the men will require extra clothing if their lots is to be made as comfortable as circumstances will permit'. Women should get to work immediately, the appeal said, to meet the 'urgent demand'. Men were asked to buy such garments or help with subscriptions to fund the production of the required number. The appeal was quickly answered, with one anonymous 'well known gentleman' offering to pay for all 600 cardigans. Meanwhile women were busy knitting socks, sleeping helmets and other items of clothing aimed at staving off the effects of cold. It was remarked upon how there was now no excuse for anyone to assist with the war effort because there were plenty of different types of work that could be undertaken.

A more formal Soldiers' Personal Comforts Depot was established at the Cutlers Hall on 25 September 1914 to provide warm, comfortable clothing for injured soldiers and soldiers and sailors overseas. Food was also required for wounded soldiers to supplement those which could be afforded by the hospitals, as were cigarettes, tobacco and a range of other gifts to help them convalesce. By 1917 the Depot was serving 15 hospitals. It was later known as the Sheffield Voluntary Organisation.

Clothing and food were also provided for wives and children of military personnel overseas, who were struggling to cope financially.

Each winter, as the weather turned cooler and wetter, appeals were made for woollen comforts including helmets, mittens, shirts and pyjamas. Mittens and mufflers were particularly sought. Although women had been regularly knitting, since the war began, for the benefit of soldiers and sailors both overseas, and those recuperating in Sheffield's hospitals, by the winter of 1915 the amount produced on a regular basis had decreased because many women were now working in munitions factories and other places of work and so were unable to knit as much. It was made clear the demand for women who could knit was as great as the demand for the work undertaken by women in the factories.

In December 1915 the Drapers Union was asked to appoint inspectors to provide quality control before the items were dispatched. Arthur Cole was appointed inspector for Sheffield. His first inspection led him to conclude that a very high standard had been achieved by the women.

Women also played a key role in organising Christmas gifts for men overseas and in hospitals. In addition to clothing, candles, games, cigarettes, pipes and tobacco were especially sought.

Mrs Bookless collected items for the navy. Especially sought were mufflers, mittens, cardigans, helmets, books and games, as well as money, which were to be left at Mr Hanbidge's shop on Fargate.

Although the work of the Comforts Depot and other individuals and groups of women carrying out comforts work continued throughout the war, it was not long before it became recognised that women could fill some of the gaps created when men joined the colours. Firms began taking on women in December 1914, although the number of women workers in Sheffield at that time was very small. Firms such as Simplex Motor Works Ltd at Tinsley and Cammell Laird and Co were amongst the first to employ women in shell manufacture and file grinding. Their work was quickly appreciated. However, as 1914 ended and the first full year of war began it became necessary for women to be more fully involved in the war effort.

An account in the *Telegraph* on 15 November 1915 gave a good insight into the work being undertaken in the factories by women. Although it was not specified that the munitions factories visited were

Munitions workers at the Sheffield Simplex Motor Works Ltd., Fitzwilliam Works, Tinsley. (*Photograph reproduced from the Picture Sheffield Collection, courtesy of Sheffield Local Studies Library*)

A painting of female shell workers at Cammell Laird and Co. Ltd., Sheffield. The lady in the centre of the picture was Elizabeth Dowde (nee Darlow). (*Image reproduced from the Picture Sheffield Collection, courtesy of Sheffield Local Studies Library*)

Women munitions workers at Thomas Firth and Sons Ltd, captioned 'And we - we feed the guns'. From The Bombshell : a monthly journal devoted to the interests of the employees of Thomas Firth & Sons, Ltd., Norfolk Works, Sheffield. Vol. 1 no. 10, Dec 1917. (*Photograph reproduced from the Picture Sheffield Collection, courtesy of Sheffield Local Studies Library*)

in Sheffield, merely being referred to as 'the North', it gives an insight into what the munitions factories were like and the work being undertaken by women. The reporter announced 'truly astonishing' results in the performance of the women, who displayed great energy, enthusiasm and hard work. Lots of difficult work was being undertaken efficiently. He found crowded workshops with thousands of women carrying out work which was not undertaken by men previously but which women had quickly turned their hands to, with training lasting between just three and 12 days. There had been a 'rapid growth in efficiency', it was remarked and although the workers had been, 'A little trying for the first few days' the women were now finding the work 'most interesting and should be sorry to leave it', according to one of the managers. Despite the heavy nature of the work, which involved moving very heavy equipment and materials, it was said that the women were working as well, if not better, than men. Indeed it was said, 'the output of the woman munition worker is double that of the man. To say this is to understate the fact. The product is not only fully double – it slightly exceeds that proportion.'

Two days later another account in that same paper stated women in the munitions works were generally found to be 'magnificent in volume and thoroughly efficient'.

Many men had originally scoffed at the idea of women working in the factories. In one factory in Sheffield the principal told his manager that it was necessary to get the factory running with women producing 18-pounder high explosives. The manager said it could not be done but only two days later large numbers were being produced. After only a few hours the manager admitted he had been wrong. 'British women are rendering aid of priceless value in this hour of stress' with 'well applied energy', 'willingness', 'enthusiasm' and 'punctuality' it was said.

Women were quickly making a good impression through their work, although accounts of female munitions workers were patronising in the extreme.

Although it was previously written that women were capable of doing double the work carried out by men, on 23 December 1915 the *Telegraph* featured a Government report which claimed that each man should be replaced by two women and if that replacement was made 'the productive power of the country need not suffer much'. In fact it was said that the loss of men had been 'largely neutralised by the more vigorous and effective work of the civilian population' and that exports were higher in 1915 than in 1909. Every woman was called to do her bit by working in the factories. 'The women have their chance. Every idle woman is worse than so much waste material. She consumes but does not contribute to the wealth of the nation. If all capable women will work, then the power of Great Britain to meet her own expenditure, and the sums needed by her Allies, is very great', the report continued. According to the report women had the capability of helping win the war by liberating men and by running the country until

The Girl Tommy Atkins left behind him has enlisted in the great Munition Corps with "barracks" all over the country. There are now few processes in shell and cartridge manufacture with which women cannot be trusted. Above, percussion caps are being fitted, and below is a section of the testing room, where girls are gauging the shell cases as they pass along on a travelling belt.

201

This page appeared in the 30 December 1915 issue of the English war magazine "The War Budget" and shows women in English munitions factories. Above: Percussion caps are being fitted. Below: final inspection of shell cases on a travelling belt.

The City Council hopes to erect a bronze memorial called 'Women of Steel' on Barkers Pool if sufficient funds are raised. This image is a scale model of what the memorial will look like. (*The Author*)

Thousands walk over this small plaque which is set into the pavement at Barker's Pool close to the Balm Green Gardens without realising its existence. (*The Author*)

IN RECOGNITION OF THE WOMEN OF SHEFFIELD WHO SERVED THEIR CITY AND COUNTRY BY WORKING IN THE STEEL INDUSTRY AND FACTORIES DURING WORLD WAR I AND WORLD WAR II

THE PEOPLE OF SHEFFIELD WILL ALWAYS REMEMBER WITH GRATITUDE THESE WOMEN OF STEEL

2011

the men returned. By doing this they would prove the old fashioned views were wrong. The article ended by saying:

'The war demands the strenuous cooperation of every man and woman, youth and maiden in the country.'

In January 1916 there were concerns that the health of women working in the munitions factories was suffering due to the conditions they had to work in. A memorandum that month, written by the Health of Munition Workers Committee, wrote, 'If the present long hours, the lack of healthful and sympathetic oversight, the inability to obtain good wholesome food, and the great difficulties of travelling are allowed to continue, it will be impracticable to secure or maintain for an extended period the high maximum output of which women are undoubtedly capable.'

In November 1917 a women's canteen was opened in Sheffield to provide moderately priced food for women employed in munitions factories. It was located at the corner of Hoyle Street and Morpeth Street.

Although women had a greater responsibility as well as earning money, with most women earning the same wages as their male counterparts, there were some women who were unhappy with their working conditions and not just because of the noise, dirt, smells and long hours. On 19 January 1917 a woman appealed to the Munitions Court for a leaving certificate so that she could leave her job because she objected to having to wear trousers when operating machinery.

Another role carried out by women in Sheffield during the First World War was tram conductress. Due to their public presence they encountered some difficulty when undertaking their work. They were somewhat patronised early on with claims by male passengers that conductresses struggled to carry the heavy bags of coppers. On 17 December 1915 the Tramways Committee of the council prosecuted a number of individuals who were taking advantage of female staff on the trams. Mr HG Adams, speaking on behalf of the Committee, said it was becoming common for men to avoid buying a ticket from conductresses who were viewed by some as 'fair game' and this resulted in them having problems when fares were not collected. The

Sheffield's first female tram inspector. (*Photograph reproduced from the Picture Sheffield Collection, courtesy of Sheffield Local Studies Library*)

Sheffield tram workers in 1917 or 1918 showing the prominence of women workers. (*Photograph reproduced from the Picture Sheffield Collection, courtesy of Sheffield Local Studies Library*)

magistrates were asked to make an example of those who had been identified as failing to buy a ticket. Three men appeared before the magistrates and were fined between 10s and 20s each.

Another way in which women helped the war effort, described as an 'Opportunity for Women Patriots' by the *Telegraph* on 16 November 1915, was to replace approxi-mately half of the 300,000 or more men in England and Wales who were working in clerical and commercial work but were required in the forces. Men below and above military age, and wounded soldiers and sailors with previous experience, also filled some of the vacancies.

Rapid training and organisation was needed in order to make sure the new workers had the necessary skills. It was therefore recommended that every commercial centre create a body made up of representatives from higher education and those with commercial experience, to assist in providing training, support and to seek out and encourage women who already had skills and qualifications. It was suggested that employers should give preference to educated women and women who were the wives or relatives of men already employed by the firm. It was to be made clear that the women would only be employed for the duration of the war, until the men they had replaced returned from active service. Importantly it was recommended that where possible and where warranted every effort must be made to ensure that the women received the exact same wages as the men whom they were replacing. In the case of banks it was recommended that the working hours should be reduced to help ease any staffing problems.

In Sheffield Sir William Clegg told the Education Committee that more was needed to be done in order to train women. By November 1915 Sheffield had for some time been doing much in this area, with about 1,500 girls and women attending classes for commercial education at 35 of the evening classes in the city with the expectation that most would soon be undertaking work. Further new classes were planned. Appeals were to be made to women who were educated to secondary school level, had free time and wanted to qualify for commercial or clerical work. Clegg hoped that there would not be such a huge influx of women attending training so much so that women would be competing for jobs and be willing to be paid below a reasonable wage. Women were, however, encouraged to attend the classes in order to liberate men capable of fighting.

During the festive period in 1915 women students from the Sheffield Pupil Teachers' Centre helped deliver letters and parcels across the city; so many had put their names forward that it was not possible to employ them all. They worked eight hours per day throughout the week and were paid an unknown amount for their services.

In addition to their efficiency, which has been remarked upon, further words of praise were given on 14 December 1915 when it was written that women were bringing many other admirable qualities into the workplace.

> 'The coming of woman into the man's world of work has had a decided effect on the amenities of life. There can be no question that there is more politeness about than there used to be. In many directions the short, sharp, business-like mode of question and answer usual between man and man has given place to a greater suavity and courtesy which, befit the relations of man and woman. And this is certainly the woman's doing. Her attitude towards the public is amiable. She looks as if she would give a pleasant reply to a question, would probably take a lot of trouble to help you, and might perhaps smile when you thanked her afterwards.'

It was said that women were nicer than men because they had not seen the rougher side of the world.

It was a somewhat patronising view that would undoubtedly cause great offence but it showed that women were becoming increasingly respected, compared with the previous view that women were incapable of 'man's work'.

Women also worked on allotments and on farms in the Land Army in and around Sheffield. By July 1917 the value of women on farms was realised, with women having been willing volunteers. Training depots were set up for women and a demonstration for the benefit of local dignitaries and the press was held where women were seen to be working and 'the most extraordinary results were shown' according to the *Telegraph*.

On 2 November 1917 it was decided that two female police officers should be recruited on a probation period of six months, at the weekly remuneration of £2 2s, with uniform provided. The Bristol Training School for Women Patrols and Police were asked to supply two capable women. Women constables had been employed earlier in the year, but only in relation to dealing with women and children rather than general police work.

In 1917 the Women's Army Auxiliary Corps (WAAC) was formed to provide work in areas including clerical officers, cooks, waitresses, storekeepers, drivers, mechanics, fabric workers, needlewomen, tailoresses, printers and domestic workers within the army. Several hundreds of Sheffield women joined up. The Women's Royal Naval Service (WRNS) and the Women's Royal Air Force (WRAF) were also formed and involved some Sheffield women. In February 1918 the WAAC paraded in Sheffield, accompanied by a small number of members of the Women's Land Army, in order to encourage more women to join the two services. They were greeted by large crowds at the Midland Railway Station and the streets were lined with spectators. The Lord Mayor spoke that the people of Sheffield welcomed them and were proud of them, recognising that without their efforts England would be 'in very sore straits'.

Nurses were employed in Sheffield hospitals prior to the war, but their importance and number rapidly increased as those hospitals, and new ones, began to treat the war casualties. Several women made a particularly outstanding contribution in the field of nursing. On 16 April 1918 Miss MA Brown received the Military Medal for her services in treating wounded soldiers. It was a unique recognition for a woman. On 22 June a number of Sheffield nurses were awarded the Royal Red Cross by the king.

Although often women were paid the same as men, this was not always the case, resulting in some men fearing for their jobs. The local branch of the Associated Society of Locomotive Engineers passed a motion to request the General Secretary to act on their behalf if women were introduced to working the footplates. In such an event it was

Nurses at Wharncliffe War Hospital. (*Photograph reproduced from the Picture Sheffield Collection, courtesy of Sheffield Local Studies Library*)

requested that the committee of officers of the society should immediately meet and determine what steps should be carried out in order to protect male staff from losing their jobs to women, with strike action not being ruled out.

Dr Scurfield of the Ministry of Health in Sheffield believed that women with children should not work. In March 1917 he said that day nurseries in the city were 'a confession of failure' by the community in not insisting that mothers should look after their own children, at home.

However, the following year the Sheffield Education Committee set out plans to provide nursery places for children aged between three and five years. Miss Cleghorn spoke of their necessity, especially in the slum areas. It was said that eight or nine years previously three years olds had attended schools in the city and this had only changed due to a lack of space. Although some schools had a nursery room for those aged three to five, dedicated nurseries were needed in each infant school. Crèches were intended to look after children up to the age of three. To succeed it had to argue against the Executive Committee of the National Union of Teachers who believed that the appropriate place for children under the age of five was at home with their mothers.

During the war the Women Workers' Interests Association had an office at 36 Campo Lane. From this location it campaigned for better support for working mothers, including childcare and Mondays off work so they could do the washing.

On 3 November 1917 a women's conference was held at Montgomery Hall. The room was packed with women, and some men. Six million women nationally were to be given the vote and it was now necessary for them to consider how they could use the great power to be bestowed upon them. It was particularly hoped that women would contribute to an improved education system. Equal pay was also something that could be achieved by women playing a part in democracy, it was argued.

In February 1918, by which time the Representation of the People Act had been passed, a meeting was held by women at the Town Hall to discuss the issue in light of the enfranchisement of women. The

111

president of the National Union of Women Workers, Ogilvie Gordon, expressed her surprise that a city such as Sheffield did not have any women councillors. She believed there should be at least one female councillor on each of the Education, Health and Watch Committees. She hoped women would stand for election but that a women's party would not be advisable, with the need for women to collaborate with men. In terms of work, adequate training for all women working in industry through to domestic work, a decent wage and good morale were essential. To try and achieve these aims a Women's Citizens Association was formed in Sheffield as a consequence of the meeting.

The Women's Citizens Association met on 27 March 1918. In addition to discussions about whether women should look after their own children at home rather than sending them to a nursery, it was acknowledged that women being given the vote was the culmination of the hard work they had undertaken during the war and that the war had hastened the suffrage movement. Now women were anxious, it was said, about proving themselves worthy of this great trust placed upon them.

In addition to the roles women played in helping the troops in terms of comforts and in supplying them with weapons to enable the war to be carried out, there were women in Sheffield who were campaigning to abolish war.

Miss Maude Royden addressed a meeting at Mappin Hall on 17 November 1915 under the auspices of the Sheffield Workers Education Association, on the subject of Women and War. It was attended by a 'moderately large audience' most of whom were women. She expressed her belief that the women's movement would be a great instrument in the final abolition of war. Although 'staggered' by the war fever displayed by women who were displaying 'that senseless and blind hatred which one sometimes found among men'. It was her belief that by gaining influence, especially in public life, women would be in a better position to help prevent war. 'Feminism and militarism were so unalterably opposed that one would have to die,' she announced, adding that the women's movement stood for moral force governing the world and not physical force. It was her hope that women would find new forms of serving and new powers within themselves but that they should strain every nerve to gain any employment they wanted, on equal terms to men. She hoped that following the war in which women had done so much good and achieved a greater degree of responsibility and recognition, there would not be a 'sex war' between men and women which would result in women's rights being attacked.

Once the war had ended and men returned to Britain large numbers of women were no longer needed and so they lost their jobs. Although it was a step backwards they had showed they could perform difficult jobs including those in heavy industry. Importantly women of 30 or more had secured the vote and the ability to stand in elections, which saw the start of the long journey for greater influence in the political system. Much, much more needed to be done but a significant step had been taken in the advance of women's rights and changing attitudes towards them.

CHAPTER 12

1915

As 1915 commenced the issue of conscription reared its head. In fact, 1915 began and ended with conscription being a major topic of conversation, interest and concern. On 8 January it was considered in the House of Lords but it was remarked that; 'We do not regard the possibility of compulsion as being within the landscape, as we now see it.'

The argument was increasingly raised throughout the year. In April Lloyd George spoke that; 'The Government are not of opinion that there is any ground for thinking that the War would be more successfully prosecuted by means of conscription.' Yet as the new year began the number of new recruits was significantly below that which was needed, and many of those who were joining the army and navy were more desperately needed in the munitions factories.

The hopes that may have been raised at the close of 1914 by the *Telegraph and Star*'s optimism that the war might be over before long, with the great advance being not far off, were dashed as those on the Home Front realised they were at increased risk of attack. No longer was it just on the battlefields, or even the coastal towns like Scarborough, Hartlepool and Whitby, that were in danger. On 19 January two German Zeppelins flew over Great Yarmouth, Sherringham, Kings Lynn and the neighbouring villages, dropping 24 high explosive bombs and several incendiary bombs. Four people were killed and 16 injured, along with buildings damaged and destroyed. A feeling of terror began to spread, and those in Sheffield began to think maybe they would be hit.

With growing intensity of war overseas there were greater demands on the munitions factories and a growing anger towards those in cities, such as Sheffield, who were not working as hard as they should. In February 1915 Lloyd George spoke at Bangor saying:

'Most of our workmen are putting every ounce of strength into this urgent work loyally and patriotically, but that is not true of all. There are some, I am sorry to say, who shirk their duty in this great emergency. I hear of workmen in armaments works who refuse to do a full week's works for the nation's need. What is the reason? They are a minority. The vast majority belong to a class we can depend upon. The others are a minority. But you must remember a small minority of workmen can throw a whole works out of gear. What is the reason? Sometimes it is one thing, sometimes it is another, but let us be perfectly candid, it is mostly the lure of the drink. They refuse to work full time, and when they return their strength and efficiency are impaired by the way in which they have spent their leisure.'

This fuelled resentment. In December 1915 Lloyd George reacted angrily when the media accused him of tarring all workers in the munitions factories as being drunkards and shirkers. He reiterated what he had said at Bangor.

Workers were encouraged to entirely abstain from alcohol consumption, with those who did so saying they had taken the King's Pledge because the King had led the example by giving up alcohol and requesting that it should not be consumed within the Royal household.

Sheffield continued as it had previously since the outbreak of war, with hard work, fundraising and recruitment to the forces, although the initial war fever had passed, without significant event until May.

On 13 May 1915 the majority of the City Battalion, the exception being the reserves, was transferred to Cannock Chase in order to continue their training in preparation for going to war. It came with only a few days notice but great excitement was felt by the soldiers who had endured several months more at Redmires than they would have liked and were keen to actually fight.

More than 5,000 gathered to see them off despite a change of time with only a few hours of notice. A platform was assembled for

'Good-bye to Sheffield' - the Hallamshires stepping out into the unknown. This is how they left Sheffield in October 1914. They were then bound for Gainsborough, preparatory to leaving for the war. (*Photograph reproduced from the Picture Sheffield Collection, courtesy of Sheffield Local Studies Library*)

speakers, including the Lord Mayor, who wanted to wish them well and express the hope that they would bring glory to the city.

The following day a second reserve company was formed in anticipation of the possibility of a large number of deaths once the men went into battle.

Towards the end of May two German gun carriages captured on the battlefields which had been on display at Fitzalan Square were returned to the Royal Arsenal in Woolwich. People were encouraged to see them before they were taken away.

Housing was a serious issue. The Rent Restrictions Act of 1915 was passed to prevent large rent increases. Rent increases in Sheffield, where most houses were rented, were kept to a minimum but this restricted revenue for the corporation, putting pressure on finances to build new homes.

Councillors learnt the population of the city was increasing by approximately 5,000 per year and it was estimated that at least 1,000 new houses had to be built to accommodate this rapid growth. However, given that 24,000 houses were considered to be unsanitary, with slum dwellings, it was thought a minimum of 2,500 new houses had to be built to accommodate the rising population and to replace homes unfit for human habitation. Sadly it was not until many years later that the slums were cleared, with efforts focusing on the development of new housing for those moving to the area. For now, the majority of those who were unfortunate enough to live in slum conditions had to make do.

On 3 September violent thunderstorms plagued the city for two hours. Some may have viewed it as a sign of what was happening in the war. Certainly there were heavy losses and injuries and on 14 September two convoys of wounded soldiers consisting of 450 men arrived into Sheffield Midland Station. It was the largest convoy so far.

Morale was boosted towards the end of the month by a Royal visitor. On 28 September 'loyal demonstrations' greeted King George V on his arrival in Sheffield for the start of a three-day visit to Yorkshire where he also visited Leeds and Rotherham. The visit was unannounced, in a bid to prevent people from leaving their work to greet him. On the contrary it was hoped his visits to munitions factories and other businesses and institutions concerned with the war would encourage workers to redouble their efforts. He arrived at noon, having travelled by train to the Midland Station. He wore the service uniform of Field Marshall and was welcomed to the city by the Lord Mayor, Councillor Oliver Wilson, and Town Clerk, Mr WE Hart. Up to three thousand people, mostly women, had assembled outside the railway station. Handkerchiefs and red scarves were waved as the King approached.

As the news spread of the Royal visitor, crowds began to form along his anticipated routes, although the crowds were restricted to those who were not working. Nonetheless there were large groups of enthusiastic people to be found everywhere that the King moved despite the cold weather. Prior to the King's arrival Sheffield was, according to the *Telegraph*, 'a dull city' with only flags hanging from the Town Hall and Cutlers' Hall. However, soon after his arrival the Union Jack, and the flags of the Allies, sprang up across the city's most prominent buildings. Despite having no time to prepare them, shopkeepers and other individuals began creating makeshift bunting and flags. Even in the poorest areas, such as Charlotte Street close to the university, the streets began to be decorated with glittery flags and as much colour as could hastily be created, with the waving of hats and handkerchiefs and a 'storm of cheering'. The efforts were acknowledged by the King who waved and appeared to be in 'perfect health and was evidently in excellent spirits'.

It was his first visit to the city as king, having previously visited in 1909 as the Prince of Wales, in order to open the University of Sheffield's Edgar Allen Library on Western Bank. From the Midland Station he was taken by car once again to the university, but this time to the Applied Science Department, passing the library and the Royal Hospital, a wing of which he opened in 1896 when he was Duke of York.

The king was greatly interested in being shown the Applied Sciences Department, which was one of the most equipped departments in the world. He spent half an hour being toured around the laboratories, tool rooms and machine rooms, viewing the technology used to develop metallurgy and engineering. In the non-ferrous laboratory one of the platers silvered a penny and then gilded it. Professor Arnold, who was helping the university officials in the guided tour, remarked that he was unsure whether to do such a thing was to break the law, by defacing one of the King's coins. The King, whilst laughing, said he did not know the law in that regard. The King was then shown fragments of poisoned shells created by the Germans and recovered at Ypres, sent to Sheffield for analysis. He was greatly interested to view the fragments and was pleased that they had been recovered so that more of the German's methods of warfare could be learnt.

Before leaving, he paid tribute to the value of the department in developing science for the benefit of technology and industry. The university was, he announced, playing a great public service during this time of war. He said he was pleased also that the university was fulfilling a modern role and had moved on from being an institution that concerned itself only with learning facts from books. As he left he was watched by thousands, who gathered in the streets and in the yard of St George's Church. The children from St George's school were highly vocal spectators.

From the university he travelled to the East End factories, where he spent the afternoon, with thousands lining the streets as he proceeded. Approximately six hundred children from Carlisle Street Council School heralded his arrival by singing and waving Union Jacks, so much to the pleasure of the King that their headmaster, Mr JJ Grainger, was presented to the King by the Master Cutler so that his thanks could be passed on to the children. He viewed the steel workings, taking great interest in the different processes used to produce a range of weapons and tools. He asked many questions of the workers in a bid to understand their work and he was particularly keen to meet the older workers. He remarked to one man, 'Why you were working here a year before I was born, and you look as though you have plenty of work left in you yet.'

Three generations of workers from the same family were presented to the king, the oldest being 74 years old and the youngest 20 years of age, each having spent their entire working lives with the firm. Another worker, named Charles Young, had been with the firm for 50 years. The King was pleased to be told the story by one of the older workers of the King's father, King Edward VII, visiting the works in 1875 whilst he was Prince of Wales. He recognised one of the workers as a man with whom he had served as a midshipman on HMS *Bacchante*.

Pleased with how much work was being undertaken, the King remarked to one employee, 'I am glad you realise the importance of the work in hand. Without an adequate supply of shells we cannot expect to win.'

The *Telegraph* found it amusing, and later referred to it as 'a war joke of the year' that the King viewed shells being made which were going to be used to kill Germans on foreign soil by means of guns also made in Sheffield.

The King enjoyed lunch in a 'beautifully decorated' room, with large amounts of food including vegetables grown in Sheffield. He was surprised that such a variety of vegetables could be grown in such an industrial city.

After lunch he travelled by car to another large works, with two thousand people lining the streets and forming a crowd at his destination. A worker had climbed high up on the roof of one of the buildings to unfurl the Royal insignia, which was said to have 'floated gracefully in the breeze'. The King saluted the crowds, with a smile on his face acknowledging the displays of patriotism. He then spent an hour in the works, viewing the workshops.

Before leaving the city he was asked to visit another works, which had not been part of the schedule. There being a small amount of time available, he agreed to a quick visit. Again crowds of enthusiastic workers gathered to see the monarch and he was encouraged to enter a packed reception in the show room. He was shown the visitor's book where he saw his own signature from a previous visit as the Prince of

King George V visiting war wounded at Wharncliffe War Hospital during his visit to the city in September 1915. (*Photograph reproduced from the Picture Sheffield Collection, courtesy of Sheffield Local Studies Library*)

Wales. He was also shown the entry made by his grandmother, Queen Victoria.

He also visited the Wharncliffe War Hospital to speak with some of the wounded soldiers, wishing them a full recovery, and speaking with the staff nursing them.

Even greater crowds than those which had formed during the day gathered at Sheaf Street to wave the monarch goodbye and cheer to him, receiving a salute in exchange. The road was kept clear, by the City Defence Corps, so that the car could travel to the station without hindrance. When arriving at the station the King found another large crowd and he saluted to them. Before the Royal train departed at 5:35pm, with a large number of spectators gathered on the platform opposite, the King remarked to the Lord Mayor how much he had enjoyed the day and how he had been interested in all that he had seen.

The Royal visit was a much needed boost to the morale of those on the Home Front. However, the following day some disappointing news affected the City Battalion and by association the whole city. On 29 September 1915 Colonel C V Mainwaring retired from the City Battalion. It came as a great surprise to the battalion and the city as he had always expressed the strongest of desires to be the man who would lead his men to battle when they were finally sent to fight the enemy. He gave a farewell address in which he told his men that he had been deemed too unfit to participate in active service. He was replaced by Lieutenant Colonel J A Crosthwaite.

The King's feast during his visit to the city was the consequence of a large amount of food being available at that time. Just two weeks later, the markets in Sheffield had what the *Telegraph* described as a 'bountiful supply' of almost all types of fruit and vegetables. This was due to the cereal crop harvest having been completed, allowing farmhands to work on the harvesting of the fruit and vegetables. Tomatoes and potatoes, however, were in short supply. Fish were in short supply due to the poor weather resulting in fishing trawlers being unable to sail as frequently.

The local papers gave advice on how to grow vegetables including marrows, which were abundant, and how to store them to prevent waste. Those who had even a small amount of land were encouraged to grow their own food, and many did so.

The King's visit to the munitions factories highlighted the value of the work undertaken by the workers, but, as Lloyd George had said earlier in the year, not everyone saw the importance of the work sufficiently to do their best and to work their hours. In one department of Messrs Edgar Allen's, the men lost almost 600 days and nights worth of work in a period of just seven weeks. Fourteen men were prosecuted at the Sheffield Police Court for being absent from work without proper notice between 7 July and 22 September. Mr FW Scorah, speaking on behalf of the firm, said he believed the absences were 'appalling'. The foreman and manager spoke to the men to resolve the matter but despite several warnings it was necessary to prosecute. Any improvements were only brief. All defendants were fined, including one man who lost 277 hours. 'For the last month he has not been at work, and as far as the firm know he has simply been walking about the streets and going into public houses and singing. His mates, and I think they are quite right, say his conduct is simply scandalous,' Scorah told the court.

The initial war fever which had led to thousands of Sheffield men signing up in a matter of days had long passed. The dead and wounded needed replacing and the intensification of the war compounded this shortfall.

With the pressing need for more recruits, the Lord Derby scheme was introduced, which was a final push to encourage men to join the forces voluntarily with the recognition that if it failed some form of compulsory service would follow. Lord Derby became Director-General of Recruiting in October 1915. He immediately set about asking every man aged between 18 and 41 whether he would attest under the National Registration Act (to pledge his services to King and country if called for, but until that time continue as before with work and life), with all men being divided into two classes; married men and single men, with the classes divided into 23 groups depending upon age. When required the younger single men would be called up first, with married men being called up last.

On 22 October 1915 a letter dated 15 October was printed in the

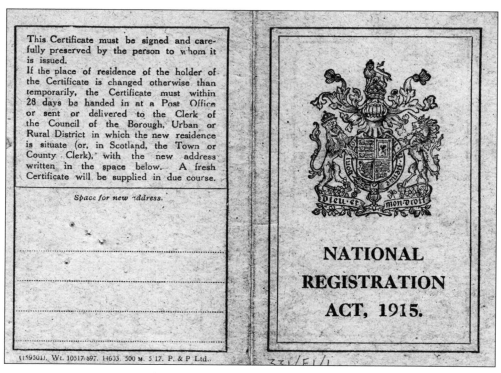

This Certificate must be signed and carefully preserved by the person to whom it is issued.

If the place of residence of the holder of the Certificate is changed otherwise than temporarily, the Certificate must within 28 days be handed in at a Post Office or sent or delivered to the Clerk of the Council of the Borough, Urban or Rural District in which the new residence is situate (or, in Scotland, the Town or County Clerk), with the new address written in the space below. A fresh Certificate will be supplied in due course.

Space for new address.

(19501). Wt. 10517 897. 14603. 500 M. 5 17. P. & P. Ltd.

NATIONAL

REGISTRATION

ACT, 1915.

National Registration Certificate for Joseph Parkinson, turner, of 473 Barnsley Road, Sheffield. (*Photograph reproduced from the Picture Sheffield Collection, courtesy of Sheffield Local Studies Library*)

Telegraph and Star, it was written by Lord Derby regarding the issue of whether compulsory recruiting of unmarried men would take place. It read:

> 'Sir,- At my request the Parliamentary Recruiting Committee representing all political parties, working in conjunction with the joint Labour Recruiting Committee, are organising a great recruitment campaign to induce men who can be spared to come forward voluntarily for service in the Army. If this effort does not succeed, the country knows that everything possible will have been done to make the voluntary system a success, and will have to decide by what method sufficient recruits can be obtained to maintain our armies in the field at their required strength.

Mr. Asquith pledged this country to support our Allies to the fullest extent in our power. It was a pledge given on behalf of the nation and endorsed by all parties. Every man of military age and fitness must equally bear his share in redeeming it.

May I, as Director-General of Recruiting, beg you to consider your own position? Ask yourself whether, in a country fighting as ours is for its very existence, you are doing all you can for its safety, and whether the reason you have hitherto held valid as one for not enlisting holds good at the present crisis. Lord Kitchener wants every man he can get. Will you not be one of those who respond to your country's call?

I am, yours faithfully,
DERBY
Director-General of Recruiting'

The same day saw a letter, written also by Lord Derby, encouraging employers to allow employees to enlist and keep their jobs open for when the war ended. If by leaving the company it would cause tremendous difficulty, the employee could be put into a later group. He stressed that employees should be advised that if the voluntary system of enlisting failed then conscription could follow.

A letter in the *Telegraph and Star* could not have been better timed to be printed on the same page as Lord Derby's statement. 'Sir, - As the recruiting band was playing past the new Town Hall at 12:20pm today, what a number of men gazed from its windows! Are they all old men, cripples, or do they belong to the SVDC?'

Whilst the call for more men was made, people began to ask why it was not yet over. JEF Sherington of Sheffield wrote to the press, on 15 November, referring to a popular novelist having a second set of poems published, in which the following lines appeared:

'As sure as God's in His Heaven,
As sure as He stands for right,
As sure as the Hun this wrong hath done,
So surely we win this fight!'

The correspondent questioned whether because Britain had right on its side it was sure to win, which was being said in churches. There were, he believed, two dangers in maintaining the belief that we would win because God was on Britain's side. Firstly, it made the British less enthusiastic about fighting the war if they believed they would win anyway, resulting in people being complacent and not playing their full part. Secondly, what if Britain lost the war? Would that mean it was not on the right side or would it be a sign that people should abandon their faith? 'We shall win the war – if we mean to, and if we refuse even to consider the staying of our hand until we have won. But we shall not win simply because we are right and our enemy is wrong. Let us – even the poets and preachers among us – try to think and talk sensibly about the war, and to avoid anything which tends even in the least to make our people less keen on obtaining a swift and complete victory,' he concluded.

Certainly there were people in Sheffield and elsewhere across the country who were complacent and unwilling to do what they could to obtain a swift and complete victory. The view of one soldier writing to the *Telegraph* in November summed up the frustrations of the military and the reluctance of large numbers of Sheffield in doing their bit.

The soldier was Canadian, fighting in the C section, 4th Canadian Field Ambulance in France, who received the newspaper from a brother living in Sheffield (who was too old to fight). He wrote to ask why men eligible for service hung back until they were forced to enlist. 'The more men we get the more rest our men can have when they are relieved in the trenches,' he wrote. He recounted how, when on leave he visited Sheffield, visiting the Hippodrome where he was surprised to see a full house, made up largely of young men in civilian clothes. 'Wake up, Sheffield eligibles, don the uniform,' he urged.

It was this frustration and the recognition of the lack of numbers of men in the forces which led to the serious contemplation of compulsion.

On 15 November a report was printed in the *Telegraph* of a speech by Walter Long, the President of the Local Government Board, who had spoke at the annual dinner of the Unionist Dolphin Society at

Bristol. He said the Government would be glad to end the war under the voluntary system of enlistment. However they were 'absolutely determined that the married men in this country with their wives, children, and other responsibilities, should not be allowed to give their lives in the trenches in order that young unmarried men might be able to take their places and enjoy their wages and enjoy privileges for which others were fighting'. He made it clear that if needed the single men would be called upon and forced to join the army and he hoped that they would be forced to reflect badly on themselves for the remainder of their lives.

As plans were set in place for more men to be called up to fight the enemy overseas, the ongoing campaign to tackle the enemy at home gathered pace. By reducing, or even prohibiting altogether, the consumption of alcohol, more work could be achieved.

On 15 November Philip Snowden MP attended the Wesleyan Temperance Convention in Sheffield to express his belief that the Government's alcohol control measures would aid the temperance movement. He was certain public houses would never return to their pre-war opening hours and he expressed his delight that alcohol consumption had been halved in many districts. He hoped that much more would be done and that lessons learnt so far during the war would encourage temperance supporters to be more active and more aggressive in achieving their aims. Councillor Neale, who also attended the conference, expressed his belief that abstinence was right and that it had been proven during the war. He hoped the Government's stance on abstinence would continue after the war was won.

Later that night Snowdon was the chief speaker at a 'large and enthusiastic' temperance demonstration at Victoria Hall. He expressed his view that when the war was over Britain would have to compete in a more difficult economic market and that 'the nation could not tolerate the economic waste which was involved in the destruction of £200 million worth of capital every year on drink'. Reverend E Bromage remarked that drink was a menace which would not be removed with anything short of total abolition. He expressed his frustration that those who worked in the alcohol industry were opposing the Government's measures which, he believed, were in the interests of the nation during this difficult time. This, he believed, disgraced and discredited the alcohol trade.

Such concerns about alcohol resulted in further regulations by the Central Control Board to restrict alcohol, which were first outlined in the *Telegraph* on Monday 15 November and were to come into force a week later.

The regulations required consumption on a licensed premises during the week to be restricted to between noon and 2:30pm, then between 6:30pm and 9:30pm, and between 12:30pm to 2:30pm and then again between 6pm and 9pm on Sundays. Consumption off-premises was between noon and 2:30pm, then between 6:30pm and 8:30pm, and between 12:30pm to 2:30pm, and then again between 6pm and 8pm on Sundays. The sale of spirits for consumption off premises was restricted to between noon and 2:30pm Monday to Friday only. Treating customers to free drinks was prohibited, as were lending money to buy alcohol and credit. Liquor was not to be consumed or leave the premises until paid for. The 'long pull' was also prohibited. The premises could remain open under the licensing laws for the previous opening hours but during the extra hours only non-alcoholic drinks, and food, could be purchased. Any breaches of these regulations could result in a £100 fine and six months imprisonment with hard labour.

There were inevitably mixed feelings on the issue, with letters in the *Telegraph* highlighting the differing opinions.

JB Wallis wrote that the 'evil' of drink undoubtedly existed and that there was a huge increase in drunkenness despite attempts to restrict alcohol consumption. He believed, however, that whilst restrictions had to be in force for the war effort, harsh restrictions were 'evil and retrograde' and should not be used hastily or needlessly. '…cannot the incurable cases be weeded out, and placed under restraint? Why burn down the house to roast a pig? Which is a greater interference with the liberty of the subject, to restrain the madman [he believed alcoholics were insane] or (because of him) to fetter all the sane?' The blame should be with the drinker, he thought, and not the publican or brewer so they should not be penalised. 'We do not blame the gunsmith, or the cutler, when some wretch has shot himself or cut his own throat.' The system of rules and regulations governing the ability to drink was 'wrong' he believed. 'It makes us all subservient to laws designed for the most degenerate members of the community.' He thought that unnecessary regulations had begun before the war and would continue after the war.

One city centre publican felt the new order was unnecessary, unfair and would lead to job losses. 'It is no use mincing matters. The order has come on us something like a thunderbolt,' he said. 'We expected an order, but we were under the impression that after the satisfactory way in which Sheffield men have behaved it would not be very drastic. We have often heard that the various drink regulations would ruin the trade, but really I can say confidently that this order will mean the shutting down of many houses which have already been badly hit by the measures which have been adopted against the licensed trade. This new order is unfair to the trade and grossly unjust to the public who, be it remembered, are not all teetotallers.'

A spokesman for Garnet Bros Ltd, Wine and Spirit Merchants, agreed that it was unnecessary. 'The Sheffield working men, and indeed, all classes, are steady and temperate, and because of a small minority it is unfair to brand them in this public way as drunkards...' He believed it would not prevent those wanting to get drunk to do so. Drunkards would still have three and a half hours to buy alcohol and could take it home to continue drinking. He agreed it was bad for the trade. 'The order is cruel and crushing to the Trade. We pay rent, rates and license duty for a possible 84 hours per week: this order allows us 12 ½ hours only for spirits, and 14 hours for wine...' Wine traders could not deliver wine to all pubs in the time allowed, he argued. Speaking of the benefits of alcohol he wrote: 'The moderate use of pure wines, beer, and spirits, taken with meals is beneficial, and no better drink has yet to be invented: it is an ancient habit of the British race, and they will have it. Surely they should not be compelled to obtain it under such servile red tape laws?'

He added that the regulations would be bad for the country, saying duties and licenses for selling alcohol generated £70 million.

The reference to there being no better drink invented may be amusing to modern readers, but in 1915 it was believed beer was a good source of nourishment. In fact in December that year another correspondent wrote, 'Our commissioners remind us that if the worth of a food is measured by its calometric value, the fact is that a glass of good ale is approximately as nourishing as a glass of milk.'

Trade leaders in the city also believed it was too harsh and would be opposed. 'During the time which will elapse before the order is put into force, representations will be made to the Board in London, though with what success, if any, it is difficult to say,' one representative said.

Councillor A J Bailey, district secretary of the Amalgamated Union of Labour, which had thousands of members in Sheffield, said, 'So far as Sheffield is concerned I do not think there was the slightest need for this restriction.' Councillor W L Angell was surprised by the stringent nature of the regulations. He hoped that that it would not lead to more drinking at home, which could not be adequately controlled, unlike in public houses. He felt, as many did, that the previous regulations had worked well, and landlords might be tempted to break the law and sell alcohol during prohibited times, if they were open anyway to sell non alcoholic drinks and food. He was pleased that clubs were being restricted in the same way as public houses.

Dr George Franklin, a former Mayor of Sheffield, felt the regulations were unnecessary and went too far. He said if the restrictions had taken place at any other time, 'I think it would have excited a good deal of resentment amongst the working people. They are pretty powerless now, but the time will come when more will be heard of it. It is a great restriction upon the working people. I can only assume that the Board have tied up Sheffield with other places where the need is greater than in Sheffield. I don't know anything about places outside Sheffield, but I do know something of Sheffield, and I do not think that there is any need for this repressive legislation.'

A manufacturer gave his very different opinion of the regulations to a *Telegraph* reporter:

'It was badly wanted. People have little idea what trouble we have had with some of our men. Don't, please misunderstand me. We have thousands of men at our works, and the great majority have done their best to meet the demands made upon them. They have worked overtime, have turned their hands to that work which was most urgently needed, and have done all they could to assist us in carrying out the requirements of the Government. But there are others – and although they are only limited in number they can and do cause serious loss of time – who come to work in a "fuddled" condition, and never get really sober all the time they are on the job…These men frequently find a quiet corner and there sleep until some comrade wakes them. It is disgraceful to think that men will act thus at such a time.'

Were the regulations too drastic? 'They are certainly very severe,' he thought, 'but I am convinced the work cannot be done so long as the men have such free access to the drink shops. As they leave here in the morning, they go straight to the public house, stop there for hours, sometimes all day. How can a man do his work under such conditions? Of course he cannot! And the men who go off at night; many of them walk straight from the shop to the "public" and stop there until closing time. It was quite time something was done.'

A leading official at Cammell Laird and Co also agreed with the order, which he felt was much needed especially because it prevented the sale of alcohol in the mornings. His experience was that men who started work at 6am had a five minutes break later in the morning, during which time some of the men had gone to the nearest public house for a drink. In some cases his employees had remained there for more than their five minutes, for sometimes half an hour. It resulted in a lack of work being performed. He was keen to emphasise that only a minority of his staff were responsible for such behaviour but that the problem was sufficient enough to warrant these new regulations.

It was not only civilians who were the cause for concern. There were requests made in December 1915 to prevent soldiers from getting drunk.

However, the rules were relaxed from 20 to 24 December, to allow a little more festive cheer, with consumption allowed between 12:30

until 5:30 and then between 6:30 until 9:30. Wines could be bought for drinking off premises during the same period. Spirits were only available for off-premises drinking until 5:30pm.

Towards the end of November Sheffield folk will have been intrigued and excited to see what was described as a 'war trophy' arrive in Fitzalan Square. It was a 77mm German field gun, captured at Loos in September. It was particularly popular with the young with their romantic thoughts of warfare, but was widely viewed by the Sheffield populace. It was removed by the Northern Command at York shortly before Christmas, to be exhibited for the pleasure of the people of Huddersfield.

In December deliveries of fuel and materials were affected by snow and fog. As a result some managers in Sheffield were uncertain whether or not they would be able to keep their furnaces operating beyond that working day and some departments could not do any work. The Christmas break was all the more welcome due to a lack of materials but there were fears that the required items would run out before the break began.

Attestations had resulted in a large amount of lost time for the workers. Even those who could not serve in the forces due to their jobs were still required to spend half a day, and in some cases a full day, at the attesting stations. There were now fears that even indispensible men could be called up.

The value of November's exports was higher than at any time since the war began, with most exports going to France, resulting in increased profits for some Sheffield firms. The metal industry in Sheffield had earned approximately £2 million.

Despite the wealth generated by Sheffield industry it was a time of great austerity. It was recognised that once the war had ended, and even before it was completed if the duration was long, there would be a huge financial burden to the country and probably high unemployment, high prices and a general lack of money in peoples' pockets. It was therefore recommended that people should try and save as much money by cutting down on unnecessary expenditure. As part of the general 'Thrift campaign' a 'Thrift Week' was planned. On 11 December, in advance of 'Thrift Week', several prominent members of Sheffield's society wrote their thoughts on the necessity to save.

Charles Hobson, President of the Sheffield Federated Trades Council, outlined the financial problems which would follow the war. 'After the war there is sure to come a period of bad trade such as has not been experienced in England for 50 years or more,' he claimed. Furthermore there would be a 'heavy burden of debt contracted during the war' which would have to be paid through increased income tax and/or voluntary or forced levies on income or possessions. 'In either, and in both cases, the wage earner will be called upon to contribute his quota,' he added. He advised that the poor should save now in expectation of hard times to come

The Lord Mayor, F A Warlow, wrote:

'Thrift is one of the cardinal virtues needful at all times but never so necessary as at present. If wisely practiced now by all within the State, certain victory is ours with the blessings of a lasting peace.'

The Bishop of Sheffield, Leonard H Sheffield, urged Sheffield people to give 'thoughtful and careful consideration' to the campaign. 'We are engaged in a gigantic struggle which is costing the country millions a day,' he said, 'We are told by those who have the best means of knowing that only by strict economy can we hope to pass through the financial difficulties which such an expenditure entails. After the war it is the opinion of everyone that there will come bad times, caused by the depletion of capital and lessening of employment. Therefore save now...'

HAL Fisher, Vice-Chancellor of the university, explained that thrift meant wise expenditure, not starvation, not hoarding but not reckless spending. He added, 'If the rich are extravagant and the poor thrifty, then at the end of the war the rich will be poor, and the poor richer. But if the rich save and the poor spend, then the gulf between the classes will be greater than ever. Let us then all save as much as we can. It will be best for us, and what is infinitely more important, it will be best for the country.'

Barnet Cohen, Rabbi of the Sheffield Hebrew Congregation, agreed that saving money would mean victory would come sooner, but he hoped that people would not try to save money by cutting down on the donations to charities helping the war effort. 'The more waste now, the longer will be the duration of the war, and the greater the subsequent distress. Not to practice economy now is a crime against the whole of humanity. But to begin to save by reducing your contributions to charities will be artificial economy. Look to your own persons, your homes, your pleasures. Save these, and you will save the country. Economise – and win the war.'

An appeal was made for children to understand the need to save. The daily cost of the war was said to be £5,000,000. 'To obtain this money it is necessary for every one, even little children, to try to save all they can,' readers of the newspaper were told. They were told to avoid spending, and encouraging their parents to spend large amounts of money by asking for lots of toys and sweets. This would help bring their fathers home sooner and ensure that when they came back, they would be able to cope financially when there were the expected lack of jobs.

The aim was to save money but also to ensure that all efforts were made in producing the 'necessities of life' and work for the benefit of the war effort rather than creating items of luxury. A lower demand would lead to men who worked in producing luxuries to instead produce items for the war.

A small but vocal group of individuals believed that the example of thrift should be set by those at the upper echelons of society. They argued that the wages of Ministers should be reduced, which would save more for the country than that a large number of working class people could cumulatively save.

One of these individuals living in Sheffield wrote a poem attacking the wages earned by Government ministers who were encouraging the public to practice thrift:

'It was a British Minister
And he stoppeth one like me
"By thy long frock-coat and glistening hat
What may thy business be?"
He holds him with his ringed hand
"There is a war" quoth he,
"And you should practice, sir, I urge,

Extreme economy."
"I always do," the other said,
"For, as old lore explains,
Needs must when one is in the shafts,
And Old Nick holds the reins!"
"But may I ask," continued he,
"What you yourself have done,
That I may then, pro rata dock
My weekly one pound one?"
"God save thee!" cried the Minister,
"Thou hast a healthy cheek!
Why, man alive, I save the State
Some thousands every week."
"And, if you mean my salary,
That sir, is my affair,
I exercise, as Asquith said,
My private conscience there.'"

The editor disagreed, however, stating his belief that Ministers were worth every penny they received and that he would rather they be overpaid 'than risk any interruption that might occur to their work through financial pressure'. He did believe, however, that MPs were grossly overpaid.

During the festive period, with religion playing its role, it was apt that a question was raised about whether ministers should fight. Several Methodist ministers had already attested and the matter was discussed at the quarterly meeting of the Scotland Street United Methodist Circuit in Sheffield. Those present hoped the Government would be more explicit in its guidance as to the eligibility of religious ministers.

The Reverend JE Rattenbury, speaking at the Victoria Wesleyan Mission, said he did not believe that ministers should have any rights more than any other Christian. 'If it was wrong for a preacher to fight it was wrong for a layman to bear arms. If it were true of any minister that he dare not kill and dare not stain his hands with blood, then it was utterly wrong for any Christian man to fight, and how could any minister dare to ask for himself privileges that he denied to the whole church?' He spoke about the concerns of many Christians who believed that the war proved the failure of Christianity. He agreed that Christianity had yet to succeed because the war involved countries, all of whom were Christian, or claimed to be, and yet if they were truly Christian there would be no war. Once Christianity made a real impression there would be no war. He believed the war was right, because although he was uneasy with the terrible sufferings and death, he felt that if Britain had not gone to war the suffering of Europe would have been greater.

The work of the church was considered to have value during the time of war. On 11 December 1915 Mr CB Stuart Wortley MP opened the third day's sale for St Mary's and St Saviour's Churches in Walkley. He praised the work of the church, with the need for ministration being greater than ever whilst people were trying to cope during the war. He felt the churches of the city cultivated the higher virtues and spiritual welfare of the community. 'Sheffield has done its part nobly in this war, and is continuing to do so. In Parliament, or wherever men meet together, the part Sheffield is playing, in the fulfilment of its share in the prosecution of the war, was highly spoken of.' Addressing those who had not yet joined the forces he said, 'I would suggest to them, that if ever they are in a tight corner in regard to what is their duty, let them see before their eyes the image of a British soldier. And whatever serves the soldier's interests best is the right thing for them to do.'

On the second Sunday of Advent a number of the city's churches held musical performances of an 'exceptionally attractive character'. Handel's *Messiah* was performed at the Petre Street PM Chapel and St Paul's in Norton Lees, Mendelssohn's *Hear My Prayer* was performed at the Queen Street Congregational Church, with the congregation hoping that God would hear their prayer for an end to the war. A special musical service was held at the Albert Hall Wesleyan Mission during which Handel's *Largo* and other music was performed. The annual choir sermon of the Mount Tabor Methodist Church on Wellington Street had its primary performance of a cantata named *Earth and Heaven*.

A special advent preacher gave a sermon at Sheffield Cathedral later that evening. Reverend Dr Frere, spoke of the lessons of the war. He based his remarks on early verses of Issiah, Chapter 28. Issiah's words 'other lords have had dominions over us' were true of the current situation. He urged that people should pray with a new intensity to carry out the prayer of desire and to learn righteousness. Prayer was something which everyone could do to help end the war, irrespective of age and health, he claimed.

At the meeting of the Sheffield Wicker Congregational Men's Own on 12 December the Town Clerk spoke of the importance of nature and the value of tranquillity, patience and faith in God, their cause and themselves. When evil seemed to dominate they should remember that evil could not triumph for ever.

There were requests made by church leaders to pray to call for the end to the war. The Archbishop of Canterbury requested that the end of the year and the beginning of the New Year should be set aside for deepening the spiritual life. To this end, the Bishop of Sheffield issued a letter suggesting that 31 December should be a day of fasting and penitence, with prayer in the cathedral and a solemn midnight service. On 1 January a letter was delivered to every home asking all to pray and make a special effort to attend any place of worship on Sunday morning, with the afternoon for entertaining the children. The Bishop's letter concluded, 'This effort may seem to some too much to expect from our people. I do not believe it will be if we give the lead. The war in which we are engaged is abnormal, extraordinary, stupendous, on a terrific, unexampled scale. Our Christianity must be in proportion. Our penitence, our prayers, our communion, our self-sacrifice must also be on an unexampled scale if we are to overcome the world.'

Leaders of other Christian denominations in the city, and also the Chief Rabbi of the Sheffield Hebrew Congregation wrote a letter to the *Telegraph* adding their support for the day of intercession, which had also been suggested by the Lord Mayor and was to be held on 1 January. 'Another year has passed,' the letter began, 'The end of 1915 finds the world still in the terrible grip of war. The infinite issues still hang in the balance; the hearts of men and women all over the world are in suspense and pain. Again the first Sunday of the year is suggested as a National Day of Prayer [the Jewish synagogue held a day of prayer on 1 January and a second on a later date], when we may bring all this very humbly into the hands of God. This is no moment either for criticism or doubt. We are all of us out of our depth; a stronger hand is needed to save us. A greater Love behind is saying to us, "Be still, and know that I am God."…'

The *Telegraph* gave a somewhat pessimistic view in order to encourage more to do their bit. On 15 December it wrote, 'Since the German attacks in the West, apart from the first rush in August against unready foes, have all been unsuccessful, the prospects do not seem bright now that the allies are better prepared in all ways than ever before. In addition the winter season is unfavourable to attack. Frost has its difficulties, so has mud; and the alternation of frost and mud of which the western winter is usually composed unites to a certain extent the difficulties of both.' However, it was not all bad, with the Allies now 'superior' to the enemy, both in manpower and in munition power, although the war needed more men to undertake the sustained effort needed.

To this end, Asquith was questioned in the House of Commons regarding what should be done about the men who had not enlisted. Mr Hohley, the MP for Chatham, asked whether if insufficient unmarried men answered the nation's call on a voluntary basis, whether compulsion would be used. The Prime Minister responded that it was his hope and belief that the question of coercion would not be needed. He believed that the request that men should carry out their patriotic duty would be enough to obtain the numbers needed, from all classes and especially young, unmarried men.

The *Telegraph* believed Lord Derby's scheme had been, as of 14 December, 'a splendid success'. Bad news and a 'stormy outlook' its editorial claimed, had encouraged men to enlist, which was against one of the reasons for censorship of the press. Once all single men were called up the married men could be next. 'A very simple form of compulsion for the remnant of single men is all that is needed, and if the Government hesitate on that they will range against them every married man in the country between the ages of 19 and 41. It would be wicked to call up the classes aged, let us say, 30 to 41, while young men of 20 and 22 strolled about free,' the editor believed, before adding that conscription for single men was now a 'foregone conclusion'.

The editorial received great support. One woman reader wrote, 'I read with entire agreement your remarks regarding compulsion for the single men. I hope you will keep at it. I have an idea that the Government will not dare to bring in any form of compulsion and so will say that the "vast majority" had volunteered. What can we do in such a case? I suggest a league of married women to deal with the matter. My husband has attested, though he is near the limit, and all my male relations of military age are doing their bit. If my husband is called up I shall have to go back to business, a nice prospect at my age, especially seeing as scores of eligible men with no ties whatever seem to have not the slightest intention of helping their country. It will be only by the weight of public opinion that these men will be forced to take their share.'

Another correspondent was worried by the vague nature of Asquith's pledge not to call up married men unless the vast majority had already attested. How large did the majority have to be she wondered.

The *Telegraph* believed the debate about conscription versus voluntary-ism was 'unfortunate' in an article dated 18 December. It was said that the results of the review by Lord Derby should be known before the opponents began to be so vocal. 'Their eagerness to get the ear of the Prime Minister indicates that they are nervous about the result of the Derby effort.' The editor believed a deputation of opponents to see Asquith was 'useless'. He believed that if all the young men capable of fighting had joined the forces then there would be no need to introduce conscription. However, if there were still men who could fight but were refusing to serve their duty, then it was necessary for them to be forced into action, unless they were involved in essential war work. 'The country owes it to every man who has attested to see that those who have held back are not allowed to escape their liabilities.' The editor went further than arguing for conscription. It was his belief that school children should be given military training in the event that the war was still being fought when they reached military age.

A week before Christmas large numbers of Sheffield's attested men learnt they would soon be off to war when a proclamation was made by Lord Derby, summoning groups 2, 3, 4 and 5 of the Army Reserves to the colours, with the calling up process beginning on 20 January, and a gradual recruiting process taking place to prevent excessive workloads at the recruiting offices. Any man who wanted to join a later group, for example due to being employed in essential civilian war work, had to make an application to the Town Clerk within ten days of the issuing of the proclamation. Lord Derby promised that all married men would only be called up if they were required, though they could enlist should they wish to do so. The displaying of a poster in a parish was considered sufficient notice that the services of the men in those groups were required, even if the men did not receive a notice paper through the post because they had changed address since their details were added to the Attestation Register. Notice papers were sent to all those to be called up, giving details of where and when they should present themselves.

Many men in Sheffield were uncertain and anxious when they learnt of the proclamation calling four of the reserve groups to the colours. They were uncertain whether or not they fitted into those groups. Hundreds of men visited the Corn Exchange on Saturday, 18 December and Monday, 20 December to ascertain whether they were needed. The *Telegraph* printed a clarification stating that the men who had to join up were those attested men aged 19 to 22.

The Press Bureau also issued a statement of clarification. Men who had attested, and were in one of the groups given the call, would be called up for service unless they belonged to a reserved occupation or were engaged in essential war work. Whilst ever the man remained in such work he would not be called up. In order to ensure that the rules were not abused, a man who was exempt from being called up would, upon receiving the call up notice, immediately be required to see his employer who would send the notice along with a certificate stating the precise occupation of the employee and return it to the recruiting officer. The notice would then be provisionally cancelled. The recruiting officer had the power to investigate any potentially false claims and have them referred to the Home Office, Ministry of

Munitions or Local Tribunal. Cases of misrepresentation would be reported to the War Office.

The recruiting authorities issued instructions for the benefit of men who had been called up for military service but who were considered indispensible due to their work, with these men forming 'a considerable proportion of the city's attested manhood'. Men were told they could request exemption from the armed forces or they could be asked to be relegated into a later group. Men in groups 2 to 5 who were wearing munitions or Admiralty badges were required to inform their employers immediately. The employer would then contact the Recruiting Office giving details from the man's Attestation Card.

On 23 December appeals were lodged at the Town Clerk's Office to appeal against enlistment. Many asked to be put into a later group due to family commitments or work. Appeals were strengthened if the employer could verify the man was engaged in work for the war. The appeals process involved an appellant completing forms and returning them to the District Recruitment Officer. Forms were obtained from the Town Clerk, to be filled in duplicate and forwarded to Recruiting Officer who considered the claim in conjunction with an Advisory committee made up of people with expertise in the trades carried out in the city. They made a recommendation and the Recruiting Officer made the final decision. If the Recruiting Officer did not believe there was sufficient grounds to prevent the man from being called up, it went before the Tribunal, where the applicant and (if appropriate) employer had the opportunity to present their case. If the applicant or Recruiting Officer were dissatisfied it could be referred to the Central Tribunal in London. Clerical staff were harassed by people wanting forms to appeal, before the tribunal's work had properly started. These were likely to just end up in the rubbish heap, it was said.

On the industrial front, there was what the *Telegraph* described as a 'lull' of activity, with a short festive break for workers. Thousands of munitions workers who had been working since the last Bank Holiday 'will rejoice in the welcome relaxation' it was said. The decision to suspend operations concerned those who understand how much munitions needed 'but it is a wise decision. The Sheffield industrial captains appreciate the truth of the old adage that "All work and no play makes Jack a dull boy."' It was also realised that prolonged heavy work had put great strain on the machinery and that a break would prevent the machinery from failing. The break would be used to carry out essential maintenance and cleaning.

None of the works completely shut down; some carried on producing certain essentials. Arrangements were made so that everyone had some respite over the festive period. Most firms gave four days of holidays, but some firms such as Hadfield's, Jessop's and the Brightside Foundry and Engineering Company were expected to have less holidays because they had major orders to fulfil. Most firms did not allow a holiday for people to see in the New Year.

Others had unofficial absences. Michael McGrail was fined 40s plus costs for eight days of lost time. 'He cheeks his manager when spoken to,' said FW Seorajh who prosecuted for the firm. James Ellis was fined £3 and costs for eight and three-quarters days off and Enoch Whitehead was fined 20s and costs for 19 ½ days of absence. All three worked at John Wiley and Sons of Norfolk Bridge Works.

In addition to losing hours, there were some workers in Sheffield's munitions factories who were unhappy with their conditions and workloads, so much so that they went on strike. On 29 December 1915 a Munitions Tribunal hearing was held to look into the circumstances of, and punish those involved in, a strike at the Weeden Street Works of Messrs T Firth and Sons.

In total 73 men stood accused of breaching the Munitions of War Act for going on strike over pay and conditions without giving the Board of Trade the required 21 days notice. They were employed on three shell presses, which were worked continuously over the course of three shifts. The case was, according to Arthur Neale who represented the firm, the first case in Sheffield where a strike had taken place which needed referral to the Munitions Tribunal. 'I am exceedingly sorry, that such a case has arisen in Sheffield, and I am glad to think that these men were not acting under the advice or control of any Trade Union.'

The men were angered by low wages. A meeting with the management resulted in small pay rises for all but five of the men, plus a bonus on all shells once 200 were produced in a shift, and a small bonus on all profits.

On 26 November the men demanded that the pay rise be implemented immediately, sending a note, 'We in the press shop insist on having our money at five o'clock, if not, no work done after.' The general manager, Mr Morse, told the men that there were severe penalties if they went on strike without following the required procedures. The men wrote a letter of apology and expressed the hope that the management would come to an agreement with them. They were informed the new pay rates would come into force on 15 December. Those who did not receive a pay rise were extremely angered and on 16 and 17 December the situation became serious. The 'ringleader' was Thomas Wilkinson. He was asked in a note to bring some materials out of the store but refused to do so, instead giving the note to one of those who had received a pay rise. When confronted by the assistant manager (Mr Micklethwaite) and foreman he was defiant. Micklethwaite was followed around the works by Wilkinson and 14 others who had not received any rise, but they were told he was too busy to deal with them. Wilkinson led the workers who had not received the increase, out of the works and the strike commenced. Those who had received a wage increase refused to join the strike. Those affected who were working on other shifts refused to go to work and sent in notes stating their reasons.

The strike only ended on 20 December when the men were notified that proceedings had commenced against them and they were ordered back to work. Wilkinson was sacked.

At the Tribunal Wilkinson defended himself by arguing that he had not gone on strike at all. When he had refused to obtain the items from the store and had been confronted by the management, he was told to clock out. He was adamant that he could not have been on strike if he was told to leave the premises. The other men, he said, had been advised not to go to work by the foreman of the company.

George Thomas Todd, another employee who joined the strike, was asked why he had gone on strike. 'Why, because I was an Englishman,' was the response. When told that there were many Englishman in Europe fighting in the war who were unable to go on strike and were in worse conditions he replied, 'I would sooner go there than go back in that shop.'

As the second Christmas of war got ever closer, women were urged to make Christmas as happy possible for the children, as if nothing was wrong. One means by which they could do this was to take the children to the *Babes in the Wood* pantomime at the Theatre Royal. The pantomime was described as having 'new and delightful scenery' and 'unique electrical effects' to provide 'an abundant amount of rollicking fun'.

Christmas was certainly made more enjoyable for hundreds of the city's children who attended special parties. On 22 and 23 December the Lord Mayor and Lady Mayoress held a party for children of Sheffield soldiers who had died thus far during the war, with 482 children and mothers on the first day, and 565 children and mothers, with a larger proportion of mothers, present on the second day. The parties were held at the Town Hall, in which 'merry entertainment' was performed, including a display by Professor Duval's ventriloquism, lots of singing and a Punch and Judy Show, and despite a few tears when the younger children were temporarily separated from their mothers, a good time was had by all. Before the evening entertainment, a grand tea was laid on in the reception room for the children and special tramcars were provided for transport to and from the party. 'There have been few more successful afternoons than this one in the history of Sheffield' was the verdict of the party on 22 December.

A reporter writing about the second party described:

'The brilliance of the electric lights, the whiteness of the cloths, and the feast of good things on the tables made hundreds of young eyes glisten, and, for the next two and a half hours, gloom was in the background, and even recently widowed women shared in the pleasures of their little ones.'

There were some large families including around 16 families of seven children, and some families of eight children. The Reverend GH McNeal proposed three cheers to the Lord and Lady Mayoress for what was considered by all to be a success. The cheers being given there followed a rousing rendition of the National Anthem. On leaving the party, the children and mothers were handed oranges, sweets, cakes and tram tickets to get home.

Although the cry of 'Not much like Christmas' was frequently heard at schools, as it was said in the *Telegraph and Star*. According to teachers children were still 'wild with excitement' and it was just like any other Christmas in school, with children wondering what they would get for Christmas and wanting to decorate their homes with trees, mistletoe and any other item they could buy or make. It was considered a blessing that young children could not understand the full horrors of the war. One mother expressed her belief that Christmas should be happy for the children and that she hoped the soldiers would not begrudge a special effort being made for the children. 'I'm sure no wounded sojer would want little 'uns to go short of a toy 'cos teacher gives her money to 'im, surely e'd go 'alves. Of course, I'm not wantin' toys fer my kids cos o't value on 'em; it just encourages little 'uns and 'elps 'em ter 'ave a jolly Christmas,' she said.

Another issue of Xmas Cheer was produced by the *Telegraph and Star* for one penny to provide stories, pictures, games, jokes and puzzles for children and the whole family.

Sheffield firms competed to offer items that would make ideal Christmas presents. An emphasis was made on buying British made products or products manufactured by Britain's allies whilst also observing the thrift campaign. 'Never have the shops been more alluring than this year, and great efforts have been made to bring before the public notice British goods of all descriptions,' the *Telegraph* wrote, 'We should make a point of choosing something which will show our patriotism at this time of stress.'

For the children, Babyland Ltd at 19 Angel Street sold 'All British Made' toys including cars, trucks, wheelbarrows, chairs, dolls and teddy bears. Messrs FJ Bramwell Limited had 30 showrooms in the Haymarket providing novelties, toys and games.

Predominantly aimed at women, Messrs Newsholmes Limited on High Street sold perfumes including Dorset lavender water in 'dainty wickered bottles' and Messrs Loxley Brothers Limited sold fountain pens, pocket diaries, fancy leather goods including purses and albums. Also on sale were 'patriotic calendars and Christmas cards'. Mr Beal, 'Sheffield's oldest jeweller', in the Market Place sold chiming clocks, jewellery including illuminating watches, cufflinks, silver match boxes, necklets, rings, 'and the thousand and one other articles of jewellery of the pre-war days'.

Although no longer desirable in our animal loving nation, the sale of furs prior to and during the First World War was an important trade in the city. Mr Anson on Castle Street sold furs including squirrel, coney and fox, as well as umbrellas. The appropriately named Mr Joseph Fox, of 54 The Moor, had an impressive stock of furs despite having lost one large consignment when the Germans sank the *Lusitania*. These included the 'very fashionable skunk and wolf'. Rugs and footmuffs were being sought after by motorists, and could be purchased from Redgate Company on Fargate. The rugs and muffs were made of sable, skunk, wolf and fox furs. Fur coats could also be bought along with toys and miniature perambulators.

For the men, including those in the forces, Messrs Tyler and Co, tobacconists on Snig Hill, sold their brand of cigars made in their factory in Nottingham, tobacco mixtures, pipes and other smoking paraphernalia. Mr J Lomas Cockayne sold cigars, including many types of Havana cigar, from his shop at 12 George Street. He furthermore happily described to customers the processes of making the cigars, from growing tobacco to the arrival of the cigars in the shop.

For the household in general, many old pianos had been donated to hospitals for the entertainment of soldiers and so those seeking replacements were encouraged to buy from Messrs John Hoyland and Son's extensive showrooms on Barker Pool, opposite the Albert Hall or Messrs WF Cole and Sons Ltd on Surrey Street. Mr Cann, 'the music man', also sold instruments and sheet music in his shop at 4 Dixon Lane. Messrs T and T Tate were selling furniture.

In terms of food, for something special, Messrs Timothy Newby and Sons, Ltd on High Street were the 'largest retail fish, game and poultry salesmen in the North of England'. Turkeys, geese, ducklings, chickens, hares, rabbits and wild foul of all types could be obtained.

Oysters could also be obtained. Yorkshire and Derbyshire hams could be bought from Mr George Sharman at 231 to 237 Glossop Road. Cheese, including Stilton, could also be purchased from this shop along with wine, spirits, cigars and tobacco. Messrs Thomas Porter and Sons of King Street could provide 'irresistible novelties' from Stilton cheese to a Japanese vase. Fruits, perfumes, groceries, novelties, fancy chocolates, 'a huge assortment of delicacies' especially plum puddings and 'delightfully artistic crackers' could be bought from Messrs Tuckwood's Stores on Fargate. Swiss confectioner Mr Stauber of 76 Pinstone Street sold his award winning confectionary including cream toffee containing 'all the nutritious qualities of cream, butter and sugar' along with 'excellent chocolates'. Boiled sweets, including mint rock, and chocolates could be bought from Messrs W. Batty Ltd's factory on Wicker Lane. William Artindale and Sons, of High Street and Market Hall sold fruit, holly and mistletoe.

The markets were well stocked. Home reared turkeys were reasonably well supplied. Geese were scarce, but chickens, ducks, pheasants, English hares, Dutch hares and English rabbits were plentiful. There was a very small supply of fish. At Castlefolds Market business was only moderate for the time of year, with lower than expected trade given that a reasonable amount of money was around. English and American apples were plentiful and there was an excellent supply of oranges at a good price. Tomatoes were plentiful, but nuts and dates were very scarce. There were lots of vegetables. In terms of decoration there were few flowers, no mistletoe, but plenty of holly.

Christmas Eve saw 'phenomenal trade' in the city, with a desire for a higher though not extravagant standard of living. The manager of a large city centre emporium said that people were spending liberally with the attitude 'no pessimism, no parsimony' in crowded shops. It was remarked how curious it was that even ladies and gentleman were having to do their own Christmas shopping because servants and errand boys had joined the armed forces or were working in the munitions factories or other war work. The shop fronts were not illuminated but the interiors were well lit displaying the wares and well decorated. Shopkeepers in the working class areas of Attercliffe and Brightside were doing very well during the run up to Christmas because men working in the munitions factories had more money than in previous Christmases and, due to their long working hours, the workers were less willing, or unable, to travel to the city centre and so were spending money closer to their homes and places of work.

With time off work, more money than previously enabling them to buy gifts, treats and decorations, some of Sheffield's citizens were able to try and enjoy what they could of Christmas.

Christmas was made happier for those who had loved ones returning home on leave. Soldiers returned to the city for Christmas with mistletoe in their caps. They were given a good reception at Sheffield Midland Railway Station, by loved ones grateful for a festive reunion and by the city as a whole, which was grateful to see a convoy soldiers who were not wounded.

It was, of course, not a happy Christmas for an increasing amount of Sheffield folk who had lost family or friends or were worrying about the safety of those fighting overseas. On 14 December it was revealed that Private George Higginbottom of 31 Hobson Avenue had been missing in action since 21 October. He had been serving in the King's Own York and Lancasters Infantry and had been a soldier for 12 years. Just two days before Christmas, on 23 December 1915, Mr and Mrs Colver of Rock Mount, Ranmoor, learnt that they had lost their second son to the war. Captain Henry Colver was serving in the 5th York and Lancaster Regiment and had died at Flanders on 19 December. His brother, Lieutenant EW Colver had died in June, with a glass window at Ranmoor Church having been dedicated to his memory just six days before his brother's death.

The family of Arthur Stanley Vickers of Ecclesall Road were also mourning. Vickers was in Germany at the outbreak of war, where he studied the German language and business. As a British citizen of military age (he was 24 years old) he was taken prisoner. His mental and physical health quickly deteriorated as he spent time in an overcrowded prison cell, in unsanitary conditions, uncertain of when he would be released, if he ever would be, cut off from the outside world. Diplomatic efforts eventually secured his release, after 14 months, and there were hopes he would make a recovery. His health did not improve, however, and he died soon after regaining freedom, freedom in the loosest sense of the word in an enemy country. His funeral at Fulwood Church on 21 December was well attended.

For civilians, wounded soldiers and members of the forces on leave, there was entertainment at all the theatres and picture houses, with The Albert Hall showing *The Rosary*, and *Ivanhoe* on Christmas Day itself. On 23 December the Star Picture House on Ecclesall Road opened, with free entry to the first screening. All looked complete but there were still finishing touches being carried out by workmen; the café and billiard room still unfurnished. Soon it would be 'a very comfortable, very commodious, and very admirable picture house'. It was predicted by the *Telegraph* it would have a 'highly successful future'.

Festive entertainment was provided to soldiers in the city's hospitals. At Wharncliffe War Hospital the Hallamshire Band performed music, there was 'an enjoyable concert' for soldiers at the Royal Hospital and a musical treat for soldiers at the Sheffield Base Hospital with a programme 'full of good things', with singing and playing of music, including Zoe Addy who 'delighted the men' with her violin solo, Mrs F Booker sang *When the Boys Come Home*, Mrs Walsh sang *Ireland*, with the men joining in with the chorus, and others performing other songs. A whist drive raised £3 for the Western Road Hospital. The Attercliffe Wesleyan Guild of Help held its first 'patriotic Saturday evening concert' in aid of the war relief funds with a 'varied and interesting' programme which was enjoyed by a large audience. A concert for the wounded soldiers at Shiregreen Military Hospital with music and comedy proved 'eminently entertaining' according to the *Telegraph*.

On 23 December 20 wounded soldiers from the base and Greystones Hospitals were taken to the Myopic School in motorcars where they were given a tea and 'bright and very admirable entertainment'. Plays *Mildred and Patty* and *Britannia and Her Allies*, were performed. Afterwards scarves and mittens, knitted by the teachers and children, and a pipe were given to each of the soldiers. Each child was given a small gift also.

That same day there was an exhibition at the Junior Department of Manor Council School including displays of woollen blankets knitted by the girls for Serbian refugees and also warm clothing for the poorest children in the city. A large number of homemade cakes and plum puddings were brought in for wounded soldiers.

On Christmas Eve a group of wounded soldiers from the Base Hospital was entertained by teachers and pupils from the Sheffield Cathedral day school. The men were received by Reverend Archdeacon Gresford Jones, the Reverend Cecil, CW Cohen

Local school children at Woodhouse Junior School, Station Road, entertaining troops wounded. (*Photograph reproduced from the Picture Sheffield Collection, courtesy of Sheffield Local Studies Library*)

(Headmaster), Sister Horner and Nurse Arnold. The men visited each of the classes to see drawings by the children and chatted with them, a group of girls performed Morris dancing, others recited extracts from Shakespeare's works, with others singing patriotic songs. The infant school raised money to provide funds for the soldiers. The children were then dismissed and the teachers enjoyed a tea with the soldiers, whilst a Belgian refugee child handed round cigarettes and sang the *Marseillaise* in French. 'A pleasant hour' was spent talking, with music and skill games, before the soldiers were escorted back to the hospital.

By the end of 1915 13,500 wounded soldiers had passed through Sheffield hospitals since the outbreak of war. Ten and a half thousand of these had been brought back from overseas with the remaining 3,000 having been struck by illness during training in England. During December there were 2,000 soldiers and sailors in the city hospitals.

Gifts, and money to buy gifts, were sought for the benefit of those patients. On 23 December the afternoon and evening performances at the Albert Hall were included in the 'soldier's comforts' scheme. Patrons presenting a gift to the Soldiers' and Sailors' Comforts Society (excluding literature) were admitted free to the Nurse Cavell pictures. Tobacco, cigarettes and similar gifts were especially welcome. Funds were raised by performances at the Sheffield Temperance Hall of Miss Florence Lee's fairy tale play *Golden Echoes*, which was distributed to various comfort funds for wounded soldiers.

There was also a request that men who had only attested to the forces out of compulsion rather than voluntary-ism should hand over their fees of 2s 9d in aid of the comfort's fund, with collection boxes for the fees at the Corn Exchange and the depot on Leopold Street.

Teachers in Sheffield told their pupils that Santa Claus did not have time to visit the wounded soldiers and so they would have to take them presents on his behalf. They were asked to bring cigarettes, tins of fruit, tins of salmon and tins of sardines, Christmas cakes, Christmas puddings, or pennies or halfpennies. One boy, when asked what the children could do to make Jesus happy on his birthday, replied, 'A know, send 'im a gun ter shoot t' German's wi'.'

Children made a special effort for the war. Four eight-year-old girls organised a bazaar on their own initiative, which raised 24s for the Soldiers' and Sailors' Comfort Depot.

A Wounded and Sick Soldiers' Picture House War Fund was set up to subsidise tickets for soldiers in the city's hospitals to see pictures. To help raise money for the fund flags were sold, with more than 200 people selling flags with an incentive of prizes for those who sold the most.

Sheffield's lady telephonists and the lady members of the clerical staff working at the Post Office held a dinner at Stephenson's Café on Castle Street, for the benefit of 60 wounded soldiers.

On Christmas Eve 'a match of special attractiveness' was played at Bramall Lane to raise money for the Comforts Fund. Teams from Messrs Hadfield's Nos 4 and 5 Machine Shops consisted of employees and some League players, including players from Manchester City, West Bromwich, Aston Villa, Birmingham and Burnley as well as local teams. A football match at Cammell Laird's ground at Wincobank on 29 December to raise funds.

The Sheffield and Rotherham Millers' Association raised £440 as part of the national Association's efforts to obtain £50,000 for the Red Cross. Councillor W L Angell addressed a meeting of the Association where the donations were pledged. He told those present that the Red Cross did a vast amount of important work, particularly in France, treating thousands of wounded soldiers at relatively little cost. He said that every Englishman had a duty to do all that he could for the war effort and that those who were unable to fight could at least donate money to help those fighting on their behalf. It was 'up to them' Councillor Angell added, to see that the wounded were supplied with what they needed.

A concert was held at Gleadless Road Evening School, raising £5 10s to the 3rd Northern General Hospital for 20 pairs of crutches for wounded soldiers. A student sent 6s 6d for an additional pair. £5 8s was raised for the Serbian Relief Fund. £50 was raised to enable relatives from a distance to visit patients at the 3rd Northern General Hospital.

A 'monster' Christmas cake weighing 300lbs, and standing several feet high with a statuette of the King guarded by soldiers of all the Allies' colours on top and with flags on its sides and bearing the motto

'Fighting For Peace and Honour' was on display for several days in the Cutlers' Hall. It was made by a Mrs Stephenson, for the wounded soldiers at the Base Hospital. She had made a similar cake the previous year, but on a smaller scale. There was a charge of 3d per person to view the cake, with money raised going to the Red Cross.

On Christmas Eve lots of people attended the Albert Hall cinema performances in the afternoon and evening shows, bringing gifts in exchange for free entry, for the Soldiers' Comforts. Films included *The Babes in the Wood*, *Across the Wires*, Pathe's *Gazette*, *Tale of Twenty Stories* and others. The evening highlight was the film *Edith Cavell*. Gifts included fruit, cake, sausage and polony, pipes, tobacco. Five times as many soldiers in the hospitals as the previous Christmas but such was the level of generosity from those attending the Albert Hall and Messrs Johnson and Appleyards, who were also collecting, it was expected that every patient would receive a present.

The small Sheffield society known as the P.I.P.S. presented each wounded soldier at the Base Hospital and Longshaw Lodge with a Christmas present. The matron and sisters also received a small gift. The gifts for the men included razors, shaving cream, knives, strops, pipes, tobacco and cigarette cases filled with cigarettes. The sisters each received a 'dainty' penknife. In total 467 presents were handed out. Additionally ham, sausages, pork pies, plum puddings, potted meat, mince pies, oranges, bananas, tomatoes and cakes were provided by the society.

The wounded soldiers at the Winter Street Hospital received presents from the Haddon Works Relief Fund. These consisted of razors, pipes, tobacco, cigarette cases filled with cigarettes and strops. In total 85 gifts were presented. Again the sisters were each given a lady's penknife.

In addition to soldiers in Sheffield hospitals, an appeal was made on behalf of the 'wounded lads' from Sheffield at the Colchester hospital, from Sister E Andrews, and for games, jigsaw puzzles, Meccano 'which are of special interest and amusement', playing cards, quoits, draughts and dominoes, 'to while away many weary hours and brighten the Christmas days'. Cigarettes, tobacco and pipes were also wanted.

Those wanting to give the wounded merriment in the form of alcohol were prohibited from doing so. Changes to the Defence of the Realm Act which came into force on Christmas Eve made it illegal to give, sell, procure for or supply alcohol to any wounded soldier.

In addition to those efforts made to give some comfort to wounded soldiers in Sheffield, the people of Sheffield tried their best to help give a little joy to those troops fighting overseas. 'A good time' would be had by British soldiers in the trenches over Christmas, according to the official press reports designed to keep up morale back home. The Press Association's special correspondent at the British Headquarters said British soldiers would have half a chicken and half a plum pudding, many plum puddings being supplied by Sheffield folk. They would have 'a mucky old time' in the trenches with mud but at least it would not be cold. Troops were happier in the knowledge that the British army were not outnumbered and were better equipped with weapons than during the previous Christmas, thanks to the efforts of those in munitions factories in Sheffield and elsewhere. The work of the women, and some men, producing items for the Comforts Depot and other collections was also recognised. 'Compared with twelve months ago there is less exposure, and a very much more adequate system for minimising the discomforts of the wet,' it was said.

A balanced and realistic view was given but an optimistic message was emphasised that although hard times lay ahead and that winter campaigns were arduous, good times would follow.

'It may be truthfully said – and I would emphasise that point as a cheery Christmas message to the multitudes of fond, anxious ones at home – that a retrospect across the past twelve months leads to very satisfactory conclusions.'

Thus ended the official statement which would have given the greatest possible gift to those in Sheffield with loved ones overseas, short of those loved ones returning home; hope.

Such was the desire to send messages and gifts to the troops that the Field Post Office staff were being 'buried in chin-deep avalanches'. Even by 13 December half a million parcels were sent to France and Flanders and 300,000 were sent on each of the remaining days of

Advent. One million, to one and a half million, letters were also sent each day and so it was not surprising that staff were finding it difficult to cope. Six special trains and four special boats had been set aside for mail in addition to the regular facilities. Of course, these figures relate to the mail situation nationally but certainly Sheffield contributed significantly to these statistics.

With fewer trains running, due to them being used by the military, and little in the way of football, over Christmas, it was suggested that people should use that free time they had over the festive period to walking over the moors, and the *Telegraph* published a book entitled *Ramble Book* to give routes that could be easily followed.

On Christmas day the Bishop of Sheffield preached at the Cathedral, with a 'beautiful little cantata' entitled *Christmas Eve* rendered by the choir in the afternoon. The evening service had the Anthem, *Comfort ye, my people* by Handel. With the second Christmas of war, there would have been a great desire for those who believed for comfort from the divine.

Rather than preaching to his congregation during the Christmas of 1915, the Reverend H Ewbank left St George's Church to be a chaplain so that he could preach to the troops. The congregation presented him with a Communion service set and a wrist watch.

After the short festive break, life resumed with hard work in the factories as men and women returned with renewed energy. The issue of conscription, which had no doubt troubled large numbers of men over Christmas, re-emerged.

The number of unmarried men who had not attested had been found to be 650,000. This led the Prime Minister to announce that the number of unattested men was not 'a negligible number' and that therefore some form of compulsion would be necessary. It was said that early in the new year a Bill would be passed forcing unmarried men of military age, who had not already attested, to do so. As the *Telegraph and Star* said it was now 'an unescapable necessity'. Unmarried men in Sheffield and elsewhere who had not wanted to fight now realised that what they had feared but had hoped would never happen, now would. Of course, a reasonable proportion were unfit and another significant proportion were starred in that they were employed in war work, but another significant proportion were what the Government and the country as a whole regarded as shirkers. The Labour Recruiting Committee claimed these proportions were 60 per cent, 20 per cent and 20 per cent respectively. Those who were concerned with political matters feared that the Government would break up and a General Election called, causing political instability, due to the knowledge that Ministers opposed to compulsion might resign from the Government if it was introduced.

The *Telegraph* now argued, after claiming to want 'justice for married men', that married men with no dependants should be considered more eligible for military service than single men who had a mother or sisters to look after.

According to the Registrar-General's returns the birth-rate for the third quarter of 1915 was 'the lowest recorded in any quarter since the establishment of civil registration'. The reasons are obvious and it was felt that the birth rate would not stabilise and increase for some years following the war, and that it would decrease further before the war was over as more men joined the forces. This would have impacts on schools in five or six year's time.

1915 would later be described by the Medical Officer for Sheffield as a year of 'excessive mortality'. It was described in a more mixed way by the *Telegraph* who claimed it had been 'a year of war and prosperity', although the 'disturbing increase in the death rate' was alluded to.

The prosperity was the result of 'mighty efforts' to produce weapons for the war, which had made Sheffield 'perhaps the most prosperous city in the country' and had made it possible for the city to raise more than £2 million for the War Loan since June. All classes were enjoying the benefit of 'this period of artificial inflation'. Sheffield men were praised for their work in the factories which had involved extensive overtime resulting in 'exceptional wages and war bonuses'. It was commented upon with dismay that most men had spent this extra wealth on items of luxury that were unnecessary and that little, if any, of it had been saved in anticipation of 'the rainy day' expected following the war. It is interesting that the efforts of women were not recognised in the article, and is suggestive that attitudes had not changed greatly despite the thousands of women carrying out sterling work in the city.

Despite the prosperity the Local Government Board told local authorities to cut expenditure.

The district rate was reduced by one penny in the pound but the education and poor rates were increased. The total city rates for the year ending 25 March were 9s 8d in the pound, an increase of 3d.

Tempting fate, the article ended, 'Happily the city itself has not suffered from the havoc caused by the dogs of war. The blast of war has not actually sounded in our ears, as it has at places on the coast, or in the Metropolis.' This would change before the next year's end.

CHAPTER 13

Conscientious Objectors

Not everyone was enthusiastic about the war, and this became increasingly apparent as the horrors of warfare became increasingly known and when conscription began to compel men to go and fight.

During the first two weeks of the war 20,000 casualties were recorded and this understandably led to some opposition.

Early in the war a small voice of pacifists began to be heard across the country, with its numbers growing steadily as the results of conflict began to reach the Home Front in the form of convoys of wounded soldiers and news of Sheffield men who had fallen. Tales were also heard about the horror of the battlefields, with Sheffield man Private HC Sucker of the 26th General Hospital in France describing to Mr Ernie and Mrs Cooke of Sheffield, how he had 'gathered brains from the men's wounds and often taken arms and legs to be destroyed. I see some terrible sights.'

The No-Conscription Fellowship (NCF) was set up in 1915 when the issue of conscription began to be seriously considered. When conscription was introduced, originally for unmarried men, it successfully campaigned to secure 'the conscience clause' in the 1916 Conscription Act. This allowed men to claim exemption from military service on the grounds of conscience.

About 16,000 men claimed exemption nationally. In order to be exempted they were required to attend a tribunal with a panel consisting of councillors, other leading members of civic life and a military representative. Most of these were highly patriotic individuals who were motivated to obtain as many recruits as possible and consequently most claims of exemption were therefore refused.

A military representative also sat on each panel with a common aim: to get as many men as possible into the army to fill the gaps left by the dead. As a result, only a minority received full exemption.

In Sheffield one of the leading voices against Britain's involvement in the 'European war' was Edward Carpenter who lived in Millthorpe, close to the city, and who wrote essays and pamphlets airing his views. In 1915 Carpenter wrote an anti-war pamphlet entitled 'The Healing of Nations' (Carpenter/Mss/190) and in 1916 he wrote another pamphlet entitled 'Never Again!'

(Sheffield Archives: Carpenter/Mss/205-208)

In 'The Healing of Nations' he wrote:

'It is true that if the Allies win there is no alternative but to reduce Germany to such a condition that her insane Militarism shall be put hors de combat for long years to come. There is no alternative because she has revealed her hand too clearly as a menace…of barbarous force to the whole world…If Germany wins a German terror might be established through the world… freed from the nightmare claim of any one nation's world empire…But in order to substantiate this result England must also abdicate her crass insistence on commercial supremacy. The "nation of shopkeepers" thing which has in the past made her the hated of other nations which has created within her borders a vulgar and ill-smelling class, the repository of much arrogant wealth, must cease to be the standard of her life.'

He believed that Britain was being hypocritical in its empirical stance. He referred to a Manifesto of the British Empire League, which had been founded in 1895 and was patronised by Royalty and members of the aristocracy. One of the points raised in the manifesto was that the navy should be used to defend and expand British trade. 'Not a word is said in the whole Manifesto about the human and social responsibilities of this vast empire. Can we blame Germany for struggling at all costs to enlarge her borders, when that is what the British Empire means?' He had hopes that the war would bring the 'age of empires' to an end. He was against empires and nations being ruled by another nation. He believed the way to prevent wars in the future was to give these nations independence.

Carpenter was not a German sympathiser and wanted to ensure that this was known by all. Instead he simply opposed war, feeling that there were no circumstances which justified the taking of life on mass scale. 'Why should we – we the "enlightened and civilised" nations of Europe get involved in these senseless wars at all?' he asked.

In terms of conscription he believed it must be 'persistently opposed'. He believed it was deceitful to claim to secure peace through war, and that conscription would only perpetuate militarism. 'The nation says it is fighting to put down militarism. Why then make compulsory militarism foundational in our national life? To abolish militarism by militarism is like putting down drink by swallowing it! The whole lesson of this war is against conscription. Germany could never have imposed herself on Europe without it,' he wrote. It was his belief that conscription allows governments to force people to fight for any cause that the government desires, without the conscriptees understanding that cause. 'To force men to fight in causes which they do not approve, to compel them to adopt a military career when their temperaments are utterly unsuited to such a thing, or when their consciences or their religion forbid them – these things are both foolish and wicked,' he believed.

If the Government treat its soldiers and sailors badly, he argued, and paid them little when they risked their lives, it would lead to a lack of people wanting to join up, which would necessitate conscription, and then all people would be forced to fight for little and endure bad treatment. '...it is simply a scandal that the wealthy classes should sit at home in comfort and security and pay to the man in the trenches who is risking his life at every moment … no more than the minimum wage of an ordinary day labourer.'

All nations claimed they wanted peace, he noted, but they were all 'arming to the teeth; each accusing the others of militant intentions', forming alliances to try and shift the balance of power. 'What nonsense! What humbug! What an utter bankruptcy of so-called diplomacy!', he wrote of the so called desire for peace.

If diplomats and foreign ministers genuinely wanted peace then 'their utter incapacity and futility have been proved to the hilt and they must be swept away' with people, especially the working class, paying the cost.

Lots of men in Sheffield claimed to be conscientious objectors. The following two cases are good examples.

A conscientious objector refused to join the army when called up. Appearing at the South Yorkshire Appeal Tribunal on 27 July 1917 it was said that he had passed his medical examination and was ordered to drill with the voluntary reserves but he refused to do so. At the tribunal he informed the committee that he would not desire to take any life and would rather communicate with the Germans, urging them to stay away.

In February 1918 Leslie Copleston, an 18-year-old metallurgy student at the University of Sheffield, appealed against being called up to the army on account of being a conscientious objector. Both his brothers worked on the land, growing food, and had been granted exemption due to being conscientious objectors. He too wanted exemption arguing that no cause justified such violence and horror. He was offered work in the ambulance corps to allow him to avoid carrying out any combat role but he declined, saying that the purpose of such a role was to make men better so that they could be forced to return to the battlefields to be killed. He said he would happily be occupied in work such as railway work. He was challenged about this on account that the railways are used to transport munitions used in war, but he argued that he would not be responsible for what was carried. The Appeal Tribunal was unconvinced by his claims that he was a genuine conscientious objector and they considered him to be a shirker. His appeal was dismissed.

In addition to writing pamphlets, pacifists wrote to the newspapers, made speeches, lobbied the authorities and attempted demonstrations. On 30 June 1916 the police prohibited a 'stop the war' demonstration in Sheffield.

The conscientious objectors wanted an end to all wars. Edward Carpenter believed that humanity could cease to exist if the desire for war continued. In 'Never Again! A Protest and a Warning Addressed to the Peoples of Europe' Carpenter wrote, 'The time has come – if the human race does not wish to destroy itself in its own madness.' He predicted, at a time when most believed the First World War would be 'the war to end wars' that more powerful weapons would wreak more damage and that there would be more violent wars in the future even though a growing number of people were recognising the grotesque horrors of warfare. 'That human beings should use every devilish invention of science with the one purpose of maiming, blinding, destroying those against whom they have no personal grudge or grievance. All this is sheer madness.' There was, he said, no glory in war; just bloodshed, writhing bodies and people killing one another. (MSS/205-208)

CHAPTER 14

1916

With the recognition that vast numbers of men had not attested, with an estimated 343,386 of whom were able to fight, on 5 January the Military Service Bill was presented to Parliament to compel the attestation of all unmarried men and widowers without children or dependents, between the ages of 18 and 41. It became law on 27 January, with men who had not yet attested automatically being attested at midnight on 1 March. Attested single men had already been called up and now attested married men aged 19 to 27 were also gradually called up to serve. As more men were needed, older attested married men were called up and in May conscription was introduced for the married men. This resulted in a gradual large scale reduction in the male population of the city.

The period of January to September was dominated by this military growth, with only a small number of other events worthy of mention, although some of these events were of huge importance.

On the face of it the alcohol regulations appeared to be having an effect on drunken behaviour. By 2 February there had been 1,111 convictions for drunkenness in the past twelve months, compared with 1,473 in the twelve months before. This was not regarded to be because of the stricter regulation, although that may have contributed to the decrease, but instead largely because there were fewer police.

One undesirable related effect was highlighted in March, when publicans reported that they felt the need to protect themselves with revolvers against hooligans.

On 6 March a fierce gale for eight or nine hours caused much damage. However, by Easter on 12 April the weather had improved. In fact it was described as 'glorious' and allowed for a 'perfect holiday' with large crowds of Sheffielders enjoying the outdoors.

On 21 May the daylight saving scheme was introduced and was accepted with 'almost perfect nonchalance' in Sheffield according to the 1917 Year Book. At the December 1916 council meeting Alderman Cattell spoke in favour of the alteration of time during the Summer Time Act 1916 and called for the council to support it being permanent because it was 'so beneficial to the community'. The council agreed and sent a motion to the Government

On 1 July printed lists of the names and addresses of men who had not reported under the Military Service Act of Groups System were displayed prominently throughout Sheffield in a bid to shame them into signing up.

It was aptly timed because 1 July saw the greatest loss of life of any single day of the war, and featuring in the dispatches were hundreds of Sheffield men who were ill trained and ill equipped.

The City Battalion which had been at the Somme since May 1916 joined the thousands who went 'over the top' on that fateful summer day. 512 of its members were wounded and 248 were killed, 165 of whom were never identified. After the Somme the Battalion was rebuilt largely of men from Lancashire, Norfolk and Staffordshire and so it lost much of its connection to Sheffield. By the end of the war it was no longer formed chiefly of Sheffield men and it had ceased to allow only professional men to be part of its ranks. Indeed the professional and skilled men were now encouraged to carry out their war work in the factories and any other places on the Home Front which could better use their abilities.

One of those who died at the Battle of the Somme was Ecclesfield man Tom Lockwood, although he died on 6 November 1916. His letters (Sheffield Archives X1/4-5) give an insight into life on the Front and the information given to loved ones back home.

In a letter dated 24 May 1916 he described being 'in the best of health ... never better'. He was aggrieved that parcels had gone missing, especially as they contained cigarettes. Commenting on the war, he wrote, 'You ask me how I think the war is going on. Well you will know better than me I expect. I only know how things is where we are and of course I'm same as you it would be better if it was over but I never bother myself. I just take things as they come enjoying myself when I get the chance and then going in the trenches and does my bit their [sic]. We get some horrible stuff sent over at times but we give more than we get. Their [sic] is not much I can tell you but I hope I'll not be long before I'm coming to see you…'

A second letter gave a slightly more graphic account of battle, 'I am writing these few lines in my dugout about 100 yds off the Germans but things seem quiet enough but for a few shells whistling round and they're alright if they will keep going over. Remember me to inquiring friends. I'm in the pink. … I'll be pleased when I can get a few days off to see you because if I don't come soon I'll only be able to talk French and that'll make things awkward…'

Another Sheffield man's letters (Sheffield Archives: WED/310/15-16) reveal the thoughts and fears of the soldiers at this time, thoughts and fears which will have had an impact on morale in Sheffield. Fred Philpot did not expect to return home after he left Sheffield for war, having received from the city a memorable send off 'as the warriors did of old'. On 2 July 1916 soon after arriving in France he wrote of a 'chum' who had written that there were no comforts had his letter stopped, so he was being careful about what he was writing. He described the mud which 'seems awful to me now but what must it be like in winter?' and 'heavy artillery fire is going on near us practically day and night more especially at night'.

He was grateful for medication sent by family in Sheffield and requested a satchet, made by a Sheffield firm, worn on the breast 'to keep away those little animals that affect the skin under the conditions in which we live'.

He complained about the food, especially lack of green vegetables and the early starts, 'but to my mind its not as bad as I expected to find it. However, it's bad enough.'

Remarking on the war he said, only a day after thousands of the Allies lost their lives; 'According to the general chatter out here the war is going well with us although naturally not without considerable loss.' He added there were only two casualties from his group and that the 150 guns had done 'some excellent work'.

Fred was justified with his fears of death; he was killed on 16 October. His parents later wrote, 'It has come as a great blow to us all, still you know each letter that came we were almost afraid to open it thinking we might see bad news.' They were just replying to a letter in which he had expressed a degree of happiness when the news came.

On 1 August wounded soldiers and sailors convalescing in the city gained a small amount of extra leisure at this time, with the opening of the Sheffield Soldiers' and Sailors' Rest Room on Castle Street. There was a tea room and games room where billiards or bagatelle could be played, along with a Quiet Room where men could be found writing letters or reading. It was so popular that by its first anniversary 96,516 teas had been served, with 123,436 visits. In fact it was so popular that there were usually more than 400 men who visited each day.

CHAPTER 15

The Defence of the City

At the outbreak of war no one knew what to expect but the naval battles of the North Coast had led to fears of a possible invasion. Road blocks were set up on all main roads into the city. They were manned by police officers at a cost of £156 per month by July 1915.

Within weeks of the war commencing it was decided to block the retirement of police officers, in order to ensure there was an adequate number to cover increased duties and because of those who signed up for military duties. The hours worked by officers were increased to nine hours per day. In order to save costs it was decided that the increased hours would not be pensionable. Consequently once the war had ended many police officers threatened to go on strike and it is because of this that it was made illegal for officers to strike.

In addition to the regular police force more special constables were hired on a voluntary basis to increase a police presence. On 19 August 1914 61 more special constables had enrolled at the Sheffield Police Court.

In December 1914 a letter from 'Sheffield Jack' in the *Telegraph and Star* gave a somewhat tongue in cheek view of the investment into Special Constables but one which highlighted a problem; 'Sir, - In the event of the Huns arriving in Sheffield there will be no need to confront them with either Regulars or Volunteer forces. Simply show them our special constables in their rag market regimentals, viz., a pair of trousers, second hand, formerly belonging to a member of the force; a commissionaire's overcoat, costing (so it is said), 11s.; a G.P.O. cape, which after a shower of rain is closely akin to a dish cloth; a peaky sort of cap, breed unknown; boots, waistcoat, and jacket missing.

Now, Sir, hard-hearted as the Huns have hitherto proved themselves to be, I feel sure that previous to firing a shot at anybody they would take up a house to house collection for new uniforms for the specials. Of course if the Germans never come, our City Fathers can each have a stall in the market and dispose of the clothes by mock auction, or they might wear a few of them themselves.'

In addition to volunteer police, other voluntary groups were established. On 28 November 1914 a meeting was held at Wincobank Parish Room for those who wanted Home Defence.

The Chief Constable had already organised drilling for civilians who were unable, due to age or health, to undertake active service but who could help defend the city in the event of invasion. The Chief Constable's Civilian Corps (or Four Cs as it was most commonly known) consisted of approximately 5,000 men, with every member attending drills twice a week between 2pm and 10pm. They trained for the event of an enemy invasion and were taught how to use muskets. It was formally recognised towards the end of 1914.

On 1 January 1915 the Four Cs, eager to show what it was doing, spent the day marching, from 10am until late and soon joined other volunteer units to become the Sheffield Volunteer Defence Corps. In 1916 it became part of the West Riding Volunteer Regiment and in 1918 became the Volunteer Battalion of the York and Lancaster Regiment.

It was argued the Defence Corps were shirkers trying to avoid military service and that they should be forced to join the army, much to the anger of those involved in the group. On 16 October 1915, 'Compulsory Looking On' wrote to the *Telegraph* saying of the 15 acquaintances he knew in the S.V.D.C., nine were aged over 40, three had bad sight, one so bad that he would not be able to recognise someone from a distance of three yards without glasses, two worked in munitions and one had a job with such great responsibility that he could not be let go. Although conscription could lead to him joining the armed forces, it was only one out of the 15. Therefore few of the 2,000 men would be eligible if his own acquaintances were anything to go by.

Sundays were no longer days of rest or worship, much to the dismay of religious leaders. Instead Sunday was a day of marching for civilians who were undergoing military training on account of having to work for the remainder of the week.

The Year Book for 1915 criticised the training:

'Thus far sufficient attention has not been paid to shooting. Drill and marching practice are admirable. But the power to shoot is more admirable. We ought to concentrate much more than we are doing on becoming a straight shooting people. That will be worth more than any other quality we may possess in the hour of direst need.'

As air raids became more prevalent more emphasis was placed on defending the city. Voluntary efforts needed to be greatly enhanced by professionals.

During the war there were 23 air raid warnings in Sheffield. The first air raid warning was sounded on 16 June 1915, with four further warnings that same year. There were 12 occasions when the sirens sounded in 1916. During the last two years there were only six warnings, three for each year.

Searchlights were set up at Norton, Wincobank, land off High Storrs Road and Marsh House Road. Anti aircraft batteries were located at Wincobank Hill, The Manor and Ecclesall. These were popular visitor attractions.

A number of landing grounds were planned to defend Sheffield and its munitions factories. The Royal Flying Corps established two landing sites at Redmires and Coal Aston, in order to provide the means of intercepting enemy aircraft, with work started in 1915. Each ground had refuelling facilities and flare paths. The Redmires site was expanded to cover a wide area and comprised three camps providing accommodation, a Stores Depot, an Engine and Mechanical Transport Depot and an Aircraft Repair Depot. German prisoners of war were also housed on the site towards the end of the war. In March 1920 the site was bought by Sheffield Education Committee. Coal Aston continued to be used by the RAF until 1919.

Street lighting had been reduced from the beginning of November 1914 at the order of the Watch Committee to try and prevent Zeppelins from finding their way to the city. No electric flashlights were allowed

Fleet Air Arm at Coal Aston Aerodrome. (*Photograph reproduced from the Picture Sheffield Collection, courtesy of Sheffield Local Studies Library*)

and Bonfire Night celebrations were kept to a minimum and were actively discouraged. The following year even stricter lighting rules were imposed by the military. Street lamps had to be half covered and house windows covered. By September 1916 there was no street lighting.

A new order from the Home Secretary under DORA came into force on 10 January 1916, regarding the lighting up of vehicles half an hour after sunset, the requirement to carry lights, and, from 10 February, all vehicles to show a red light from a lamp at the rear. The rules were needed due to restrictions on street lighting and because of more traffic on the roads especially for the military, and the need to prevent accidents. Restrictions were in place on lighting for vehicles in areas where lights might be used to direct enemy aircraft. Headlights were prohibited but sidelights were allowed.

On 7 February 1916 in light of increased air raids the Chief Constable, Major J Hall-Dalwood issued the City Against Hostile Aircraft regulations (Sheffield Archives 295/Cl/18) which set out the 'co-ordination of the arrangements made locally…against possible attack by hostile aircraft and in order that greater expedition and efficiency of action may be ensured'. These precautions were publicised on notices from the Lord Mayor. The arrangements were as follows:

> Upon an air raid threat being recognised buzzers were sounded for three minutes in a series of triple blasts simultaneously. Upon hearing this warning all police officers on duty were to remain so and those off duty were to report to their Headquarters. Only illness or being away from city were acceptable excuses for Specials to not report for duty. They would then disperse the public and keep people moving until they reached their homes or the air raid shelters. Everyone was required to immediately seek shelter.

No traffic was to be allowed except official approved traffic, directed by a constable. Official cars and motorcycles had headlights showing a green light. Trams were to progress to the sheds with their lights off. Two motorists or motorcyclists were to go to each of the main entrances to the city and to oversee the extinguishing of road lamps, warning residents to stay indoors and to keep windows shrouded, watch cars and other vehicles and investigate possible signals. All lights were to be extinguished and no matches could be lit, with smoking strictly prohibited. Factories and workshops were to have their outside lights out, and inside lights shielded, with all doors closed. Anyone who was thought to be signalling to aircraft was to be arrested immediately.

Volunteer firemen were to go to the Central Fire Station at Rockingham Street or their designated places of duty. The 450 Royal Army Medical Corps at Hillsborough Barracks were to go to hospitals and police stations. If they were not needed for ambulance work (there being 16 ambulances available) they were to assist the police. Members of St John's ambulance were to go to the nearest police station. Ambulances were to stay at the garages until the Danger Past signal was sounded then go to the fire station to await instructions. The Danger Past signal was a continuous blast lasting one minute.

The council schools were to be used by the Queen Victoria Nursing

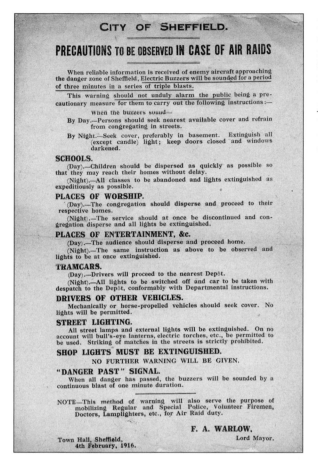

CITY OF SHEFFIELD.

PRECAUTIONS TO BE OBSERVED IN CASE OF AIR RAIDS

When reliable information is received of enemy aircraft approaching the danger zone of Sheffield, Electric Buzzers will be sounded for a period of three minutes in a series of triple blasts.

This warning should not unduly alarm the public being a precautionary measure for them to carry out the following instructions:—

When the buzzers sound—

By Day.—Persons should seek nearest available cover and refrain from congregating in streets.

By Night.—Seek cover, preferably in basement. Extinguish all (except candle) light; keep doors closed and windows darkened.

SCHOOLS.

(Day).—Children should be dispersed as quickly as possible so that they may reach their homes without delay.

(Night).—All classes to be abandoned and lights extinguished as expeditiously as possible.

PLACES OF WORSHIP.

(Day).—The congregation should disperse and proceed to their respective homes.

(Night).—The service should at once be discontinued and congregation disperse and all lights be extinguished.

PLACES OF ENTERTAINMENT, &c.

(Day).—The audience should disperse and proceed home.

(Night).—The same instruction as above to be observed and lights to be at once extinguished.

TRAMCARS.

(Day).—Drivers will proceed to the nearest Depôt.

(Night).—All lights to be switched off and car to be taken with despatch to the Depôt, conformably with Departmental instructions.

DRIVERS OF OTHER VEHICLES.

Mechanically or horse-propelled vehicles should seek cover. No lights will be permitted.

STREET LIGHTING.

All street lamps and external lights will be extinguished. On no account will bull's-eye lanterns, electric torches, etc., be permitted to be used. Striking of matches in the streets is strictly prohibited.

SHOP LIGHTS MUST BE EXTINGUISHED.

NO FURTHER WARNING WILL BE GIVEN.

"DANGER PAST" SIGNAL.

When all danger has passed, the buzzers will be sounded by a continuous blast of one minute duration.

NOTE—This method of warning will also serve the purpose of mobilizing Regular and Special Police, Volunteer Firemen, Doctors, Lamplighters, etc., for Air Raid duty.

F. A. WARLOW,
Lord Mayor.

Town Hall, Sheffield,
4th February, 1916.

Precautions to be observed in case of air raids. Issued by Sheffield City Council in February 1916. (*Photograph reproduced from the Picture Sheffield Collection, courtesy of Sheffield Local Studies Library*)

Association nurses as Dressing Stations, for first aid for any wounded.

In the event of bombs being dropped, all fragments were collected for examination. If any unexploded bombs were identified barricades were to be put up.

In the event of a crash or a shot down enemy aircraft it was required that a 'strong guard' should search and arrest any crew. There was to be no conversation with the prisoners unless medical assistance was needed. All charts, instructions and other documents were to be seized, with the aircraft itself left intact until the military authorities arrived in order to carry out a full examination.

These measures would soon be tested.

CHAPTER 16

Sheffield's First Air Raid

A s stated in the previous chapter, by September 1916 air raid sirens had been sounded in Sheffield on several occasions and prior to Monday 25 September that year there had been no danger to Sheffield or its people. Inevitably there was a feeling among the populace at large that Sheffield was safe and that the alarms were nothing more than a nuisance, causing disruption to business and people's lives.

This complacency was a major contributing factor in why, when Zeppelins flew over the city in the early hours of Tuesday 26 September, so many people lost their lives.

The raid was referred to in most documents in the public domain in 1916 as simply having affected a north Midlands town due to censorship. It was considered imperative not to confirm to the Germans that they had struck Sheffield, otherwise it would help them pinpoint their locations for any future raids. The knowledge of Britain's geography was somewhat limited and although coastal towns could be more easily identified, in the darkness especially in fog, such as that which covered Sheffield on the fateful night, it was not always possible for airship crews to pinpoint their precise location. Indeed the crew of L-22 were uncertain whether they had bombed Lincoln or Sheffield, such was the lack of accuracy.

It therefore requires an element of interpretation to ascertain the relevant facts from the contemporary newspaper accounts, especially as other towns and cities were affected in late September 1916 and it is not always possible to distinguish the different raids.

A German zeppelin resembling that which caused fear, death and destruction in Sheffield in September 1916. (*The Author's Collection*)

However, later newspaper accounts did provide clearer details and knowledge has been greatly enhanced by the contemporary accounts written by those who witnessed the airships of terror which haunted Sheffield on that tragic night.

On the afternoon of Monday 25 September the L-22 Zeppelin, a monster of an airship at 178.5m in length, under the command of Kapitänleutnant Martin Dietrich, left Germany with the intention of attacking Sheffield. It was one of seven airships heading to the British Isles, three targeting the south including London, two attacking the east and north-east coasts and the remaining two (the L-21 and L-22) ordered to attack industrial towns or cities in the North. The aluminium framed ship covered in waterproof cotton was powered by four engines and could travel a maximum speed of 60 miles per hour.

The L-22 crossed the North Sea and headed towards Yorkshire, passing over Lincolnshire with Dietrich using the seaside town of Mablethorpe as a landmark. Before it reached the city, at around 22:45, the authorities sounded the air raid alarm, alerting people to take cover and extinguish lighting. Thousands observed the warning and hid in cellars or found shelter they considered to be safe. Others ran to the woods and parks believing only buildings would be targeted. The remainder chose to do nothing. After all, previous air raid warnings had come to nothing, why would it be any different this time?

The Zeppelin approached Sheffield from the south-east, arriving over the city at around 12:20am and circled to the north, flying towards Redmires and Fulwood before turning towards Burngreave where it dropped its first bombs. The first two bombs, incendiary bombs, hit Burngreave Cemetery, but they caused little damage. A high explosive bomb then fell in Danville Street, killing Frederick Stratford when shrapnel hit him as he lay in bed. In Grimesthorpe Road a bomb destroyed a house and killed mother and daughter Ann Coogan and Margaret Taylor. At least one of the women survived the explosion, because screaming was heard coming from the house, but once assistance had arrived the building had collapsed and both occupants were found to be dead. Thomas Wilson looked out of his window in a house on the corner of Petre Street and Lyons Road and was hit in the chin by shrapnel from a bomb which had struck a nearby outbuilding. He died instantly, having been (it has been said) almost decapitated. Ironically Wilson was one of the hundreds if not thousands who had refused to take action when the air raid warning began to sound. He had not believed that any Zeppelins would find their way to the city and he had gone outside earlier in the evening to speak with neighbours about his belief. His granddaughter was scarred by window glass that shattered and flew across the room. The remaining family members who were downstairs were physically unharmed.

A bomb fell on a house in Writtle Street causing fatal wounds to Elizabeth Bellamy as she hurriedly tried to save her 11-month-old granddaughter. Her trunk was almost severed as shrapnel from a bomb exploding nearby hit her in the back, and she was crushed as the building collapsed around her. Almost all of the muscles on her back were torn. Although she was pulled from the debris, she died hours later. The child survived. Two bombs fell on Cossey Road, destroying three houses and killing members of four families who were sheltering in a cellar; George and Eliza Harrison, their two daughters and two grandchildren, and William and Sarah Southerington. Alice and Albert Newton were killed whilst they lay in bed. The second bomb killed a young couple named Levi and Beatrice Hames and their one-year-old son, all of whom had remained in bed. Selina and Joseph Tyler and four of their five children were killed when a bomb fell in Corby Street destroying their home of 136 Corby Street. The fifth child was found in the debris and was taken to hospital but later died. Eleven-year-old Richard Brewington of 134 Corby Street and Martha Shakespeare of number 143 were also killed by the same bomb. Richard had announced just moments earlier that 'the Zepps are here'. His mother and a lodger managed to escape the building before it collapsed. William Guest tried to do his part to reduce the dangers of the raid by alerting a household on Woodbourn Road to extinguish their lighting but whilst outdoors trying to gain their attention a bomb fell and he was killed. Further bombs fell close to the Washford Road bridge, near Manor Lane and in Princess Street where the primitive Methodist chapel was destroyed save for one wall bearing the ironic text 'A new commandment I give unto you, that ye love one another'.

The airship flew east over Darnall, dropping incendiary bombs, and soon disappeared into the heavy fog. The 36 bombs that were dropped left 29 dead and 19 injured, 89 houses destroyed and 150 damaged, a hotel was also destroyed. Luckily no munitions factories were badly damaged with the only affect upon them being shattered windows from the explosions nearby.

One of those who managed to escape becoming a victim was a soldier who was on leave. He heard an explosion and ran out of his house only to realise that the bomb had exploded just five houses away.

One observer recalled the Zeppelin sounding like a 'traction engine coming from Darnall. The sound seemed to go by Woodseats, Ecclesall and Crookes.' Soon after it was first heard, the explosions began. Describing the bombings, the witness wrote, 'And shortly I saw flashes of blue light and heard sharp, very loud reports. Over the Midland Station it appeared to be.' Of the aftermath it was said, 'Houses were wiped out and windows and rooms wrecked in the vicinity.'

A member of staff at the *Telegraph and Star* described, 'a vivid light blue glare followed immediately by a terrific reverberating roar.

I jumped out of bed and went to the window, and was in time to see a second flash, and hear another explosion succeeded by a third within a radius of a few hundred yards.'

A letter (Sheffield Archives: MD7126) sent by a Sheffield woman named Maggie Smith, who lived on Woodhead Road in the Highfields part of the city, to her Aunt Ellen, written two days after the raid, gave a more detailed, vivid first hand account of what occurred that night. 'Just a line to let you know we are still living, although we thought our number was up on Monday night,' the letter began. The city was 'heavily bombed; I shall never forget the awfull [sic] sensation as long as I live'.

She explained that at around 22:45 the air raid sirens sounded and within half an hour the streets were empty, apart from those engaged in patrols.

'I think we all realised it was more serious than ever before, as the soldiers, police and specials worked like Trojans + were very alert,' she wrote.

A man named Alf (presumably her husband) was at the home of a friend or relative named Alice who would not let him leave because it was too dangerous. Maggie and three people who were presumably Maggie and Alf's children, named Harry, Willie and Elsie, went to watch for Alf. Whilst stood outside talking to the next door neighbours the Zeppelin appeared. 'Suddenly we heard a droning, hurrying sound overhead, which came stronger every minute, then there were two sounds from another direction,' the letter continued.

This caused obvious fear and panic. 'Elsie clutched hold of Harry's arm and screamed out … she trembled like a leaf.' Elsie had more reason than most to be scared, having more knowledge than most of what was taking place and the danger that she and her neighbours were in. She had been in Cleethorpes three weeks earlier when there had been a raid in that town. Maggie described the scepticism which had existed in the minds and conversations of Sheffield people who had not believed that the Zeppelins would reach Sheffield.

A few minutes later 'soldiers and police were running about and ordered everyone indoors'. She returned indoors and sat at her bedroom window. It was at around midnight she thought that the bombs began to fall. She recalled, 'a great red flare go across the sky and a second later a terrific crash, then another. They were high explosive shells and they shook the earth, then a number of pale green lights like lightening with terrible crashes after each one. They lit the whole sky up, they were incendiary bombs. There were 15 bombes dropped. I sat and watched it all through. I could not move, I felt numbed. Well needless to say bed was out of the question. I was down at Alice's before it was daylight.'

Describing the horrendous damage she wrote, 'The damage is at Pitsmoor and Attercliffe right among the works, where thousands of men and women were on night work...but not one of the munition works were touched. It is miraculous how they missed them. Of course all lights are out and work stopped when the alarm went.'

The munitions factories had of course been spared, with Maggie rightly describing the poor slum houses as being the worst hit. 'But the havoc among the poor slum homes is awfull. One street, Corley Street, four houses were completely demolished and all the inmates buried. When I seen it early in the morning they had recovered the bodies, but later in the day they brought a baby boy about 3 years out alive and conscious he was buried 14 hours. The soldiers who found him cheered.'

On many streets the windows and doors had been 'blown to atoms' and she could not see the worst streets because there were cordons and soldiers with bayonets.

Some of the letter was illegible. 'Excuse the writing as I am unnerved. We have not slept since it happened,' it ended.

Although Maggie described the streets as being deserted some crowds of terrified onlookers did form in parts of the city to watch what was unfolding. There was terror on the streets, with people congregating outdoors to watch despite the police instructing them to seek shelter.

One young woman is recorded as having completely 'lost it' and ran down the street screaming hysterically, only being calmed down when someone grabbed her and dragged her indoors. The terror remained with her for the remainder of her life.

Another woman seemed less perturbed and after her home was

Following the zeppelin raid on the city came the search for survivors and for bodies. The photograph shows a search at 24-28 Cossey Road, Burngreave. (*Photograph reproduced from the Picture Sheffield Collection, courtesy of Sheffield Local Studies Library*)

damaged she was seen in a recreation ground, sat on a chair nursing a small child who was, in the recollection of an observer, 'prattling away as if there was no such nightmare as Zeppelin raids'.

There were some who wanted to make money out of the raid. Standing on a chair in a Sheffield street, a bookmaker put odds on which prominent buildings would be destroyed. A crowd formed of people wanting to place their bets.

The *Telegraph and Star* voiced the immense anger and lust for the killing of the enemy that was being thought and spoken of by Sheffield people. The editor wrote:

'the Germans cannot be accused of lack of courage in sending out Zeppelin raiders so soon after they had met with the disaster of Saturday, and we regret that their temerity has not been duly punished. Once again the devilish work of destroying peaceful people has been accomplished, and we have been given another reason for hoping not only for the defeat of Germany, but for the killing of as many Germans as possible, so that the earth may be rid of their fiendish wickedness. We hope that this latest visitation may strengthen the demand for reprisals, which are the measures most likely to prove effective, though we shall not doubt, from time to time, be able to give the raiders a lesson by bringing them down in flames to earth.'

Readers were urged to not be intimidated and do everything possible to help bring an end to the war, with renewed vigour on the Home Front and War Front being described as 'the true moral reply to a terrorist policy'.

There were questions as to why the anti aircraft guns and searchlights had not been used to shoot the Zeppelin and prevent such tragedy and why no planes had been sent to intercept the airship.

The official press view, no doubt instructed by the military, was 'to have illuminated the sky with searchlights would have merely guided the intruders on their erratic trip across the city and that they were at too high an altitude to be effectively reached'. Clearly the anti aircraft guns were ineffective. Equally there was no attempt to have planes try and shoot the Zeppelin, with no orders having been given. An unofficial view was that the military did not react to the raid because senior officers were at a ball at the Grand Hotel.

There was, however, a more innocent explanation. The visibility was extremely poor for pilots. The area around the Coal Aston landing ground in particular was shrouded in fog. An hour and a half before the attack on Sheffield Captain Edward N Clifton had been on night patrol for half an hour, attempting to intercept the L-21 Zeppelin which was in the vicinity of the city but in the eventuality flew to Lancashire, when he crash landed due to fog. He was slightly injured.

Extra searchlights and guns were installed on high areas of the city in order to try and prevent the success of any future raid. Thankfully there would be no such raid over the city during this particular war.

There were, however, raids nearby. A year after the attack on Sheffield a Zeppelin carried out a raid on ironworks on the outskirts of Rotherham. Perhaps it was one of these bombs that was found unexploded in 1961 during construction works at Steel Peech and Tozer's Templeborough works. Thankfully when undertaking an archaeological excavation on the site of the Templeborough works in 2006 I did not encounter any further bombs. There was also a raid on Rawmarsh, with the Zeppelins briefly visible over Sheffield. The explosions of the bombs could be heard in some parts of the city, once again renewing fear.

The inquest into the deaths was held two days after the raid. The coroner announced he only intended for identification evidence and evidence of injuries and cause of death to be given. It was, he felt, unnecessary at this stage to return a verdict. An inquest into another recent raid had ruled a verdict of 'wilful murder against the Kaiser'.

However, this was considered to be a worthless verdict because the Kaiser himself could not be proven to be personally responsible for the deaths. It was determined that it would be more useful to identify the crew of the airship and return wilfull murder verdicts against them. To this end it was recommended the inquest be adjourned pending further investigations. It was also hoped during the adjournment that the Coroner could confer with the authorities to establish whether any statement, key evidence or any information could be presented to the jury which could be used to reassure the public about the potential for further such raids.

The identities of the deceased were not publicly revealed, nor were the addresses, so that the Germans could not be certain they had successfully bombed Sheffield. The circumstances of the deaths, as outlined previously in this chapter, were recounted. It was also said that in one case the blast had been so severe that the bodies of a couple had been thrown in opposite directions from the building. Another body had been found thrown from a building, in the road.

Over the course of the week after the raid the bodies were buried, predominantly at Burngreave Cemetery, ironically where the first bombs fell.

On 11 November 1922 a large grey stone set into a brick wall forming a memorial was unveiled at the Baltic Works on Effingham Road. The text on the memorial reads,

'1914 1918
The Great War
Lest We Forget
On September 26th 1916
Nine Men
Ten Women
And Ten Children
Were Killed by a German
Air Raid on Sheffield
One of the Bombs Fell
Close to this Spot'

The names of those killed in the raid are not listed on the memorial. Those names are: Elizabeth Bellamy, Richard Brewington, Ann Coogan, William Guest, Beatrice Hames, Horace William Hames, Levi Hames, Eliza Ann Harrison, George Harrison, Vera Harrison, Albert Newton, Alice Newton, Elsie Mary Rhodes, Nellie Rhodes, Phyllis Irene

A memorial for the 29 men, women and children who lost their lives during the zeppelin raid on the city. *(The Author)*

Rhodes, Martha Shakespeare, Sarah Ann Southerington, William Southerington, Frederick Stratford, Margaret Taylor, Albert Tyler, Amelia Tyler, Ernest Tyler, John Tyler, two males by the name of Joseph Henry Tyler aged 14 and 45, Selina Tyler and Thomas Wilson.

When the memorial was unveiled, the Chairman of the Works told the large crowd which had assembled to pay their respects that the memorial was intended to perpetuate the infamy of the Germans as much as remember the dead. He claimed that if the Germans had had their wish the population of the city would not have survived.

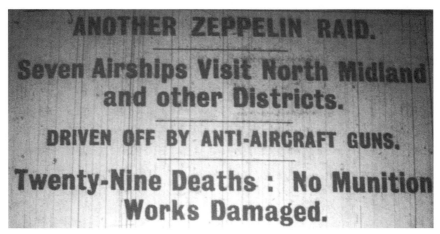

The headline in the *Yorkshire Telegraph and Star* following the zeppelin raid on Sheffield. *(The Author's collection)*

It may have failed to destroy any of the city's munitions factories, which were so crucial to the military campaigns of the Allies, but it did achieve one thing; it raised fear in the minds of Sheffield people, people who had believed that war could only affect those on the battlefields.

There was, for large numbers of Sheffield who became aware of the fact, a sense of justice when the L22 Zeppelin and its occupants saw their comeuppance. On the morning of 14 May 1917 whilst the Zeppelin was carrying out a reconnaissance mission over northern Holland near Terschelling, a squadron of naval aircraft went in pursuit. Flight Commander Robert Leckie, the pilot of a British RNAS Curtis H12 Flying Boat, shot at it and it was soon seen to be in flames. Two members of crew were seen to jump from the airship, into the sea, and within moments the ship also plunged into the water below. When the smoke disappeared after 15 minutes, there was no sign of the airship or its crew all of whom were killed.

However, the Zeppelin was just one of the enemy's weapons and its demise did not remove the fear from the minds of those who had witnessed the horror of war in their own neighbourhoods.

Fear was to return less than 25 years later when Germany once again sent its flying machines to destroy the might of the steel city.

CHAPTER 17

Further Defence of the City

Following the Zeppelin raid, there was no lighting in the city at night for a year. In the first three months this caused several accidents, resulting in seven fatalities and numerous injuries.

Further injuries were sustained during the period of blackout, including Thomas Morrison, a tailor of Curter Knowle Road, who was awarded £660 damages in March 1917 against the corporation for the loss of an eye due to the darkened streets. The corporation appealed but lost its case. On 22 August 1917 Arthur Atkin of Scotland Street fell into a pit and died, whilst at work at Thomas Firth and Sons, when the lights were extinguished after the air raid warning sounded.

With the fear of further air raids, on 25 July 1917 a letter in the *Telegraph and Star* , from 'Air Raid Reprisal', urged the corporation to start a fund for the building of bomb proof air raid shelters, especially for women and children, on spare ground in all districts.

Police papers (Sheffield Archives: SY 295/1/2/6) show the changing role of special constables.

On 19 September 1917 'a system of nightly patrols by Special constables' was organised. Each special was written to by the Chief Constable. Those in the West Ridings Volunteers were only needed for emergencies. Others were required for eight hours continuous duty per week.

From 21 December 1917 special constables had to work during emergencies and undertake a tour for one hour every week.

On 14 March 1918 the Deputy Chief Constable requested that police and special constables should be available for duty 'at the various air-raid shelters to prevent overcrowding and to regulate and control the people who congregate there'.

The police response to the threat of enemy attack was deemed insufficient from some of those who were employed as special constables. An anonymous letter sent by a special on 24 March 1918 questioned why volunteers had ceased to be asked to carry out regular patrols despite having been allowed to during the previous winter. Instead they were only allowed to carry out air raid duty. 'Do you think it is fair?' the Special Constable enquired, 'I don't and several of my friends don't like it. The men think they are had for mugs.' They wanted to do their four hours of service as they had been allowed to before and the letter writer believed it was 'a great shame' that they were prevented from doing so. He continued, 'I have only been signed on as a Special for about 6 weeks since, but I and 7 or 8 others of my friends have decided to give it up if the volunteers are not better treated.' He said that some did not have a uniform and that 'we shall all be better satisfied if all are served alike'.

Seemingly as a response to this letter the police put out a request for tender on 31 May for 265 pairs of trousers made of indigo blue cloth like that used by regular police officers.

On 13 March 1918 a letter was sent by the Chief Constable regarding the use of the Air Raid Warning Siren and when to give the all clear. 'It was noticed this morning that one of the most distinct sirens was sounded fully FIVE minutes after each of the others had ceased to give "ALL CLEAR" and as you will quite understand this belated signal caused some of the inhabitants to fear that hostile aircraft was again in the area,' the letter said. Those responsible for the sirens were instructed to use great care in line with regulations 'to ensure the smooth working of the system which has hitherto attained'. By 14 March 1918 there were 30 locations with steam sirens and klaxon horns.

CHAPTER 18

1916 continued

Sheffield tried to move on from the attack and it gave most Sheffielders a greater determination to defeat the enemy. By 5 December 1916 in excess of 480,000 War Certificates had been sold in Sheffield, accounting for £372,000.

The German air attack had caused death, injury, destruction and fear, but their naval attacks intended to hit the Home Front in Sheffield and elsewhere through causing starvation in order to bring Britain to her knees.

By the end of 1916 738 merchant ships had been sunk, destroying a massive 2,300,000 tons of food supplies, with a concentration of losses towards the spring and latter months of that year. This situation was described as being 'grave' with the potential of food shortages. It was considered that unless the situation was significantly altered then by June 1917 Britain could be forced to surrender.

In November 1916 there was recognition of the need for a Central Food Controlling Authority to secure food supplies and keep prices down, whilst increasing the amount of land for cultivation. The authority was formed in December following Lloyd George becoming Prime Minister and forming his war coalition government, with Lord Devonport appointed on Boxing Day. Locally there were appeals for people to grow their own food. In order to increase supplies, and ensure their fair distribution, rationing began to be considered in detail locally.

In Sheffield wounded soldiers were entertained during the Christmas period. There was a tea provided at Lydgate and entertained in the hospitals and schools as in previous years, with gifts and comforts provided.

There was less of a festive feeling during Christmas 1916, largely due to the heavy losses sustained in the Somme. The *Telegraph* summed up the feeling that people were less inclined to celebrate and that only the 'thoroughly selfish' would eat and drink as normal. Sheffield people were told to try and find some happiness but the message was clear that it was no occasion for the happiness that had been felt in previous years. People were advised to give to their country rather than expect to receive.

The close of the year saw further restrictions on the consumption of alcohol due to shortages in barley and to increase the productivity of workers.

It was recognised that 1917 would be the crucial year which could see the turning point in the war. The actions undertaken in 1917, and the efforts made, would be the difference between victory and defeat. Despite the losses at the Somme, as well as the losses in other battles on land and sea, there had been some small successes which, according to the *Telegraph and Star*, should encourage those hiding behind middle-aged men to join the forces.

Lloyd George told the press, 'The Allies have five men for every three the enemy can put in the field; therefore, even if we spend four lives in extinguishing three, the foe must be beaten in the end.' There were, however, fears in Sheffield and across the country that the food shortages could reverse any military gains.

CHAPTER 19

1917

If 1914 was dominated by the recruitment, 1915 and 1916 were dominated by the pursuit of victory through munitions, then 1917 was dominated by the need to produce and distribute food more efficiently to prevent defeat.

There was a prolonged frost during January and February 1917, which would have significantly affected the amount of food that was grown. During a period of two weeks the temperature rose above freezing for only 21½ hours. There was one advantage, however, in terms of leisure; for almost a fortnight skating could be performed on the ponds and lakes.

The weather was especially harsh in January. On 1 January a severe storm caused some damage to the city although earlier in the day the weather was somewhat better although damp. The day was well enjoyed by those who celebrated the holiday. There was a well attended match at Bramall Lane and theatres, music halls, picture houses were almost full by those who were treating the day as a 'second Boxing Day'. There was little travel out of the city due to harsh rail fare increases, which had seen a 50 per cent hike in prices.

On 8 January a snowstorm hit Sheffield causing disruption and damage to telegraph poles in Redmires and Sandygate. Winds raged at 38 miles per hour constantly between 9am and 9am the following day.

The theme of food production ran throughout the year dominating the news, punctuated occasionally by other events at home and on the war front.

Key news in the city in the early months of 1917 were 1,056 cases of misdemeanours at the munitions factories in January alone, and a 'reign of hooliganism' terrorising parts of the city in February.

In February there was an appeal for voluntary rationing with housewives encouraged to ensure that the household did not exceed recommended levels. The government wanted the nation to make the effort and cooperate, in order to prevent the need for compulsory rationing.

Yet often there was a complete lack of a commodity. On St Patrick's Day there was a potato famine in Sheffield, with no potatoes on sale in the city's markets.

On 6 April the USA entered the war. The *Telegraph and Star* would later remark that America was a valued ally in making its resources available to Britain and her allies. It was hoped that it would lead to Britain and the USA to having better relations with the 'removal of the historic soreness' from the War of Independence, which would be 'an immense gain for mankind'.

In April a Food Economy campaign began to teach people how they could live on food at a cost of little or nothing. On 14 May a Food Economy Exhibition opened at the Cutlers' Hall and lasted a fortnight. Women and children were especially encouraged to help grow food and on 22 May the first communal kitchen opened to provide food for those who struggled to find the time to cook wholesome meals at low cost.

The months of April and May saw what was described in the *Sheffield Year Book* as 'like a sudden burst of summer, and foliage and vegetation just raced into life'. It gave a welcome opportunity to grow more food.

The Cultivation of Lands Order gave the corporation the power to take over land that it owned and buy further land, using compulsory purchase orders if necessary, to provide space to grow food. By May 1917 Sheffield Corporation had used this power to take full control of 53 acres of its own land as well as 98½ acres of private land, including 50 acres obtained from private landowners by arrangement. Two months after the Order came into being approximately 190 more acres of land were earmarked for crop growth and were used for this purpose in 1918.

And to further prevent the poorest from having a lack of food, in June 1917, the DORA allowed the Food Controller to requisition food and fix prices. There were also efforts to prevent people from hoarding food. On 13 June Ada Nelson of Barrow Road, Wincobank, was fined £2 in the Police Court for wasting food. It was the first case of its type. On 1 July a further two women were fined for wasting bread.

It would later be said, in the 1918 Sheffield Year Book, that during the months of May and June 1917 famine was nearer than most people realised.

The Food Production Department in Sheffield made a request for more land for cultivation. The corporation would approach owners of agricultural land to come to some arrangement with them and advise on how they could increase productivity. If the owners were uncooperative the corporation had the power to seize the land for the public interest.

A proclamation by the King was read out at churches on Sundays in June encouraging people to observe a recommendation of 4lbs of bread per week. On 28 June the 'eat less bread' campaign was found to be working. Given that bread at this time was regarded as often unpalatable, it was quite easy for most to observe the voluntary ration. When bread finally became rationed, the quantity allowed was determined by the individual's occupation, with those engaged in industry and other heavy work receiving more bread.

June saw the peak of sinking of merchant ships with 398,773 tons lost, but from this month onwards the levels began to steadily fall.

At this time there were also concerns about the coal supply. It was not possible to obtain larger supplies of coal and store it in the city. It was agreed that efforts would be made to prevent people from hoarding coal. It was suggested that the tram system should be utilised at night to aid the transport of coal around the city.

Whilst the fight for food dominated the Home Front mixed news came from the war. A letter dated 23 May was sent to the mother of a Sheffield soldier informing her of the death of her son:

'Dear Madame, just a few lines to you hoping they will find you quite well as it leaves me at present. Well Madame I am very sorry to tell you that your son Leslie has got killed. He suffered know [sic] pain I was with him when the shell burst. I was very lucky to get out of it the same shell killed one more and wounded four. Madame I hope you do not take it to hard. I miss him a lot as he was my pal out here and we used to sleep together when we was out of the trenches. All the boys liked hime [sic] he was brave and he died like a hero. L/Cpl J. R. Lacey 14221 B. Coy 12th. JL. 7 Platoon. B.E.F France. Well Madame I hope you will excuse me for opening this letter I am sending back I found it to get the address and so that I could write and let you know. Well Madame I will now close my short and sad letter. From L/Cpl J. R. Lacey.'

Tom Smith of Sheffield seemed to enjoy the war. On 24 April he wrote, 'It is grand weather out here, quite a difference from Redmires and I like it very much so far.' And on 2 July he wrote to thank his cousins for chocolates and parcels before remarking, 'It isn't at all bad being out here. I shouldn't mind if I could only just pop over home now and again as I used to do before I came out here.' He was away from the front line for a few weeks on rest 'so it is just like being at Redmires again'.

The Temperance movement had long campaigned for a prohibition of alcohol for society's good. Where their speeches and campaigning failed, the war succeeded in reducing the ability of many drinkers to get beer. Due to restrictions on barley there were beer shortages during the summer of 1917, with several public houses displaying 'No Beer' signs in their windows. During the Whitsun weekend from 28 May several pubs were closed due to the beer shortage. In June more beer was produced but at a lower strength. In August the Food Controller gave Sheffield sufficient extra barley to create 15,000 additional barrels of beer by the end of September.

Food, coal and beer were not the only things in short supply. The Rent Restrictions Act of 1915 had been passed to prevent large rent increases. Rent increases in Sheffield were kept to a minimum but this put pressure on corporation finances to build new homes.

In June 224 houses were built at Wincobank and land at Walkley Hall was sought to accommodate 200 new houses. By July all 617 new houses at Wincobank had been let to 'good tenants' but across the city there was serious overcrowding of unknown scale. Notice was given to terminate the Education Authority's occupancy of High Storrs fields for further housing to be built. Alderman Cattell spoke of how the suburbs would be spoilt by large numbers of new houses. The councillors must have lots of input to avoid the suburbs being destroyed. He hoped that the corporation in competition with private enterprise would not force private enterprise out of business. Councillor Neale said it was more than just an issue of shelter; the infant mortality rate in Attercliffe was double that in Tinsley and that could only be due to housing.

On 7 July the Sheffield Estate Committee submitted to the councillors a long report on the housing problems in the city, along with a scheme for dealing with what the *Telegraph and Star* termed a 'house famine'. Preliminary plans were for three groups of working class houses at High Wincobank, the Walkley Hall estate in Crooks and land off Langsett Road in Hillsborough. There had been a marked decline in the numbers of new houses built since the century commenced. Between 1900 to 1905 112,035, 1905 to 1910 8,886, 1910 to 1914 3,924, in 1915 and 1916 only 880 and in the first three months of 1917 only two were built that were fit for human habitation. In relation to how many houses were needed, 'It is very difficult to make an estimate. For a population which increases at the rate of 5000 a year, at least 1000 new houses are required annually. Taking the last six years (1911-1916) only 3561 were built, and at least 1000 were demolished during the same period, so that there is a great deal of leeway to make up.' Twenty-four thousand homes, roughly one quarter of the total, were still in 'more or less insanitary and unhealthy conditions' as they had been in 1915. It was the opinion of the Committee that a minimum of 2,500 new houses (the same number recommended back in 1915) needed to be built each year for some years to come. It was the committee's opinion that housing should be provided by private enterprise, which could build houses at lower cost than the corporation, and that the corporation should only intervene when private enterprise has failed. They recommended the corporation build 800 houses a year for five years, and charge rents at market prices, with Government financial assistance to prevent the corporation making a loss. Whilst this was only one third of the estimate of houses needed, it was intended to provide ample opportunity for private enterprise to fill the deficit. If private enterprise did not build the remaining 1,600 houses per year, the corporation would have to do so.

The housing crisis continued and one of the consequences of it became increasingly apparent. In August 1917 one house in Bradfield Road, consisting of just three rooms, was found to be housing three families consisting of 14 or 15 individuals, along with three cats and one dog. One room alone had ten individuals sleeping in it. The house was found to be extremely filthy, when inspected, with clear evidence of advanced infestation of vermin. The circumstances were presented to the Sheffield Police Court, with fines and some prison terms given to the adults.

The City Hospitals Committee proposed an extension to the Moor End Hospital, with an open air ward for ten patients. The Estates Committee refused to allow further accommodation for the Tuberculosis Dispensary at Hawley Street. The issue of TB was a major concern and it was recommended that a sub-committee of the Health Committee be formed to work with organisations to tackle the growing incidence of the disease.

For the health of the city's youngest residents there was a Baby Week during which approximately 15,000 mothers were given advice about the care and health of their babies.

On 1 July a solemn memorial service was held at the cathedral to mark the anniversary of the Battle of the Somme.

A 'Silent Tribute Day' was held six days later, when Sheffield helped the Lord Roberts Memorial Workshops, as part of a day of national events to help carry on the work started in memory of a man regarded as one of England's greatest generals. Four hundred thousand flags were made available to sell in Sheffield, made in workshops in Bradford by men who were wounded in war, including some survivors of the Somme. The workshops offered disabled soldiers a means of earning a livelihood. The sale of the flags, and public subscriptions, was intended to raise funds to open further workshops across the country, including Sheffield.

In the July Munitions Tribunal session several staff claimed compensation for being forced to be out of work during stocktaking. One 16-year-old boy took his case to the Tribunal to claim compensation for three days of lost wages. The company argued it could not find work for all its staff during stocktaking but it was pointed out that either alternative work should be provided or compensation given. It was ordered to pay 10s to the boy.

The mother of a boy working in one of the city's factories requested a leaving certificate so that her son could leave his job in order to assist his father in his work, his older brother having been killed. Although not legally entitled to leave his job, the Tribunal agreed that he should be allowed to join the family business out of sympathy.

A puller-out working in a crucible factory requested a leaving certificate so that he could leave his job, for which he felt he was being underpaid, his wage being 9s 6d per day. On being asked why he felt he was underpaid, he claimed that the standard rate for such work was 14s per day, but he could not name any firm offering such wages. His employers argued that when he had been taken on three years earlier he had no previous relevant experience, having worked as a fruit hawker. They trained him and taught him all he knew. They claimed there was no standard rate and that the wages paid were average. The man's application was refused.

A teemer argued that he too wanted to leave his job because he was being paid only £3 1s 9d per week but he had been offered work at another factory at £4 per week. His application for a certificate to leave his job was refused but he announced he would not return to the factory anyway.

On 12 July 1917 the Police Court heard an important case in which the institution of a church would be defined and the question of whether ministers should fight was addressed.

The case centred on the alleged church known as the Incorporated Seaman and Boatman's Friend Society. Its leader, Charles Howard Bratt, a 34-year-old married man of Milton Road, was charged with failing to report for military service under the Military Service Act. He described himself as a 'superintendent minister of religion'. In order to be exempt from military service he had to prove that he was a regular minister of a religious denomination. His eligibility had been questioned and he had already appeared before the local Tribunal in February and was granted temporary exemption until 30 April. He appealed to the West Riding Appeal Tribunal and lost his case, being called up for service on 2 July. He failed to report for duty, arguing he was a minister.

He became involved in the Society 13½ years earlier whilst studying to become a Baptist minister. He decided to become a minister under the auspices of the Society instead, and began training in their theology. After studying for six months he passed an exam and became an assistant minister in Birmingham, working there for seven years, before coming to Sheffield as a superintendent, and being appointed to that position at a conference held in Sheffield. His work, he explained, was focused on the boatmen of the canal between Sheffield and Grimsby. Services were regularly held at the Corn Exchange, he said, on Sundays and three other days of the week, with additional occasional services held on vessels on the canal. Communion was conducted once a month. He could, he argued, perform funeral and burial services. He could also perform wedding ceremonies but had not yet performed such a ceremony in Sheffield.

The Society was, he argued, a genuine and legitimate religion. It had been formed in 1846 by the union of two older societies, and it was incorporated in 1899. According to the Reverend William Ward, the general recording secretary of the society, there were three assistant ministers in Birmingham, one of whom was of military age but had been granted exemption by the Birmingham authorities who recognised the religious status of the Society.

Councillor Stenibridge told the hearing that he had known the Society in Birmingham and Sheffield for approximately 20 years and he considered the work they undertook to be 'valuable'. He regarded Charles Bratt as being a reverend.

Mr H. W. Jackson, defending Bratt, argued all the superstructure of the Society was consistent with a religion. He said that it was not a case of trying to evade military service; Bratt had been doing nothing but his ministerial work, devoting great time and effort to perform his work, for 13 years.

Prosecuting, Captain Okell argued that whilst Bratt's beliefs were genuine, the Society was not a religious denomination and therefore he could not be exempt from military service. The Society was registered under the Companies Act and therefore was a corporation rather than a religion. The words 'limited liability' he said, robbed it of any religious aspect. He said that anyone could join the Society by giving a donation and therefore membership was not based upon any religious belief. He quoted from a judgment made by Lord Davey, describing a church as a 'voluntary and unincorporated association of Christians, united on the basis of agreement in certain religious tenets and principles of worship'.

It was ruled that the Incorporated Seaman and Boatman's Friend Society did not constitute a church and therefore its officials were not exempt from the Military Services Act. As such Bratt was requested to join the army and pay 4s in costs. It was agreed that he would not be arrested without prior arrangement.

There was welcome news on 21 July that food would be more affordable. 'Cheaper bread; The price of flour to be standardized; A nine penny loaf; Meat is to cost you less' was the headline in the *Telegraph and Star*. Prices were to be reduced and fixed by the order of the Food Controller, Lord Rhondda. From 1 September meat prices would be reduced and could be 6d cheaper by Christmas. Local authorities were expected to cooperate with the Food Ministry to ensure the price reductions were brought in locally. Powers were given to the corporation of Sheffield and other councils to ensure the butchers' profits were controlled so that the benefits of reduced prices will be passed on to the customer. Local authorities were expected to assist with the fair distribution of food stuffs and to administer the scheme locally.

The *Telegraph and Star* editorial on 27 July stated one of the major concerns was the shortage of food and high prices which put some foods out of the reach of the poor. 'It cannot be doubted that prices have risen by reason of the snatching of profits from the necessities of the people. Strictly speaking all war profit is a crime against the state and should have been forbidden from the first.' Action by the Food Controller would reduce the price of food, subsidising it if need be.

There were threats of heavy fines and imprisonment for those who made large profits out of the selling of food, with acceptable profits being in line with those made prior to the war. Many regarded profiteers as the enemy within.

That same day Lord Rhondda, outlined a new scheme for the control of food in short supply, with the provision of sugar cards for all households but no rationing of it. The household should register at a particular shop so that the shopkeeper could ensure they could obtain sufficient sugar to meet the needs of the customer. Rationing would be avoided if there was cooperation from the public and sensible usage of sugar. Milk prices would remain the same. All flour mills would be nationalised and would work on Government orders, with flour sold to bakers at a standardised price. The middlemen would be cut out in the purchase of foods such as wheat to drive down costs. All wholesale and retail dealers would have to register and have their accounts monitored to ensure they were not making unreasonable profits.

One luxury in short supply was chocolate, due to restrictions on sugar. As such there was an increasing reliance on imported chocolate, resulting in increasing costs. Previously there had been a ban on imports of chocolate, at the request of British chocolate producers, but eventually the restriction was relaxed so that imports only totalled 25 per cent of pre war levels. The estimated half a million people who worked in chocolate factories, the distribution of chocolate and shopkeepers whose incomes partly depended upon the sale of chocolate, requested that the ban on foreign imports be reintroduced.

There was an excess of vegetables, so much so it was feared people would eat too many and there would be a scarcity in winter. There were, however, fears of a shortage of potatoes.

Despite the optimism about food prices, the Prime Minister warned the country about submarine piracy affecting imports of food but Sheffield folk were relieved to know that whilst the risks remained German efforts were not as successful as they hoped. The Germans had conceded that they were unable to disrupt food supplies sufficiently to bring Britain to her knees. Its new method would be to disrupt the manufacture and distribution of war supplies. To waste food would be 'a crime against the State' it said, 'Piracy has failed to beat us, and it has brought us an enormous powerful ally.'

On 10 July, 92 shopkeepers and their assistants were summoned to the Sheffield Police Court because, it was argued, they had breached the Sunday Trading law known as the Lord's Day Observance Act, which had been passed more than two centuries earlier, in 1671, during the reign of Charles II. The Deputy Town Clerk, E. B. Gibson appeared for the prosecution, with Mr Clem Edwards MP defending most of the accused. The courtroom was completely filled, with the defendants alone occupying most of the limited space, and several spectators fascinated to see such a large number of accused in one place at the same time. Edwards made a clever, albeit an extremely brave, move in opening his defence, by requesting the summons of the Lord Mayor, the owners of the *Telegraph* and other leading citizens of the city. They had all worked on Sundays, the Member of Parliament announced and therefore they too should be summonsed. George Edward Stembridge had printed the Monday edition of the aforementioned newspaper and he had been aided and abetted by several individuals who had collected copies of the newspaper earlier on Monday morning. The same was true of the editor of the *Sheffield Independent* and those who had assisted in the distribution of the newspaper printed on Sunday, and the editor of *The Monthly Magazine of St Michael and All Angels, Neepsend*, on account that it could be purchased on Sundays. Other individuals to be summoned were a milkman for delivering milk on Sundays and the owner of Sheffield Motor Company at 218 West Street for being open on Sundays and the landlord of the Angel Inn for selling for consumption off-premises a pack of cigarettes on a Sunday.

Back to the cases of those already summoned, a butcher of South Street was fined 5s for selling a piece of brisket, another butcher sold two pieces of beef, several convicted and fined 5s. One had the prosecution withdrawn as it was shown meat was delivered on a Sunday to the customer but it had been paid for the previous day. There were too many cases to be heard, and some lengthy legal arguments, and so the remainder of the cases were heard on a later date.

It was asked why these cases were being prosecuted. It was not for religious reasons apparently, but a matter of principle. Until 20 years ago few shops were open on Sundays. Now 3,000 were open. The proceedings were only commenced after long and careful consideration. Many shopkeepers had been petitioning the corporation to enforce the law for the past 15 years because they could not compete with shops open every day. In order to escape prosecution the shopkeepers had to prove that the items they were selling fell into the category of 'works of necessity and charity' under the law. He argued that no one could accept that the sale of two pounds of beef, or an underskirt, or a ribbon, were necessary. No one could need to buy such things on a Sunday when they could be purchased on any other day of the week.

Edwards argued the law was only introduced for the better observance of the Lord's Day, therefore it was religious, but it was being abused with small butchers being prosecuted by the petition and lobbying 330 other butchers in order to put those smaller shops out of business. 'What right had the City Council, the Watch Committee, or any other public officer in the city of Sheffield to use an instrument of oppression in this way as a mere competitive weapon in the interests of certain other traders?' it was a scandalous abuse of their public and municipal positions, he argued. If the munitions factory workers, the farmer and the other individuals working on war work could work on Sundays then why could no one else?

As the third anniversary of the war approached, and food shortages made things harder on the Home Front, people were more desperate than ever for its end.

People in Sheffield wanted peace but only if it took away every right of the Germans.

'Walker' of Sheffield wrote in the *Telegraph and Star* on 23 July, 'There appear to be so many kites being flown in the search for a way to peace on the lowest possible terms that it has struck a way faring man to look casually at the subject and of the bill that Germany and her condjutors will be required to foot…Germany and her condjutors must pay indemnities to every offended nation…The whole people cannot be locked up and confined in a penitentiary, but no German can be accepted in any Christian community to roam at will. So no German can be allowed outside his own country, only under license, and as to the freedom of the sea she enjoyed before the war, she cannot be permitted to enter any port other than her own, only under strict permit and under substantial dues and tolls, and the longer the settlement is deferred, the longer she retains possession of her unlawful gains, the heavier the penalty of dues and tolls on the movements of her people will increase, and as to guarantees, her country, or a portion of it, must be held in pawn, as she held a part of France, until the last payment of the indemnity is made.'

By the end of July the cost of the war was increasing so much, with the figures so large, they were incomprehensible to most Sheffield people. There was 'an immense wiping out of real wealth' according to the *Telegraph and Star*, which would have to be remedied by very high taxation and a reduction in spending. It was not only the money itself which was being lost, but the greatest resource available; human labour through the tremendous loss of life.

There were many who were unperturbed by the cost of the war and the financial implications for future generations. 'We are being told that we ought not to place so great a proportion of the cost of the war on our great-grandchildren. A colleague of ours says that his great-grandchildren do not interest him. He doesn't know them and he doesn't want to know them,' it was said in the *Telegraph and Star*.

The warm temperatures during July and August 1917 provided the ideal weather for a short break to the seaside, and large numbers flocked to the coast as a result despite increased rail fares.

The Sheffield Food Control Committee was established in August 1917 to control the supply of food, with milk supplies of particular concern. The Committee considered that too many men were carrying out milk rounds, visiting a few homes on each street, having to cover large areas over a long period of time, with multiple companies sending out several men to each street when only one was necessary. It was felt that such manpower could be better spent and so the corporation set rules to ensure all residents of a particular street obtained their milk from the same firm. This problem would continue for the remainder of the year. The issue of having healthy men of military age delivering milk and spending several hours each day delivering on average to between 100 and 150 homes was of particular concern because it was felt their time could be better spent and, even better, they could be replaced by women so as to free them for military service or work in the munitions factories.

On the eve of the third anniversary of war a special report from the select Committee on the Military Service (Review of Exceptions) Act 1917, found that the task of undertaking medical examinations and re-examinations for military recruitment should be transferred from the War Office to a new civilian department in order to restore public confidence in the system. Lord Derby believed all of the recruiting process should be handled by a civilian body. The report found that the War Office had been asked to undertake an unprecedented task in mass recruitment 'a task of which they had no experience, for which they were unprepared, and for which our military system was not designed'. It was hoped this would make the response to the nation's call more efficiently handled.

One man who thought he had got away with evading the nation's call was caught out. Abraham Cantor of St Philip's Road was fined £2 and ordered to be handed over to the military as an absentee under the Military Service Act, after losing an appeal. In order to try and evade military service he had managed to get a job in a factory despite having been informed he would have to join the army. Believing he had now escaped military service he began boasting.

Another man who tried to evade doing his service, though this time in the munitions factories, was Stanley Ward of Lansdowne Road. Ward, aged 17 years old, provided false certificates of illness to excuse his absence from Messrs Tyrack, Sons and Turner's munitions works. The forged certificates were presented at an earlier hearing at a Munitions Tribunal, when he was fined £2. The certificates were immediately discovered to be false and he was brought before the Sheffield Magistrates Court where he was fined £5.

In July there had been 113 cases of lost time from employees of the munitions factories, when employees were late for work or were absent for the entire working day, compared with 86 cases in June. The total of lost hours in July had been 9,555½ hours, compared with 6,717 lost hours in June. In July the number of lost hours, on average, per employee who faced the Munitions Court, was 83.08 hours. There were also instances of gambling during working hours and cases where employees had refused to follow orders. Two 18-year-old men had left work without permission. They had long been regarded as out of control, refusing to carry out their duties and generally misbehaving. They were fined 20s each. Fines of between 20s and 100s were imposed on those guilty of not working their full hours.

On the third anniversary of war the Reverend CC Thornton held an intercessory service at Sheffield Cathedral. He told the congregation that when Lord Kitchener had stated his belief the war would last three years, few had believed it. They had expected the war to end much sooner. Over the course of the three years there had been much 'sorrow and horror' and sometimes 'humiliation and disgrace'. He asked the assembled mass to thank God for hope, for strength, for friendship and essentially for the miracle of human nature. These gifts would enable morale to be maintained, he said. Naturally a growing number would have struggled to accept that human nature was a miracle when the death toll was ever increasing, but the message of hope would have been well received by the faithful majority.

The Reverend continued that the war involved fighting to free Europe by altering the hearts and minds of the people of the Central Powers. He expressed what may have been a controversial view by saying that there was something in both the teachings of the Old Testament (to crush the enemy, with the view of a vengeful God) and the New Testament (to love they neighbour, with a forgiving God). He announced his own view that the enemy could only be forgiven if the evil spirits within them had been cast out. 'If the things we were fighting for were ideals we had to go on till we attained them. If we could achieve that end only by crushing the enemy then we must do so.'

However, the Reverend believed that negotiations should be held to bring a peaceful end to the war without further bloodshed, if at all possible. He said that if Britain and her allies were justified in the military campaign when they should be the victors through diplomacy or conquest.

The editor of the *Telegraph and Star* was also optimistic despite the temporary paralysis of the Russian army and the increased pressure on Britain 'If we support the Army with undiminished firmness the day may soon come when the Huns will see the futility of carrying on a struggle that in the long run must end disastrously for them.'

One of the effects of the ongoing war was that boys wanted to play soldier. In July a 15-year-old boy shot Frank Shepherd, also aged 15, in the eye with a pistol. Both boys worked at Messrs Barker and England, on Colver Road. Shepherd had to go into a room to undertake his work duties, but he found it to be locked. He looked through the keyhole and saw the unnamed colleague. Shepherd asked the colleague if he had the key for the door. There was some insolence given and whilst still peering through the keyhole, requesting to be let in, the boy took out his pistol, held it to the keyhole and pulled the trigger. Although the cartridge was a blank, there was sufficient residue to cause injury when the shot was discharged. The boy claimed he had shot Shepherd accidently. He was charged with causing bodily harm

Other criminal activity was plaguing the city. On 11 August the *Telegraph and Star* claimed 'Sheffield appears of late to be a happy hunting ground for the shopbreaking fraternity'. In just one day £1,400 worth of jewellery was stolen when John Merrill's shop on The Moor was broken into. The dog which lived in the shop had not barked or made any noise, which neighbours and its owner felt was highly unusual because it always barked when the slightest noise was heard. It was therefore believed that the burglars had drugged the dog to make easy their entrance and escape. That same night The Black Boy Cabin Chocolate Shop on South Street was also targeted, unsuccessfully, with the belief the same culprits were responsible.

Long butter and tea queues became common during August 1917 as shortages in supply led to panic buying and desperation.

Meanwhile there were concerns about the use of horsemeat as food. During the August council meeting the applications for licenses to sell horsemeat were considered. Councillors had mixed feelings. If it was to go ahead, it was argued, it should be regulated with a special slaughterhouse. Sir Clegg raised concerns that facilities should be created for it. He did not want to create legislation for people who were refugees, and therefore not permanent residents, and were well paid. Some of the councillors believed the horse was a good meat option because it was a clean feeder. It was pointed out that some decades earlier horsemeat had been a not uncommon food, and that was long before the Belgians arrived. Councillor Neale opposed any measures to make horsemeat available. He believed that it could be used as ammunition against Britain, by the Germans, who could claim that Britain was struggling to feed its people and had therefore resorted to eating horses. He further believed that unscrupulous meat producers and merchants would sell horsemeat to the poor and claim it was beef. History often repeats itself, with the horsemeat scandal of 2013 seeing the realisation of fears expressed almost a century earlier.

In September 1917 two shops opened to sell horse flesh on Westbar, either side of the Westbar Hostel. By November five horse flesh shops were trading in the city. At less than half the price of beef, it was no wonder that horse flesh was so popular among Belgians.

In addition to food shortages, there were shortages of petrol resulting in other methods being sought for transport. On 15 September a taxi powered by gas began to be used in the city. Imported non-food items such as textiles, soap and petrol were also rationed.

In October 1917 the Coal Committee voiced concerns about the scarcity of coal and it was decided that prices should be regulated.

Three years of giving had not dissuaded the city as a whole from further fundraising for the war. By 6 September the Sheffield war savings amounted to £1,554,590 and on 29 September the city presented a plane to the Newfoundland Government for use on the Western Front.

Sheffield schools were also doing their bit. Schools donated four motor ambulances to help transport wounded soldiers, with an impressive £1,625 raised.

As winter set in, in November, teachers and school children were asked to assist the Comforts Committee in providing knitted face cloths for hospitals at the front, as well as providing other woollen garments for soldiers overseas and those in Sheffield hospitals.

In November members of the Candidates' Section of the St Luke's

Girls' Friendly Society held a bazaar to raise funds for those at St Dunstan's Home for Blinded Soldiers. Plants, fancy goods and pottery raised £5 for the Home.

Generosity came at a price, however, and workers felt they deserved a pay rise due to increased costs of living and the increasing pressures upon them.

In September 'stiff fines' were given for Sheffield firms who failed to comply with war bonuses. Time would show that this problem would escalate towards the end of the year.

On 13 October the Skilled Timeworker (Engineers and Moulders) Wages Order 1917 resulted in fully qualified and skilled engineers and moulders being granted a 12.5 per cent bonus on their earnings. An application was made by the National Amalgamated Union of Labour for an increase in wages to counteract the effects of the increase in the cost of living due to the war. Most corporation staff were also granted an increase. It was agreed that all employees of the police and fire brigade would receive a pay rise of 5s per week as of 13 December, but that their special war allowance would fall.

December saw increased fears of food shortages and the need for a new approach. On 8 December a Food Vigilance Committee was formed and shortly before Christmas a Women's Committee of Food Experts was formed to further the cause of food economy in the city, which included well known female figures, including Miss Gillott, Superintendent of the Hoyle Street Canteen who was the author of two volumes of *War-Time Cookery*. The Committee's first task was the establishment of the SOS (which was originally intended to stand for Save now and not Starve later but was later changed to Save or Starve) week, which was to commence just before the close of the year and would end on 5 January. During SOS week all domestic servants were invited to the Cutlers' Hall to learn how they could exercise food economy in the residences they worked in. Appeals were made in all churches and chapels in Sheffield calling for people to exercise food economy. At banks, offices, shops and leading stores people were encouraged to sign up to a 'League of National Safety' vowing to follow the Committee's ideals. The League aimed to prevent compulsory rationing by encouraging people to observe recommendations as to how much they should consume of foods in short supply and if possible to go below the voluntary ration, and not to waste food. A badge and certificate bearing the anchor symbol of the League was given to all members, who signed up for free. Women in Sheffield were sent cards through the post urging them to sign up and make food economy their New Years' Resolution. By 14 January 10,000 people had signed up in Sheffield.

In December 1917 the first prosecution in Sheffield occurred for selling tea at overprice. Ellen Waller, a grocer whose shop was at Attercliffe Common, was fined 40s for selling tea at a price of 5s 4d per pound, over the maximum price of 4s per pound. It was actually her young assistant who sold the tea. Waller was warned that the offence could be punishable by a fine of up to £100. She had, the magistrates believed, influenced the assistant to give false evidence by claiming that the girl had provided the tea from Waller's own personal tea caddy in order to satisfy the customer's needs and that she had mistakenly charged too much on account that loose leaf tea was not sold in the shop normally. The customer, however, maintained that the tea had been taken from a pack on a shelf.

Fears were increased with news that German destroyers had sunk six merchant ships and four armed trawlers in the North Sea as the convoy sailed from Scotland towards Norway on 12 December. In total approximately 8,000 tons of shipments were lost. Protection vessels which should have been in the North Sea, for some inexplicable reason, were not present. There was an exchange of fire. Help came but it was too late. The ships had sunk and the enemy had fled. There were, however, some survivors who were able to give accounts to the inquest and subsequent inquiry. A further trawler was sunk, and a second seriously damaged, close to the mouth of the River Tyne. This would understandably have increased concerns about food shortages and made people question what next could happen around Britain's shores.

Discussion took place at the Sheffield Local Food Committee conference, of a ticket system for food rationing, likely to be introduced in January 1918. There were many who had not yet registered for sugar and so it was felt a coupons system would be the best way of ensuring that people could obtain rations. It was amazed that there were hundreds, if not thousands, of houses in Sheffield where milk could never be found. It was also concerned about food queues, which were a serious problem, and they were frustrated that the Food Controller was not taking any action. In consultation with shops in the city, the committee had considered rationing and felt it was likely to be needed. Plans were created for the implementation of a compulsory, simple system for the city. Plans were also set up for a coupon/ticket system would probably be introduced for margarine and tea on 1 January. They wanted to ensure there was equal supply across the city especially for the poor, because the rich would be able to better obtain provisions. It was said that in one week a company had sold a month's supply of tea because of panic buying due to publicity that there might be a shortage.

The Sheffield newspapers believed rationing was not necessary. It was thought that shortages in Sheffield were no worse than any other town or city and in fact districts surrounding Sheffield were affected more seriously. There was, however, a need to reduce consumption below the pre-war levels and that by reducing the consumption, and recognising there was a shortage, the people of Sheffield could help solve the problem, perhaps more than what the Food Controller or Government could do.

Rationing was created locally but the Government hoped there would be enough food if more could be grown. The Government hoped to obtain around 30,000 labourers to carry out cultivation of the land, including a number of women. The Prime Minister wanted to assure the public that there would be enough food for the whole population. Seed potatoes and other crops were distributed to those with allotments. He also wanted farmers who had land that was not currently cultivated, to cultivate it and make the most of periods of good weather to grow as much food as possible. He felt that farmers sitting on land that was not being used, were guilty of treason. He believed the way to win the war was to save ships and that required food to be grown at home in order to reduce the amount of imports needed, so that more ships could be used for essential war work.

From 18 December Sheffield school teachers assisted the Local

Food Control Committee in implementing the rationing of tea, butter and margarine, supplying cards to every household. A census was undertaken to ensure everyone requiring goods could be catered for. Due to the requirement to have the work completed without delay it was recognised that large group of individuals would be needed to help, with teachers being the most suitable large body of people who were available. As a result the corporation run schools were closed early to allow the 11,000 teachers to visit every home in the city. A card was left and the householder required them to state which shopkeeper they would use to obtain their provisions. It did not need to be the same shopkeeper for all three items. Headteachers supervised the teachers working in each ward, with one headteacher supervising between 20 and 25 teachers. The work had to be completed within three days and as such each teacher had to visit at least six houses per hour.

On 19 December the Food Controller, Lord Rhondda, said that his biggest concern regarding food control was the huge queues at shops. 'The question is mainly one of distributions. The queues are only temporary, but, they have been going on for some weeks now, and they will continue for some weeks longer. They are doing harm that is likely to be felt for some time afterwards.' His policy had been to give powers to local committees because conditions varied across the country. Any authority who had made efforts to reduce the queues would receive encouragement. 'I have under consideration at the present time, a proposal for compelling every customer for, say, butter or margarine, to register one shop. The retailer will be obliged to devote his supplies proportionately amongst his registered customers. Local committees would have the power to prevent retailers from accepting more customers than they can conveniently serve. ... I want you to consider, and be ready to put any general schemes that may be made into practice as quickly as possible.' Sheffield, as shown, already had such a scheme. Lord Rhondda added that a compulsory scheme would 'probably' be introduced nationally. He added that the Germans wanted to starve the country but Britain would undoubtedly win the war if it could only tighten its belt.

The following day saw talk of a meat ration and how it should be implemented. On 17 December the Meat (Maximum Prices) Order had set maximum prices for home-killed beef, all mutton, all lamb and home-killed pork. Lord Rhondda had said, 'The food position generally is causing us great anxiety for the future. There is no danger of a famine in meat, but there is likely to be a great shortage.' A ration of 2½ pounds of meat per week was suggested. The wealthy in Sheffield particular felt hard done by. One 'well to do woman' in the city said, 'We have not had bacon for breakfast for two years. My husband stopped it directly the meat shortage began, as he said we couldn't have it and keep within our just allowance.' Another well off man said he had to have bacon twice a week and porridge on the other days. People were encouraged not to have meat every day so that good portions could be provided on certain days. The suggestion was to have meat at dinner and vegetable soup, fish and a pudding for lunch, with a pudding of stewed fruit which was plentiful. A vegetable entrée could be had instead of fish, which although not rationed was often scarce.

On 21 December the Sheffield Food Control Committee was given powers to ensure supplies of margarine were controlled to prevent shortages and to reduce what the *Telegraph and Star* called 'the evils of queues'. Retailers were forbidden from selling margarine, butter and where necessary other foodstuffs to customers who had not registered with them. Shopkeepers were not allowed to register more customers than what the Food Committee believed was appropriate for the shop so that there was not higher demand at some shops and less demand in the others. This would help ensure that every shop had a similar level of business, reducing queues accordingly.

A speech by Lloyd George in the run up to Christmas was reported by the *Telegraph and Star*. He argued that there was a danger of making a peace with Germany which left them so strong they could wreak further havoc on Europe. He was willing to make peace in order to bring an end to the war, but only on the terms of the Allies, which was complete victory. The Prime Minister criticised the pacifists for arguing that Germany had learnt its lesson, 'We are entering on a period of supreme crisis, and if we are to pass it safely there must be not only no slackening of effort, but a readiness to bear an even greater strain during the next few months. There lies before us a period which will test the fibre of every man and every woman.' An unfaltering determination would result in a peace that was just and fair for Britain and her Allies.

The accompanying editorial summed up the position: 'The fourth Christmas of the war has come, and the end is not yet. In the nature of things, the war is nearer by a year to the close than it was twelve months ago, but it is not to be denied that the immediate situation is far less favourable than it seemed to be a year ago.' The Germans had had some successful military campaigns, most notably with Russia having surrendered but although the Kaiser boasted that God was on the side of the Germans, it was to be emphasised that the Russians were not 'knocked out' of the war but due to internal problems exacerbated by the workings of German spies. The Russian defection could have resulted in the loss of the war for Britain and her Allies, but the Americans entering the war had brought a new force which replaced Russia and would lead to victory.

Heavy snow blizzards swept across the country. On 16 December snow fell all day in and around Sheffield, followed by a fierce gale with a snowstorm during the night. This affected road and rail traffic, with country roads impossible to be used. There was a quick improvement in Sheffield once salt had been distributed. Two buses were stuck overnight, however, between Lodge Moor and Crimicar Lane due to the engines freezing.

There were bright Christmas offerings in the markets in Sheffield despite less variety of produce and higher prices, but plenty of holly and mistletoe at Castlefolds Market. There had been fears that the restricted railway service would reduce the supply of such decorations. They were only a quarter of the price as the previous year. There were plenty of potatoes, onions and English apples. There were very few oranges. Bananas had made a welcome return after a short absence. A small number of pears could be found. There were no tomatoes.

The Fitzalan Market was well stocked with meat and poultry, including turkeys, geese, chickens, ducks, pheasants, hares and rabbits, but it was not expected to be able to meet demand. 'I shall probably have little or nothing left by four o'clock tomorrow afternoon,' said one butcher on 23 December. Bacon was scarce and expensive. It was now considered a luxury along with butter, margarine and tea. Fish were only in moderate supply, but there was a wide variety.

There was another penny special of Christmas Cheer to add light entertainment to the home, with jokes, stories, puzzles and cartoons.

There was an extended break over Christmas for most of Sheffield's workers engaged in commerce and industry, with three days off, although some of the smaller shops and firms might only have two days holiday, with drapers also having New Year's Day off work. The Grocer's Association decided to have Christmas Day, Boxing Day, New Year's Eve and New Year's Day as their days off, with some grocers having further days of rest. The East End steel work companies in some cases had a week long break due to Christmas falling on a Tuesday. It was felt that starting the furnaces only for the Monday (Christmas Eve) was extravagant. A considerable amount of repair work would be undertaken whilst the machinery was not being used. Where orders had to be met, a rota was drawn up to allow all workers to have a few days of holiday.

The time off formed what was described as the longest Christmas holiday on record, especially in the munitions factories in order to give the machinery a break from the tremendous strain it had been under for the past year and once again to allow for maintenance work. Although there was not such a festive exodus to holiday resorts as there had been in previous years lots of Sheffield people did travel to the coastal towns, especially in the south of England.

For those remaining in Sheffield there was, as usual, plenty of entertainment in the city during the Christmas and New Year period. The Cinema House on Fargate showed *Love's Old Sweet Song*, *The Crimson Dove*, *Jackie in Wonderland*, *Tom and Jerry Mix* and a documentary about the York and Lancaster Regiment. The Electra Palace showed performances including *The Gun Fighter*, *Whose Baby?* , *A Good Liar* and a Christmassy comedy entitled *Kitchenalla*. The Picture Palace showed *Little Shoes*, *The Little Hero*, *Dough Nuts* and an 'excellent detective drama' called *The Mystery of the Grand Theatre*. The Star on Ecclesall Road showed *Tess*, *The Persecution of Bob Pretty* and *The Fall of a Nation*, which was the story of what could happen if Germany invaded Britain was described as being 'one of the most elaborate and realistic' pictures to be shown in Sheffield for some time. Its production involved 25,000 men, 10,000 women and a fleet of ships. Lansdowne Pictures on London Road showed *Richelieu*, *My Lady's Slipper* and *The Little Volunteer*. The Lyceum showed the 'daintiest, happiest and sweetest of plays' known as *Daddy Long-Legs*, the Theatre Royal showed the 'tremendously popular' *Mother Goose*, the Empire Palace showed the 'excellent' *Little Bo-Peep* and the Hippodrome showed *Jack and Jill*, which was described as 'one of the most successful pantomimes on tour'.

For the soldiers and sailors who could not return home for Christmas, an impressive 1,256 gifts were received in the form of woollen clothing and other comforts by the Sheffield Voluntary organisation.

There was a 'striking success' of a Christmas scheme for gifts for soldiers on the war front. There were 10,000 soldiers for whom gifts were sought. They were sent to France in the tons. 'Each gift will not only remind the lads of their many friends at home, but will assist in making life more durable during the cold and darkness of winter,' the *Telegraph* said. Gifts were also sent to the navy. Items included candles, books, along with donations of money. By 13 December the *Telegraph* had raised £1,831 11s 2d for presents for soldiers. Common presents included woollen clothing, tobacco, cigarettes, pipes, candles, trench fires, chocolates and handkerchiefs.

Readers of the *Telegraph* were, however, reminded that whilst Christmas does not last for very long, the adverse conditions faced by the soldiers do persist and therefore gifts should be given throughout the year.

Charitable work for the military was made more difficult by the increase in women who were now working, with closures to buildings and a general decline in enthusiasm the longer the war continued. It was also made more difficult by Charles Walker who appeared in court on 28 December charged with being absent from the 3rd East Yorkshire battalion and for fraudulently obtaining alms and attempting to obtain charitable donations through false pretences. He had collected money supposedly for the Independent Soldiers' and Sailors' Christmas Fund and collected small amounts of money, but he kept it for himself. He had fought in the Dardanelles and in Egypt and France, with active service amounting to 21 months before he absconded. He was fined £5, bound over for good behaviour, and remanded in prison to await recall to his regiment.

For the wounded soldiers in Sheffield gifts and entertainment on the same scale and of the same nature as seen in previous years took place. Additionally a 'Flag Day' was held to raise funds through the sale of flags in order to pay for relatives of the wounded, who hailed from all over England, to visit their loved ones in Sheffield's hospitals. A massive 2,388 relatives were helped through the fund to come to Sheffield, with transport and, in many cases, accommodation being paid for.

The treatment of the war wounded caused financial problems at the Royal Infirmary. An appeal was to be made for help from the public to remedy this. Presiding at the quarterly meeting of the Board of Governors, Henry H Bedford said that 2,832 servicemen had been treated and up until very recently that treatment had been provided at no cost to the country, saving the Government approximately £14,000. Although many generous donations had been made, the increasing costs of food and treatment had caused serious difficulties. They had relied upon an overdraft at the bank to fund the hospital, and it was now becoming a serious burden. A donation of £200 had been made by the Workmen's War Fund at Messrs. William Cooke and Co and it was hoped that this would set an example to be followed. A matinee at the Empire Theatre in October had also raised £230 for the hospital. The work being undertaken was of a high standard and all staff were to be congratulated.

The cost of the war was becoming a major concern. To help raise funds National Savings Bonds were offered with promises eventually of returns on the investment. Potential investors were told soldiers and sailors had given their all, but what had you done? 'This is a war of money as well as of men.' Sums of £5, £20, £50 or more could be lent. 'If you have £100 in the bank and another man has £100 in War Bonds he is better than you. He is drawing £5 a year more. If you have not £100 buy what you can. There is no risk. There is no trouble…'

There were those who were cynical about financing the war. In the

West Riding Police Court in Sheffield on 28 December, William Henry Evans, aged 67, stood accused of being unpatriotic by making statements which would undermine the public confidence in banks and the British currency which would threaten the success of any financial measure taken by the Government for the successful completion of the war. The charge was brought under the Defence of the Realm Act. On 12 December, whilst on a train, the accused had spoken about the visit of a tank to Sheffield. There had been great generosity during the tank's visit, with £1,326,613 raised in subscriptions to fund tanks, as well as sparking fascination about the new method of warfare.

Evans had apparently said, 'The war will never be over as long as people give their money…You may get your interest all right, but you will never get your money back from the Government.' Other passengers argued with him but he refused to back down from his views, arguing that he had a right to express his opinions. Evans was not a pacifist but he claimed he, like many, was anxious about the

In order to raise money for the war a tank visited the city. The tank, a Mark IV male tank Nelson, training number 130, is shown at Fitzalan Square in December 1917. (*Photograph reproduced from the Picture Sheffield Collection, courtesy of Sheffield Local Studies Library*)

growing cost of the war. He expressed his regret for what he had said, now realising that he was not entitled to speak his mind. He was fined £5 plus costs and was told that any repeat of his views would be more severely dealt with.

In addition to the financial cost there were, as ever, worries of the cost to human life. A memorial service for those who had died during the past year was held at the Holy Trinity Church on the Wicker and it was believed that there had never been such a sombre or impressive service in the city before. The Lord Mayor read the sermon and many in the congregation were seen weeping. He said that it was occasions such as this that showed just how short life could be. The bereaved should not sit with their heads in their hands and weep and mourn as if the men who had died had died in vain. Their deaths were to save others. He expressed his belief that the dead soldiers would want Sheffield folk to maintain their efforts to achieving victory, through hard work, not by striking, not to be greedy with food given the shortages, to honour the dead, to nurture the children and above all to finish off the work started by those who had laid down their lives.

At the Nether Chapel the Reverend EH Titchmarsh preached that there was a good future ahead and that God would bring them through.

Despite the Lord Mayor's belief that the war dead would want Sheffield men and women to work hard and not strike, 1917 saw a winter of industrial discontent, and it was this discontent which dominated the year's close, and threatened to damage the city's contribution to the war effort.

The roots of the discontent extended months back. After a meeting held on 30 October 1917 at the Victoria Hall, it was believed there would be industrial peace in Sheffield. Approximately 1,500 people assembled to discuss how employers and employees should negotiate in order to prevent disputes. Socialists were blamed for disrupting the discussions throughout the meeting, arguing against capitalism and booing and hissing at Charles Duncan MP who addressed the crowd. Trade unionists were accused of behaving like hooligans as a result of the constant interruptions. However, it was agreed that there should be a policy of justice and fair dealing between men irrespective of wealth. However, this was in danger due to a lack of cooperation between employers and employees and this needed to change to secure peaceful working relations.

Peaceful relations were far from being achieved at this time. A meeting of engineering workers was held at the Coliseum on Spital Hill on 4 November 1917 to discuss the issue of pay. It was felt that heavy labourers deserved a 7s a week pay rise. Higher paid engineers had been granted this sum as an increase and it was felt those doing the most physical work should therefore receive the same.

That same day a meeting of the allied trades passed a resolution that the 12½ percent pay rise should be awarded to every section in the engineering industry, but it was not paid.

On 11 November unskilled engineering and foundry workers demanded a 12½ per cent pay rise otherwise they would strike.

'Treat all Alike' wrote on 13 December that clerks were annoyed they were not receiving the same war bonuses granted by the Ministry of Munitions as other workers, including munitions workers. Some clerks in engineering were receiving the bonus but not clerks in other areas of the munitions factories.

At the end of the year a conference was held at the Tivoli Picture House to resolve the issue of workers who were demanding their 12½ per cent pay rise. Councillor Bailey spoke that many men were not intending to return to work after the Christmas holiday and he had some sympathy for them. The men had accepted a pay rise offer but the government had intervened and they had not received the money they were promised. He urged the men to refrain from striking for 14 days to allow for the Government to be lobbied.

A meeting later that same day for those working in rolling mills and forgers had a different outcome. Those men and women had demanded the same 12½ per cent pay rise but were offered only a 5s rise. They felt they should be entitled to the same rise as other workers. Councillor Bailey agreed that the guidelines about the 12½ per cent rise were vague. It was agreed unanimously that industrial action should commence immediately.

On 31 December the local sugar rationing scheme commenced, with a ration of half a pound of sugar per person. There was plenty of sugar in supply with the belief that it could not run out any time soon. There was a rush of customers at the beginning of the day, especially in the city centre. A large number of customers had failed to fill in their papers with their details to obtain the rations. Many of these made threats and were aggressive and troublesome in a bid to persuade the shopkeepers to supply the sugar but they left the shops empty handed, although shopkeepers were able to use some discretion if they believed the customer had made an honest mistake. Sugar rationing was welcomed at the outset, because most customers were able to obtain more sugar than prior to rationing because previously a small number of people had been stockpiling it, thus reducing the amount available to everyone else. Every shop was also supplied with an adequate amount to supply the customers registered with it.

By introducing the scheme Sheffield was a pioneer because national food rationing did not commence until March the following year. The local scheme limited the amount of sugar, and eventually butter and margarine, with tea soon being added to the list. The Food Office at Carver Street Wesleyan School assigned people to certain shops to reduce queues and to ensure each shop had a sufficient amount to meet the ration quotas for its customers.

There was hope that 1918 would be the year that the darkness of war would retreat. In December 1917 it was announced in the Sheffield newspapers that Lord Derby believed that the war would end the following year. In the House of Lords he stated:

'The fourth Christmas since the beginning of the war finds the British, French and Belgian soldiers in the trenches fighting side by side against the common enemy. The determination which animated them in 1914 still animates them. Each succeeding year has brought the Allies greater confidence and increasing trust in the valour of their troops. First the Portuguese troops joined us; now the American soldiers are with us. We hope and believe that during the coming year we shall see all troops back home, having ensured for the world the triumph of right over force, a peace which shall last not only during our time, but during that also of our children and grandchildren.'

216

1917

On New Year's Eve the *Telegraph and Star* summed up the past year and prospects for the coming year; 'When we compare our war position with that of a year ago, there is some excuse for regarding it with concern.' People were feeling the effects of the attacks on food shipping. The battles on the Western Front have not been as successful as hoped but Germany was weakening and the involvement of the Americans would turn the war in the Allies' favour. There were positive signs. 'We may regard the future with calm if we make up our minds to meet with fortitude whatever difficulties and disappointments the New Year may bring us.'

CHAPTER 20

1918

The New Year was quiet in Sheffield, but the theatres, music halls and picture palaces were busy in the afternoon and evening. Cold weather kept people indoors. It also led to increased deaths caused by pneumonia and influenza.

On 1 January the Bishop of Sheffield wrote in the *Diocesan Gazette* that the year ahead would see the supreme test of faith and resolution of the country. If the country maintained its tradition of doing what was right then all would be well and the enemy could not be victorious, he believed.

Due to the shortage of meat, New Year's Day was a compulsory meatless day and from that date on one day every week no meat, cooked or uncooked, could be sold.

The following day an agreement was reached to bring more meat into the city. Members of the Local Food Committee, the Town Clerk, and others met with the authorities in London to secure a deal to allow more food to be sent to the city. A very large consignment of frozen meat was obtained. It was acknowledged in the January council meeting that 'it was of course unavoidable that in Sheffield as elsewhere there would for a time be a necessary diminution in the quality of meat available for the public'.

The industrial discontent reached boiling point on 1 January when 10,000 men were on strike in the city over the 12½ per cent pay rise dispute. It paralysed the steel industry and affected the ability to provide munitions for the war. It was hoped a conference held in the city would resolve the issue. By 3 January 20,000 men were on strike and workers of the Sheffield Gas Company gave 14 days notice that it too would go on strike if they did not receive their pay rise.

218

A woman writing to the *Telegraph* expressed her disgust at the strikers. 'What makes the strike the more shameful is that thousands of the men who are striking and have previously done so are young men of military age – men, who even if they were doing their best, yet ought to feel how small is that best beside a soldier's or sailor's. I never thought the day could have dawned on which I am almost as much ashamed of being English as I should be of being a German. The Germans do keep their treacheries for their enemies; the striker bestows them on his own kith and kin and his own nation.'

On 5 January a bonus settlement was reached but some strikes continued, although by 7 January the strikes had ended and the gasworkers received their 12½ per cent also.

In January 1918 Corporal Arnold Loosemore returned to Sheffield for a period of leave and Sheffielders were encouraged to give him a 'hearty reception' on account of him having obtained the Victoria Cross. He had been given the commendation after attacking a strongly held enemy position, during which he climbed through a partially cut wire, dragging his Lewis gun with him, and killed approximately 20 Germans single-handedly. His Lewis gun was then destroyed by a bomb but he fought on, killing three men with his revolver He later shot several snipers and risked his own life when he rescued a wounded comrade and dragged him to safety. He was given a formal welcome by the Lord Mayor, councillors and corporation officials.

The 7 January was the first day of the local scheme of rationing tea and butter. Some shops did not have any butter or margarine to ration. It was said that although the first day of the scheme was not an unparalleled success, it was evident that shopkeepers were of a far better temperament due to the rationing than they had been for several months. The queues were greatly reduced and in most cases there were no queues at all.

There were concerns in Sheffield of food being hoarded leading to a desire for increased powers for Local Food Control Committees to search premises.

On 14 January Joseph Hill and William Cooper were both fined £100 for food hoarding, but in April their convictions and fines were quashed at the Court of Appeal.

The efforts to reduce meat consumption failed. On 12 January the streets of Sheffield were presented with the 'deplorable' sight of meat queues, according to the *Telegraph*. Butchers' shops were, by and large, shut and had notices stating that they would not be open until the afternoon due to the lack of meat. Vast queues formed as customers waited for the shops to open. The customers behaved until the doors opened and word spread down the line of people that there was no meat left. 'Where's t'Food Committee?' cried one woman, 'Isn't this their job?' A male passerby shouted, 'It's a cursed shame.'

A communal kitchen at Burngreave Vestry Hall opened, enabling people to buy a more affordable good quality meal. It enabled women in particular to be able to work, or enjoy some leisure time, without having to worry about spending time cooking for the family.

On 26 February women were encouraged to form a Food Bureau in the city. One of these existed on Chesterfield Road in Woodseats, where women made and sold cooked or prepared food, the most popular of which was bread with uncooked grated potato. Potted beans were used to replace fat. Mashed potatoes mixed with bloater paste was suggested as an alternative to butter or margarine. Leaflets produced by the Women's Committee of Food Experts provided simple and affordable recipes. Such was the popularity of the Bureau that requests for assistance in their establishment were received from other towns.

Canteens were set up in munitions factories, to ensure workers received a good meal during their work.

In addition to food shortages there were concerns that smokers would be unable to practice their habit due to an increasing scarcity of tobacco. However, Sheffielders were assured that if they exercised a little more restrain there should be sufficient amounts for all smokers. The Government took 40 per cent of all tobacco, for the Forces, but Sheffield was assured the 'working-man's supply' would not be greatly interfered with.

On 28 February the City Battalion was disbanded, having never been able to fully recover from the huge losses at the Somme. In its short existence approximately 3,000 men had served in it, almost 700 of whom died.

During March, with the need to fight off starvation on the Home Front, Sheffield could be forgiven for neglecting its tradition of enthusiastic fundraising for the battlefields. Sheffield was expected to raise £1.2 million in a week to meet the government required money for the war. Each city, town and district across the country was expected to raise £2 10s per person. The *Telegraph* had no doubt that the city's people would rise to the challenge despite only being informed of the need to raise the money two weeks earlier. It was hoped business men in particular would contribute by buying War Bonds. In order to eliminate the fears of the wealthier members of society who were considered they would have their wealth taken from them, the City Treasurer urged the Government to send a leading Minister to explain the situation. If people were less concerned that their wealth would be taken against their will, they would be happier to give more generously it was believed. In order to raise the money a 'monster procession' was held with representatives of all forces, the WAAC, the Land Army, Girl Guides, Boys' Brigade, teachers and pupils. Additionally door-to-door canvassing took place, as did meetings where MPs addressed the crowds on the importance of the appeal. The money from the city was spent on buying three cruisers, costing £400,000 each.

As March came to a close there were huge losses of British soldiers fighting in France and Flanders. Field Marshall Sir Douglas Haig made a statement to the Forces describing a period of 'crisis' with 'very heavy loss' over the past two days. Although counterattacks took place, with the Allies inflicting losses on the Germans, there was not enough in the way of munitions to challenge the huge number of Germans advancing.

On 28 March a six-hour long 'impressive' period of prayer running from 6pm until midnight was held at Sheffield Cathedral for men on the front, who were 'undergoing the most trying ordeal ever imposed on British soldiers'. There was a service from 7:30pm until 8:30pm led by the Reverend J. K. Mosley, and occasional hymns, but otherwise those present knelt beside one another in earnest prayer.

Munitions workers decided to forego their Easter holidays in order to make good the losses sustained by the Britain during the German offensive. In addition to a great loss of life, guns and shells had been left as British soldiers fled, and these were now in the hands of the enemy. Firms across the country offered to work through the Easter period. However, it was felt that due to the limited rail services to transport materials and munitions, only those whose work was of crucial importance should work during the holiday period otherwise the railways would not be able to cope with all the goods that need to be transported. Sheffield firms were, of course, amongst those companies which were required to work and they were notified by official telegrams. Churchill, as Minister of Munitions, appealed for workers to continue through the holiday and the trade unions encouraged them to do so on the understanding that most workers would have friends or relatives fighting and that they should not let them down. Sheffield workers needed little encouragement. A telegram was sent from Vickers stating, 'We beg you will feel assured of the most enthusiastic co-operation of the whole of the Vickers' organisation.' A spokesman for another leading, but unnamed, firm said, 'The men and women have responded splendidly to the call for help at this time of great national crisis.' Despite needing rest, the employees of all firms passed resolutions to work even harder than previously to produce more weapons to overturn the German advantage. It was believed that four days of extra work on manufacturing cannon and machine guns would replenish those which had been lost. Only a small number of men were unwilling to work and these were condemned as troublemakers who were part of the 'stop the war party'.

The editorial of the *Telegraph* tried to give hope and encouragement:

'The Germans are still fighting desperately. There is nothing surprising in that. They are struggling as a drowning man struggles, with every muscle in their huge army…They have come to the conclusion that trench fighting may never give the decision they want. By hurling every available man against our armies, and by ramming in every gun, and every other appliance they have been able to invent, they hope to rush a conclusion after the pattern of their 1914 effort.'

The editor argued that the British army could not be defeated and would continue to kill Germans until the German army was crushed. He accepted that it hurt to acknowledge that Germans had taken land occupied by the British, at a great cost to British lives, but that the Germans could not crush the British spirit to win. The Germans would continue to attack, he wrote, and their numbers would be maintained and possibly increased. It was therefore essential that Sheffield folk 'strain every nerve to strengthen and sustain our sorely-tried troops'.

That same newspaper also urged all people to refrain from having a holiday. 'We do not know how men at home can holiday while their sons or brothers are struggling unshaven and unwashed, day and night, against overwhelming odds to save Britain from defeat.' The public were also urged not to take trips to the coast or elsewhere, because the trains were needed to transport munitions.

On 8 April meat rationing commenced and workers engaged in heavy work in munitions factories were given additional allowances but these were only supplied from 15 April, meaning that workers had to go short for the first week.

On 6 May a six-hour long service was held at Sheffield Cathedral asking for divine intervention to end the war.

Prayers were partly answered when American troops arrived in the city in preparation of their war efforts. Large crowds gathered in 16 May 1918 to watch the arrival of approximately 450 American troops. They were led by a band from the Royal Flying Corps which played American music. The crowd cheered them on their way to the Town Hall, where the flags of Great Britain and the USA flew side by side. Inside the Lord Mayor and Lady Mayoress gave a civic welcome to the men, shaking hands with them all and introduced them to leading members of Sheffield society. A tea was held for the men, following which the American consul in Sheffield, Mr JM Savage, thanked the Lord Mayor and Mayoress for their welcome and stated the determination of the USA in helping fight for liberty. The speech received great cheers from the Americans, with Lieutenant Manship, who was in command of the men, adding that they could not wait to get to France. Lieutenant Crewe stated his belief that having been known up to that point as cousins, Britain and the USA would soon become known as brothers and that any differences would be put aside. It was hoped that the whole of Sheffield would give them hospitality and good will.

Food shortages continued although the local rationing schemes allowed a fairer distribution. On 15 May the Government bought all potatoes which could not be sold through other means at a fixed price so that they could be sold at affordable prices.

By June, 352 acres had been appropriated for corporation war allotments, consisting of 4,203 plots, which it was hoped would make a significant difference in the amount of food available. As the year continued further land was acquired at Monckton Road, High Hazels Park and 222 allotment plots were created at Woodseats Golf Course. There were also hopes that the harvest would bring greater amounts of food than in recent years, as a result of more land being cultivated, more hands to work on the land and good weather. Soldiers, volunteers and prisoners of war worked the harvest. However, the harvest was poor. In fact it was described as being one of the worst on record.

A man who wrote to the *Telegraph* in June thought the local rationing of tea was unnecessary and he urged for more tea to be brought into the city. There was plenty of tea, he claimed, but it was not being brought into Sheffield because tea merchants found the attitude of the Local Food Committee to be too harsh. Consequently other towns and cities had an abundance of tea whilst Sheffield had a severe shortage. A national scheme of control of distribution of tea was introduced on 14 July.

A feeling of optimism was expressed in the *Telegraph* on 19 June in order to boost morale at a time of food shortages and tiredness of the length of the war, based on Bonar Law's claim that the 'next few months will produce the supreme hour in this struggle'. The *Telegraph* emphasised the need to maintain hope and not doubt that the war would end favourably. The cost of the war was now reported to be £7,342 million; the equivalent of £180 for every man, woman and child in the country. It was emphasised that everyone should give what ever they could to the national effort.

On 1 July an 'impressive' service was held at the cathedral to mark the anniversary of the Somme. There was a large congregation of relatives and friends of those members of the City Battalion who lost their lives. Also present were some of those who had against the odds survived the onslaught, with a small reunion taking place after the service at the Church House. The service opened with Chopin's *Funeral March* and concluded with the *Dead March* followed by the *Last Post* played by buglers of the Sheffield Volunteers. Hymns played were *For all the saints* and *O God, our help*. The service was led by the Archdeacon of Sheffield, Reverend H Gresford Jones. He preached, 'The eternal God is thy refuge, and underneath are the everlasting arms.' He praised the battalion, most of whom were sons of the city and was largely trained within the city, speaking at length about their bravery. He offered spiritual words of comfort, that those who had fallen were now at rest in Heaven.

At a service at Chapeltown Parish Church, given in remembrance of all of those who had died thus far during the war, the Reverend W Surtees praised the heroism of all of those who had died and also all of those who had suffered bereavement, especially women who had exercised great courage.

In addition to the war dead there were still concerns as of June 1918 that the death rate in the city was too high. The Medical Officer gave the following death rate information to the Corporation in a report: in 1913 the death rate was 16.6 per thousand; in 1914, 17.3 per thousand; in 1915, 17.0 per thousand; in 1916, 15.1 per thousand; in 1917, 14.5 per thousand.

Whilst there was clearly some improvement, it was minor, and Sheffield was lagging behind other towns and cities which were seeing great strides in terms of health.

It was questioned why Sheffield's health position was not better given the amount of expenditure. It was thought that one chief reason was that because of the war sanitary work had not been carried out in Sheffield whereas other cities had begun to make improvements in housing, sewerage, drainage and general cleanliness.

On 4 July there was novelty at Bramall Lane when American troops were provided with entertainment including music and a game of baseball was played in front of a crowd of 20,000 spectators, including wounded soldiers in the recently converted pavilion which was now used as a convalescence home, along with other sports. The bands of the Sheffield Volunteers and the Royal Air Force performed American patriotic music. An 'exceedingly pretty sight' was the dancing of 2,500 school children, which was described as one of the highlights of the day. Judge Charles Hunt of Minneapolis gave an energetic address to the troops saying that more Americans were on their way to give the Germans hell. The game of baseball was played with two teams; comprising members of the army and a team from the navy. The Lord Mayor threw the first ball. The navy team won the game. Other events included numerous races of varying lengths, including relays, the high jump and a tug-of-war. Individuals and teams made up of Americans and British soldiers and civilians competed, with the Americans winning all but the 100 yards and half-mile races. The event was closed with a rendition of the *Star Spangled Banner* followed by *God Save the King*. One of the most unusual aspects of the day was the introduction to several leading Sheffield dignitaries of chewing gum which was described as being 'a truly American custom, the joy of which is said to become intensified by constant practice'.

Other events to give a welcome to the American 'brothers' included music performances at the Central Secondary School. The American flag was also prominently flown from buildings across the city.

The industrial discontent which plagued the city at the start of the year resurfaced. On 18 July 1,500-2,000 moulders went on strike, ending on 13 August. A strike by corporation staff had been averted. On 21-22 August coalminers went on strike, further affecting the low supplies of that fuel.

As the fourth anniversary approached there was a period of reflection. It was noted that few in 1914 could have thought the war would still be waged in 1918. The *Telegraph* questioned whether, had the events of the past four years been anticipated, would the decision to go to war have still been made? 'History will have some hard things to say about the folly of the Government and the people who made so little preparation to meet a blow so long threatened.' Despite the dark days that had been experienced there were positives; Britain's relatively small army had fought courageously against a vast army. It encouraged readers to have faith that as the fifth year of war began Britain and her allies were in a strong position, especially given the support of the USA.

Every seat was taken, and large numbers stood in the aisles, during a service at the Cathedral on the anniversary. In fact there were an estimated 1,800 in the congregation, with 500 unable to get into the building. Leading figures in the city played important roles during the service, with the exception of the Lord Mayor who was not present. The hymn *O God our help in ages past* opened what was a very solemn service. There was great and enthusiastic prayer and singing. The service was led by the Archdeacon Gresford Jones, with the sermon read by reverend FT Cooper, the chaplain at the Base Hospital. It was said that in fighting for righteousness and freedom they were fighting for the very spirit of Christ. It was a fight for righteousness over materialism. Prayers were given for those who had died and for the benefit of those fighting.

At Ecclesall Church during the morning of 4 August Canon Houghton said there was much to give thanks for, including the justice of the cause, the unity of the nation and the Empire, the involvement of the USA and the courage and devotion of Britain's soldiers. An afternoon service was given for children, and in the evening a memorial service was held for the 94 men of Ecclesall who had died thus far during the war.

There was some light relief from the anniversary. Hundreds of Sheffield folk flocked to the coast on Saturday 3 August to make the most of their Bank Holiday break. At both the Victoria and the Midland railway stations there were 'unparalleled' scenes as long queues of people waited to buy a ticket. The Great Central station approach appeared like a fair all day long. The first train departed at 1:57am and a huge crowd had gathered to embark it. Trains were packed throughout the day. Popular destinations were Blackpool, Bridlington Morecombe, Scarborough, Whitby and Skegness. Closer to home trains ran to Matlock and Buxton where people enjoyed the Peak District. Perhaps it was a feeling of optimism that encouraged people to enjoy the Bank Holiday weekend like never before. In fact so many people headed to holiday resorts that those towns did not have sufficient places for them to stay and so some had to return to Sheffield with a feeling of disappointment.

Shortly after the anniversary, on 7 August, there were also growing hopes that the war was coming to a close. A comprehensive review of the war effort, based on a speech by Lloyd George, was printed in the *Telegraph* under the subheading 'ALLIES' GROWING PROOFS OF VICTORY'. On 22 August official battle pictures were exhibited at Weston Park to show the Allies' advance.

Despite this boost for morale there were still problems on the Home Front. Early in August the Food Control Committee planned a jam and marmalade rationing scheme. There were difficulties implementing this scheme, resulting in delays. The scheme for marmalade was finally put into practice in September, as a local scheme and not the national scheme. Honey, treacle and syrup were later added to the scheme. The jam rationing scheme could not be enforced, however although the committee continued to persevere in its attempts to obtain the power as the war came to an end.

According to the Sheffield Food Control Committee minutes for 23 August 1918 (Sheffield Archives: CA162) there was as much home-killed meat in Sheffield as Leeds, yet despite this, on 30 August, extensive queues were reported outside the pork shop of the Brightside and Carbrook Cooperative Society, Attercliffe Road, the Firvale branch of the Cooperative Society and other shops in the city.

There were plans to reduce the meat allowance to enable meat supplies to go further, which resulted in dismay and anger. The Secretary of the United Society of Spring Fitters and Vicemen in Sheffield wrote to the committee saying his organisation had protested to the Ministry of Food regarding a proposed reduction in the meat allowance. The committee agreed to support the protest.

In addition to meat queues October was dominated by bread queues. Bakers struggled to get staff to produce more bread and as other foods became more scarce there was an increased demand for bread.

Yet despite these problems the British advances continued.

On 30 September Mr JF Hope MP addressed a meeting of his constituents in the South Street school. After discussing the possibility of a General Election, and changes to the constituency which would now include 14,000 women voters, he gave a speech entitled 'The War and the Home Front' in which he spoke of the advances being made on the battlefields but that the war was very far from being finished and that there should not be any relaxation of efforts. It was essential, he said, that a peace should be achieved which guarantees peace for themselves and their children. He praised those in Sheffield who produced the means by which the tide had turned in favour of the Allies. He expressed a hope that ways could be found to quickly resolve issues between employees and employers to prevent strikes which had threatened the chances of success.

It was inevitable that efforts would be relaxed, especially when on the same day, GH Roberts, the Minister of Labour, addressed the Advisory Committee in Sheffield on the demobilisation process.

The following day Sir Samuel Roberts MP addressed a well attended meeting at the Ecclesall Conservative and Unionist Club in the city. He spoke of the need for a peace that guaranteed security and peace for the future. He said people should rejoice that the war had seemingly turned in favour of the Allies and would soon be over. He warned that although the war had come at a huge cost and had and would continue to result in high taxation, it was worth every penny to ensure freedom.

Also that day JH Whitley MP spoke of the end of the war and how it would see the creation of a new society. Speaking at the Hartshead (Sheffield) Lecture and Debating Society he claimed that there would now be a valuation of every man and woman irrespective of class, with more powers to workers. He emphasised the need for workers to work for the good of the nation during peacetime as they had at war.

Hard work was the message also, when on 10 October Winston Churchill, Minister of Munitions, arrived in the city to tour the munitions works. There had been no advanced official announcement of his visit although city dignitaries and representatives of the press greeted him upon his arrival by train. That night he stayed at the Royal Victoria Hotel where he spoke about the conditions that would be required in a peace treaty and spoke also of the important role Sheffield had played by supplying the means of war. Furthermore he praised the involvement of the USA as well as all of those many people who had made peace possible.

The following morning he visited three munitions factories. First he visited Templeborough where 2.5 million shells had been produced since January 1915 and he met some of the 5,000 women and 700 men who worked there. At the works he recognised a former soldier whom he had previously met at Ypres. 'Yes we have gone a good deal further now,' the Minister remarked. He then visited Attercliffe where aeroplane cranks and guns were manufactured. The Attercliffe works was an extension of the Vickers works and it had yet to be completed. German prisoners of war were assisting in the construction work. He then moved on to the Brightside works also of the Vickers company, where he spent an hour and a half viewing the machinery used to manufacture heavy guns and armour plates. In the afternoon he visited Hadfields works at Tinsley. He then left the city at around 5pm.

Churchill was impressed by all that he saw and left workers with the motto 'No relaxation of effort, keep on strenuously until victory is attained'.

At the Templeborough works he had made a speech which was not too dissimilar in style to those which he was to make as Prime Minister in the later World War.

'As you know, we are slowly but surely moving forward into a position of unimpeachable security. It is not for us to relax our efforts, for when you are cutting a tiger's claws, and pulling fangs out of his jaws, you have got to observe every precaution; you have got to move forward on your task with the utmost care and resolution. We have at any rate reached a point when we may be quite sure that, if we continue to work in unity and comradeship in this island home of ours, we shall succeed once more in triumphing over those who have menaced and nearly shattered the peace and liberties of Europe and the civilisation of mankind.'

There were claims that Sheffield had relaxed its efforts, at least in terms of financial assistance for the war. During 'Feed the Gun Week', Sheffield's funds were a long way behind the average provided by other cities. Birmingham had provided £2 million more and Newcastle had provided double that of the steel city. Sheffield Corporation had provided £100,000, the Providential Assurance Company had provided £25,000, Peter Dunn & Son £20,000, Arthur Balfour and Co, £10,000, and others had provided varying small and not so small amounts.

However, the *Telegraph* was extremely unhappy with the city's contributions as a whole. It remarked that every time the 9.2-inch howitzer fired a shell it did so at a cost of £25, for an 8-inch shell £11 and for a 6-inch shell £6 10s. If Britain was to win the war it required every Sheffield person to contribute and feed the guns. It seemed that after four years of contributing Sheffield was becoming complacent and perhaps despondent and so was unwilling to continue to contribute with such enthusiasm. The *Telegraph* argued that so many people had made money out of the war, especially munitions workers, by having plenty of work with higher than usual wages, and therefore it was only right that they should pay into the fund.

To encourage people to contribute, guns were displayed in the city, with children in particular fascinated by them. There was great intrigue about camouflage. Entertainment was provided, with bands from the King's Own Yorkshire Light Infantry. There were illuminations, with Verey lights and parachutes being fired at Barker's Pool and lights on many buildings. Large crowds gathered but the *Telegraph* felt they were of the 'hear all, invest nowt' type who only served to block footpaths. Nonetheless within two days £536,309 was raised and by 25 October more than £1 million was raised, with the Sheffield Banking Company donating £100,000.

With sustained efforts on the battlefields and on the Home Front in terms of raising money and producing arms, an end to the war was to come soon, a Sheffield MP claimed. On 24 October Sir Samuel Roberts MP voiced his prediction of an early finish to the war in a speech during the annual tea and entertainment of the Ecclesall Primrose League at the Cutlers Hall, at which there were 350 guests. He spoke first of the new legislation giving some women the vote and the right to stand for election for parliament, though he expected there would not be very many who would take the opportunity but that those who did would be welcome. He spoke then of the housing crisis and the imminent need for approximately half a million new houses in the country. After the briefly discussing the possibility of a General Election, he turned his attention to the war. He praised Woodrow Wilson's attempts to carve peace. If Germany failed to meet the terms of the Allies it was felt that her own allies of Austria and Turkey would desert her and Germany would have to fight alone. 'Then the end will very soon come. That is the position tonight,' he concluded. His wife, Lady Roberts, also addressed those present, thanking the soldiers for all of their efforts in bringing the war towards a successful close.

October saw plans discussed for a public memorial hall for Sheffield's residents, to be known as Memorial Hall. It was decided it should stand in a proud location and it was decided to construct such a hall opposite the Albert Hall facing Barker's Pool, along Holly Street towards Orchard Lane. It was to be a hall worthy of the city to emphasise the importance the city's armed forces personnel and civilians had played during the war and its war dead. The building is better known as City Hall.

Clearly the city was expecting the war to end at any time. This is evident especially from the council meeting held on 9 November when the council expressed 'profound gratitude' to the navy, army and air force. The Lord Mayor, Alderman William Irons, was asked to send telegrams to the heads of each of the armed forces and to the President of France and the King of Belgium to express appreciation to the French and Belgian troops.

Sheffield's City Hall was built to act as a symbol and memorial for the lives of the city's men lost in the war and to commemorate the military and civilian efforts which had made victory possible. (*The Author*)

CHAPTER 21

The End of Hostilities

Although the end of the war had been in sight for some time, the Armistice was of course not signed until 11 November 1918.

When the news was first announced, on a large board reading 'End of the War' outside the offices of the *Telegraph* on High Street, there was a degree of scepticism. Rumours had been created in the past claiming that the war had come to an end. However, once the doubters were placated the excitement began and soon crowds gathered to see what the matter was. Before long it was impossible for anyone to make their way along the street. As the crowd grew in size and vociferation a Union Jack was raised on the *Telegraph* building and began to sound its siren.

There were 'great demonstrations of delight' according to the *Sheffield Year Book* of 1919, when the news of the Armistice spread. Crowds quickly formed in the streets and flags began to adorn buildings, vehicles and, even, cats and dogs. By nightfall most streets were decked with flags, filling the city with 'radiant colours'. The crowds were not jubilant for victory as such, according to the *Telegraph*, but more thankful of peace.

One man was spoken to by a reporter of the *Telegraph*. He had been interviewed two years earlier by the same reporter and, at that time aged 70, he had expressed his belief he would not live to see the end of the war. He was now happy to have outlived his expectation and due to having seen the end he said he no longer cared what happened to him.

A woman who was interviewed summed up the thoughts of many. 'I am glad it is over and that we have won,' she said with tears in her

Yorkshire Telegraph and Star 'The World War at an End'. (*Photograph reproduced from the Picture Sheffield Collection, courtesy of Sheffield Local Studies Library*)

eyes, 'If only my boy had been here to see it.' Her son was buried in France.

The steam powered buzzers which had acted as air raid sirens were sounded to proclaim the news and the bells of the Cathedral and other churches were rung in celebration. The anti-aircraft guns around the city began to fire. One wonders whether there was anyone in the city who had believed upon hearing the warning and the guns, and had not heard the good news, whether Zeppelins were once again striking the city.

News spread quickly from the centre to the suburbs. The tale of the driver of one motorcar travelling from the moors towards the city summed up the excitement. Before the edge of the city had been reached the driver was struck by the sound of ringing bells, before even the smoke of the city could be seen. He noticed what was described as a 'crescendo of excitement' and still on the edge of the city, even before Totley was reached, was overcome with emotion when a young boy holding a Union Jack announced 'The war's over, Mister'. It was said that there were so many flags adorning the houses that those houses without flags stood out greatly. Vehicles were also covered with flags and patriotic messages.

At 10:50am, ten minutes before the Armistice agreement came into effect, Dr Swann, vicar of Pitsmoor, stood on a chair outside the offices and called for the National Anthem to be sung. Following the song Archdeacon Gresford Jones called for everyone to go to the cathedral to give thanks for victory and peace. A 'great wave' of people duly flocked to the cathedral which was soon too full to accept any further worshippers. It remained open until 11pm.

'Peace has not come yet,' the Bishop of Sheffield announced at the Cathedral, 'God grant that we may not lose the fruits of victory in talk and diplomacy.' He was, of course, referring to the fears that although fighting had ended it would come at a cost to Britain at the eventual peace talks which would take place at Versailles. He hoped that the world would now follow the teachings of Christ and evil would be destroyed. He wanted all to praise God and to thank Him for delivering them through the dark days of war. It was an impromptu service with lots of singing and high emotion. A more formal, civic service commenced in the afternoon and was attended by the Lord Mayor and all of the councillors. The service opened with the hymn *Onward Christian soldiers*. Although there was happiness there was a noticeable element of sorrow and large sections of the congregation were in tears as they recalled lost ones.

At Victoria Hall the Reverend GH McNeal held a series of thanksgiving services. The services at the Victoria Hall ran without pause until 7pm, ending only then for a Temperance movement demonstration.

The Lord Mayor told a reporter from the *Telegraph* that he believed it was the greatest day in history. 'At long last the dreadful nightmare through which we have been passing has gone from our minds. It is news of unspeakable importance and it will be very welcome in Sheffield, for Sheffield has played a mighty part indeed in the war.' He congratulated the people of Sheffield for all they had done. He added that he offered his sympathies to those who had lost friends or loved ones, stating that he too had suffered bereavement. 'To the citizens generally, I say rejoice with all heartiness, but in doing so I ask them to observe moderation and restrain themselves from excess. Above all I ask them to maintain good order.' He also asked them to thank God for delivering them from evil.

The Lord Mayor had become Chief Magistrate for the City on Armistice Day. At the Police Court that morning, in celebration of the end of the war he dismissed the case against the first defendant put before him.

Shops were closed and work ceased across the city with the exception of those selling flags and newspapers. The munitions works closed and did not open until Wednesday morning, or in some cases Thursday, to allow for a holiday. Workers were not given permission to leave but they did so anyway and the management made no effort to stop them. People flocked to the centre from the suburbs and the munitions factories, and it was remarked that Sheffield centre had never seen so many people. Indeed it was considered whether Sheffield even had so many people the streets were so full. By 1pm Fitzalan Square, High Street and Fargate were described as being 'one seething mass of humanity'. Fitzalan Square became an impromptu concert hall with singing, dancing and merriment. By 3pm vehicles had great difficulty driving through the city centre. There was cheering and singing and processions everywhere. Cheers were given to the King, the Prime Minister, the Government and the leaders of the Allies. The National Anthem was proudly sung and overhead could be seen planes carrying out celebratory flyovers. Throughout the day military bands paraded throughout the city.

At night for the first time since 1914 the streets were ablaze with light, although due to coal shortages lights that were dependent upon coal were to be limited, and the clock on the Town Hall was illuminated. It was decided that fireworks and bonfires would be allowed and fireworks were seen over the city, as were fire balloons. At Rockingham fire station fireworks and a bonfire were enjoyed. Trumpets and whistles were blown enthusiastically, although they were in short supply. After more than four years of fear, contemplation and often silence in the long nights, people were keen to make as much noise as possible.

The celebrations went on into the early hours and similar scenes were observed for several more days. To the dismay of those who enjoyed drinking there was still very little beer in the city, with most public houses closed. The celebrations were therefore somewhat sober but much merriment was still had. Perhaps due to the lack of alcohol the crowds were described as being 'wonderfully orderly and well behaved'. However, some public houses were open and in those there was music and cheery, well ordered behaviour. For once the time regulations were not observed, with confidence that there would not be any prosecution.

It was said in an earlier chapter that some newsboys had taken advantage in the fascination in the news, charging more than they should for a paper. On this day some papers were sold for 2d as opposed to the correct penny, but it was remarked that the customers did not mind the youngsters making money out of the occasion.

The *Telegraph* hoped that 11 November would be a date that was remembered as one of the greatest dates in history and that it would be remembered as well as 15 June (the Battle of Trafalgar) and 21 October (the Battle of Waterloo). 'It will stand for all time as a sign that Right is more than Might.' Thanks were given to those who had died and it was hoped they would never be forgotten. Those who were wounded, it was hoped, would be cared for.

The following day the streets were less busy but the trams were packed full of travellers who headed out of the city and on to the moors to take advantage of the mild weather. More elaborate decorations were created to replace the makeshift flags and bunting that was quickly put up when the Armistice news was first announced. Lambert Street, Lord Street, Hague Lane and Collier's Row were key amongst the poorer areas of housing that made a special effort.

On 14 November the King and Queen were due to visit the city's munitions factories, including the Cammell Laird Grimesthorpe Steel and Ordnance Works and see the expanded works at Penistone. They were then to distribute medals and decorations to soldiers at an investiture to be held at the Northern General Hospital before visiting the Town Hall for the Lord Mayor to present to them 'certain representatives' of public life especially those engaged in war work. Cammell Laird produced a souvenir programme in preparation for the visit and its existence has led other researchers to wrongly assume the visit took place, but it was cancelled.

Instead the King gave a brief telegram to the Lord Mayor, in which he said, 'I have received with intense pleasure the greetings of the citizens of Sheffield on the greatest day in our history. I welcome this opportunity of congratulating the men and women of your city who have so faithfully devoted their efforts to the attainment of the principles of right and liberty for which we went to war, and which, thank God, we have now regained. It is a real regret to the Queen and to myself not to be able to visit Sheffield during this week.'

General Sir John Maxwell took the place of the King to present medals and decorations to a number of soldiers and friends or family of soldiers killed in action at an investiture at Weston Park.

There were concerns of mass unemployment as men returned from the battlefields and the thousands of men and women lost their jobs in the munitions factories as a result of there no longer being the need for the production of the means of war. It was decided that there was to be no immediate discharge of workers and that when the discharge took place an unemployment pay would be provided, although it was much smaller than the generous wages that had been enjoyed during hostilities. Men were to receive 24s per week and women 20s. The first dependant child would receive 6s per week with each subsequent child 3s. Those aged over 15 but below 18 were to receive 12s per week for boys and 10s for girls. Partially disabled out of work men received the benefit on top of their pensions. It was aimed to tide them over until they found new employment, though with fewer jobs and increased numbers of those seeking work unemployment inevitably became a long term issue. To try and reduce the numbers of unemployed the demobilisation from the forces was made gradual, with only 'pivotal' men to be released form the forces in the short term. Those who had positions to return to would be discharged before those who had no certain prospects of employment. Overtime and Sunday working was also ended for most firms. It was hoped that the difficulties of unemployment could be overcome if employers, workers and officials worked together with that common aim. Although jobs would still be available in manufacturing steel for shipbuilding, tools, cutlery, trams, railway equipment and other equipment and items necessary in peace, this was a belief which history has shown to be very naïve.

On 16 November six war shrines were erected at St Cuthbert's Church, Pitsmoor for the dead, and memorials soon began to be erected elsewhere across the city. Trees were planted as living memorials.

On 17 November a thanksgiving service was held and on 21 November school children attended thanksgiving services in churches all over the city. Little would they know that 21 years later they would face yet another war.

A special honour was granted in the form of the Honorary Freedom of the city, to Woodrow Wilson, the President of the USA, such was the gratitude to the Americans. He was invited to visit the city to collect his honour, but the American ambassador informed the Lord Mayor that a visit would not be possible. Lloyd George, Field Marshall Foch, Admiral Sir David Beaty and Field Marshall Douglas Haig were granted the same honour.

A gun captured by the 2nd Battalion Duke of Wellington Regiment was offered to the city at the request of those men within the regiment who hailed from Sheffield. It was captured on 24 October 1918. It was accepted by the city and was to be placed on display with a suitable inscription.

Christmas 1918 was characterised as a period of 'old-time heartiness' with seasonal weather including some snow not preventing enjoyment with family reunions where loved ones had returned from war. Large numbers had returned permanently, with most of those who had not been demobbed having been granted leave. Of course there were large numbers of empty seats at tables in Sheffield and this was a grim reminder that victory had come at the heaviest of prices. Yet, with war over, people generally bought all they could to make Christmas extra special, although some rationing was still in place. People were looking forward to a long festive break from work, with no shops or businesses working. In addition to religious services, there were dances and shows in most of the city's public buildings, and entertainment provided at all the hospitals for the benefit of wounded soldiers and civilian patients. Despite the merriment it was acknowledged by most that the war had caused such a huge transformation in peoples' personal lives, working lives and in society in general, that Christmas would never be the same again.

Some merriment was to be held the following year, however. On 20 May 1919 King George V paid another visit to the city. Companies

A 'happy crowd' at peace celebrations in Sheffield. (*Photograph reproduced from the Picture Sheffield Collection, courtesy of Sheffield Local Studies Library*)

Peace celebrations in Summer Street. (*Photograph reproduced from the Picture Sheffield Collection, courtesy of Sheffield Local Studies Library*)

were strongly encouraged to give their workers the day off in order to greet the King and enjoy a day of holiday. The King later wrote to the council expressing his thanks for the welcome and loyalty which he received. He remarked, 'The armies were the spearpoint with which the enemy was overthrown, but the people at home were the good haft without which its blow could not have been successfully delivered.'

On 19 July 1919, approximately three weeks after the Treaty of Versailles was signed, a day of national celebration was held. In Sheffield the peace celebrations consisted of music, military parading by serving and discharged soldiers, with each discharged soldier receiving a card signed by the Lord Mayor, dancing, including Morris dancing and a gun salute. Tea and entertainment were provided across the

World War One Victory Cake. *(Photograph reproduced from the Picture Sheffield Collection, courtesy of Sheffield Local Studies Library)*

city for war widows and children of fallen servicemen. Bonfires, fireworks and a display of the searchlights were held at night. The illuminations of the city were timed to coincide with similar illuminations in towns and cities across the country. There were also special parties for children on 17 July at the Town Hall Square, Firth Park, High Hazels, Hillsborough Park, Meersbrook Park and Crookesmoor Recreation Ground with the council paying for tea, medals for the children, bands, music, flags and other decorations.

A tank was given to the city by the National War Savings Committee in appreciation of the contribution made by the city. It was placed in Endcliffe Woods and was well viewed. Another means of warfare that were well viewed at this time of celebration was the aeroplane. Between 23 and 26 July a Flying Exhibition was held at Coal Aston Aerodrome with 9,135 people paying for entry.

CHAPTER 22

Influenza

The great loss of lives on the battlefields and seas understandably overshadowed the loss of life on the Home Front but in Sheffield as the war came to an end, thousands died in the city due to an illness that claimed more Sheffield lives in a few months than what the war claimed over a far greater period. Influenza spread across large parts of Europe, hitting hard populations weakened due to poor diets and the strains of war.

When precisely the first victim was claimed is unknown. However, in the week ending 2 July there had been 11 deaths from the influenza. There was a noticeable rise by the week ending 15 July when there were 68 deaths.

By 6 July the virus affected the already low output of coal, having struck the ability of many miners to work and claiming some of their lives.

The virus affected schools and used them as a breeding ground, leading to its rapid spread. On one day in July 1918 142 children were absent from Beighton School. The school had to be closed when the illness continued to affect attendance, and in order to try and stop it from spreading further. The school kept being reopened but quickly closed again as it was realised that the pandemic was still present. On 11 November, the day the war ended, when reopened there were 150 children who failed to come to school due to influenza. Exams had to be cancelled because the school had been closed for so long and this was a trend throughout the city.

University students were also badly affected. The new women's hall, Oakholme, housed 36 female students all of whom caught the virus.

There were restrictions on the number of patrons allowed at cinemas which had to be continuously disinfected, and attempts to reduce the amount of congregation in other entertainment venues.

The peak of the virus and the deaths and sickness it caused, was in August to October, and by 8 August funerals were delayed due to a shortage of gravediggers as a result of the war, and because of the dramatic increase in the number of burials needed.

On 30 October it was thought that the flu was abating nationally, but there was little evidence of any improvement in Sheffield. Hospitals were full of patients and staff numbers at all hospitals had been affected, with doctors and nurses contracting the illness themselves. Even a full quota of staff would have struggled to cope. That same day a joint meeting was held of the City Hospitals and the Health committees. Due to the 'abnormal sickness' of staff it was not yet possible to open wards at Lodge Moor Hospital for the treatment of the virus. Thirty members of staff were ill and a doctor and nurse had recently died. An advert was placed in the press for volunteer nurses to work in the homes of patients and at Lodge Moor. Remuneration was offered dependent upon experience. At the Base Hospital there were 40 members of staff absent due to the virus.

The illness did not only affect Sheffield citizens in the city. At Firvale Hospital 12 German prisoners of war were suffering from the virus, and one had died of it.

By 5 November the virus had 'crippled' the tram system, with tram staff being ill and fewer journeys made as people were discouraged from embarking on crowded tramcars.

During November and December there were more than 1,000 deaths in Sheffield with so many deaths that on 9 November burials had to take place at night to keep up with demand. A lack of space and the quantity of burials resulted in mass graves.

By 12 November there were signs that the numbers of affected was starting to decline, but during the week ending 18 November there were still 246 deaths.

The death rate for the four weeks ending 16 November 1918 was 64.3 for every thousand, compared with the average of the 96 'great towns' of England and Wales which stood at 39.1 deaths per thousand,

and it would rise as high as 76.2 per 1,000. During this period there had been 2,291 deaths in the city, of which 1,332 were attributed to influenza.

In the four weeks ending 14 December 1918 there were 450 deaths attributed to the virus, showing a steady decline.

As 1918 ended the virus began to claim fewer lives. Between 21 December and 11 January 1919 there were only 31 influenza deaths recorded. For the four weeks ending 8 February 1919 there were 36 deaths caused by influenza.

Despite there being relief of an end to the war, people still had to fight battles for their lives, with more families in the city, losing loved ones, at a time when they thought death and suffering were at an end.

CHAPTER 23

A Changed City

Following the Armistice the *Telegraph* stated that it would be 'fatal' to try and return to the conditions of life that had existed in the city in 1914. People should instead, it claimed, 'rise to the opportunity of the new time'. In short it was necessary to build a new, better, changed city, a city and an era full of new possibilities.

At that time a number of leading figures spoke of Sheffield's new role in peace. Lord Stuart of Wortley wrote:

> 'We must all work hard to repair the damage that these discredited dynasties have done. Sheffield will have no small share in the work, and I doubt not that Sheffield will be as great and as loyal in the peaceful work of reconstruction as she has been in the grim work of making the munitions that have done so much to win the war.'

HAL Fisher MP believed that the steel industry would continue to be an important part of the Sheffield economy. However, he was most concerned with housing and health. He believed the Government needed to provide workers with larger opportunities for leisure and education and to create 'healthy and happy living'.

Prior to the cessation of hostilities it was widely expected that 1918 would see the end of the war and there were discussions as to what action should be undertaken to rebuild the city and move towards the future. Such thoughts had first been considered in 1916 when business leaders and councillors wondered how to sustain and build upon industry once the military demand ended.

In November that year the outgoing Mayor, Councillor FA Warlow, suggested the setting up of a committee to deal with the development of the city. The committee was established in March 1917 and its functions were to oversee and promote trade, industry, development and prosperity, to promote the establishment of factories, to check land availability for industry, to create publicity for industry, to promote travel and communications in the form of better postal services, telegraph and telephone facilities and to consult relevant and interested organisations to best achieve the aims and objectives. The committee also set out to look into the problems of housing, travel and amenities. It was funded by the Tramways Committee which appears to have been the only committee with a high amount of revenue and which found itself being used as a means to fund various projects.

The Committee began work in earnest. In partnership with the Rotherham council, Sheffield produced a publicity booklet promoting industry and trade. Adverts were placed in journals and it was hoped the huge amount of industry would not go into decline.

In August 1918 a dossier entitled 'Sheffield as an Industrial Centre' was produced to promote Sheffield's industrial strengths, with posters placed at railway stations. It was in a booklet produced by the corporation at this time that the city was described as 'The World's Arsenal'. Sheffield was now firmly on the map.

This all signified optimism; the city was looking towards the future. Despite the war and the ongoing loss of life, Sheffield was considering how it could rebuild itself and looking forward to a time when peace would return.

In August 1918 the Development Advisory Committee recommended consideration of silversmithing and cutlery, new industries, new powers to force owners to sell property for the extension of manufacturing premises, improvements to the city centre and a plan for the development of the whole city.

There were also further calls for employees to be given more security in their employment and better wages. Thomas H Firth, owner of the Sheffield firm of that name, who became president of the British Foundrymen's Association in June 1918, said that it could easily be arranged that every worker received enough in wages to keep a wife and family comfortable.

A CHANGED CITY

In terms of housing, in consultation with the Sheffield and Federation Health Association, it was decided that Sheffield was becoming so overcrowded that it was detrimental to health. Shortly before the war ended plans were drafted to create new villages on the edges of the city with open countryside separating them from the city itself. These suburban villages should have natural features such as trees and open spaces. Requests were made to improve working places and that manufacturing centres should be surrounded by trees and be within walking distance of the new villages so that workers could easily travel to work and that there would be minimal pollution, with manufacturing being dispersed rather than concentrated in the centre which was becoming increasingly smoky. It was later written that the corporation intended to buy large amounts of open space and preserve the countryside around the city. Such plans were unlikely to be achieved in the short term.

Indeed at the council meeting held on 9 November 1918, with the expectation of an imminent end to the war, Councillor Blanchard moved the following resolution: '[A special committee should] at once take steps, through the various committees of the council, to provide a scheme for an immediate resumption of a full public service in the matter of Education, Health, Housing, Sanitation, etc, with a view to make up arrears of the last four years and, if necessary, find immediate work in the event of a sudden cessation of the hostilities throwing temporarily out of work some thousands of our citizens.' The motion was seconded by Councillor Neal but after some discussion it was withdrawn without a vote being taken. It would take another, more destructive, war before real change would eventually take place with regards to these matters.

Almost a year before the end of the war, the housing issue was regarded as a highly serious matter for Sheffield. A National Housing and Town Planning conference was held in the city at the Montgomery Hall. The Lord Mayor told the conference, 'If it was an important question before the war, it was ten times more so at the present juncture. The gravity of the situation was such as to make it imperative, and no one who was interested in the moral of the people and the proper upbringing of the generations to come could fail to take the greatest interest in such conferences.'

All speakers agreed that what the country needed was more houses. The Lord Mayor, Alderman Cattell, spoke that it must have them by 'hook or crook' to end the 'disgraceful' situation with conditions in cities such as Sheffield so acute that working class families were finding it difficult, and in many cases impossible, to bring up families in what we often unsanitary and uninhabitable homes, in slum areas. In Sheffield alone it was a daily problem for the corporation. The conference was particularly keen to emphasise the need to consult women who had proven themselves to be knowledgeable and capable of making a significant contribution. Due to their role of managing the household, it was felt their opinions would be essential in deciding the strategy of improving housing, by avoiding what was considered to be the present 'haphazard housing policy'.

The conference Chairman, Councillor Harold Shawcross, stated that the Government was beginning to be more sympathetic to the housing crisis and they were beginning to revise their view that housing should only be provided by private companies. The war had shown that housing could no longer be ignored by the State and local authorities. It was now more willing to provide funding to build up to 116,000 new houses in the country on top of the 40,000 already planned. The conference hoped that the government would pledge to finance the building of 300,000 new homes immediately after the war and it was agreed to lobby the Government to this affect as well as ensuring plans for the demolition of the slum areas in cities such as Sheffield, being drawn up within six months of the cessation of hostilities and that the slum clearance should be completed within ten years of the end of the war.

Any new houses, the conference agreed, should be designed in a new way to ensure the maximum amount of sunlight and air being able to enter the house. The medical examinations during the military enlisting process had highlighted significant health problems in a large number of men and it was considered that the health issues were largely due to the poor conditions in which the men lived. Although the improvement of housing would cost considerable sums of money, it was necessary expenditure the conference agreed. The cost of the required housing was, it was said, negligible compared to the cost of the war. If the money spent on sanatoria and other attempts to ease and cure illnesses such as consumption had been spent on creating healthier homes, then the nation would be happier and healthier.

Mr Waddington, a representative of Sheffield, believed the Government's proposed housing grant should be given to builders rather than local authorities because he did not believe the provision of housing should be the responsibility of local authorities.

On 3 December 1918 the Government's offer to pay 75 per cent of the cost of new housing, was considered by the corporation. The offer was rejected because it was felt the Government needed to pay more.

With the increasing population and increased demand for water, there were fears that water supplies were woefully low. On 2 October 1918 it was discussed at the Corporation meeting that even after bringing into use the Broomhead and More Hall reservoirs in Ewden valley and taking into account Sheffield's share of the Derwent supply, the demands would exceed the total resources of existing and authorised water works by 1924 or thereabouts. A further permanent supply of between nine and ten million gallons would be required during the period up until 1927 and it was estimated a further five million gallons would be required per day for the period 1928 to 1937. One possible means of obtaining some of this water was to pump it from the River Don and have that water treated. Plans were thus put into place to make this possible.

Plans were also drawn up to extend the provision of electricity in peoples' homes and to enable it to be economical. Improvements were also planned for a higher quality of gas for domestic use.

Sheffield's roads were still somewhat primitive, with minimal improvements having been made during the war years. In fact they had deteriorated due to an increase in their use by vehicles involved in industry. Asphaltic paving had been introduced, as had some tar spraying, which had helped improve road conditions but towards the end of the war there were still many wood-paved streets. The workforce had been halved due to the increasing number of those on active service, and the sending of workers and equipment to France and Belgium to lay roads as part of the war effort, and the average age of the workforce had significantly increased. A lack of materials available had also been a problem. Indeed as late as 1926 there were some parts of the city which still had wood-paved roads.

It was announced that roads including High Street, Fargate and Waingate would be widened or that new roads would be made in order to improve the flow of traffic.

The Corporation planned on buying the canal from the railways company in order to control and increase the transport of materials and products to and from the industrial companies in the city.

Councillor Wardlow expressed his hope that a positive consequence of the war would be social changes to the city, and that this 'war of sacrifice will bring all classes closer together'.

Sir William Clegg was determined that education should improve. 'The future of education means very largely the future of Sheffield,' he wrote, once the war had been won. Children would receive better care, study in better schools and have greater access to free education. He announced that every child would be eligible to compete for a scholarship, with selected children being taken on at the age of 11. The leaving age of Junior Modern Schools would be 15.

One of the most important changes was that due to the significant role women played during the war, women aged from 30 years old were given, for the first time, the right to vote in local and parliamentary elections under the Representation of the People Act (1918). Although it would be another decade before universal suffrage was achieved, it was a massive step forward but one, which despite years of suffragette campaigning, would probably not have occurred if it had not been for the war. Women voted in their thousands in the General Election of 14 December 1918 and in the Sheffield corporation elections of 1919 and 1920. Such was the public enthusiasm for women that in that first election one woman, Eleanor Barton, was elected a councillor for the Attercliffe Ward.

Barton sought the 'social ownership of the means of life and control by the working community'. She felt that Attercliffe should be as healthy as Ranmoor and Norton and not 'the Cinderella ward of the city with the blackest sky and the highest death-rate'. She worked to re-introduce music in the parks, and the affordable supply of electricity to enable housewives to iron and wash clothes. She also campaigned

The cenotaph commemorating the two World Wars, which is the focus for Remembrance events. The City Hall is visible in the background. (*The Author*)

A close up view of the detail of the cenotaph. (*The Author*)

A memorial at the City Road cemetery for those 73 men who died in battle and who were laid to rest in the cemetery. (*The Author*)

A memorial to the men of the York and Lancaster Regiment who lost their lives during the two World Wars. It is located at Weston Park in Sheffield. (*The Author*)

for affordable education and for all banking in the city to be carried out by the Corporation rather than private bankers.

The 'public conscience is being aroused' for the care of those who were blind, according to the 1919 Sheffield Year Book: special schools, colleges and workshops were set up to provide employment for the blind and other disabled. The Painted Fabrics Ltd was set up to provide work.

Whilst it was commonly believed that the First World War would be the war to end all wars, there was a fear that improved technology and military practices could once again bring devastation. The fact the war had been fought on the home front as well as overseas, the first war involving foreign powers to affect British soil since the 18th century, introduced fear as well as causing civilian casualties and fatalities and destroying homes. Like those who had seen active service during the war, those who had witnessed the destruction caused by the Zeppelin raid, people who most probably had never seen aircraft until the war commenced, would have the images haunt them for the remainder of their lives. And that is not to mention those who died when the bombs were dropped over the city.

But of course the most important change of all was that families were torn apart and many of the thousands who had left Sheffield in a bid to protect Britain came home severely wounded or never came home at all. Sons, brothers, husbands, fathers, friends, employees were lost. The population of Sheffield in 1914 had been an estimated 476,971 and during the war 5,139 of the men had lost their lives, representing approximately one per cent of the entire population. Their absence would be felt for decades and families would face extra financial hardship as well as the trauma of bereavement. It is therefore appropriate to end this book with the words of CA Renshaw in her poem, *Sheffield's Fallen* from her anthology *Lest We Forget*, which was to be inscribed on a stainless steel flag staff forming a City War Memorial:

'We cheered you forth with smiles that hid our weeping
Bravely you went; proudly we watched you go,
The dreams of youth upon you, the deep glow

A memorial for those who lost their lives during the First World War in the parish. (*The Author*)

Of fine faith in your eyes burning and leaping,
The age-long honour of England in your keeping;
Your trust, her flag unsullied by a foe.
… We cheered you forth – and scarlet poppies blow
Over the stricken soil where you lie sleeping.
Now, in this smoky town where you were bred,
The flag you loved rides high, invincible,
The stainless thing you kept it for all years.
And we who are left, look up to it through tears,
And give you greeting – O most glorious Dead,
We shall remember! – Hail! – Hail and farewell!'

A memorial to the men of Fulwood who lost their lives in the war. The memorial is located immediately outside the graveyard in which Charles Haydn Hanforth and other Fulwood men were laid to rest. (*The Author*)

Index